GERMANY

TOP SIGHTS, AUTHENTIC EXPERIENCES

THIS EDITION WRITTEN AND RESEARCHED BY

Marc Di Duca, Kerry Christiani, Catherine Le Nevez,
Tom Masters, Andrea Schulte-Peevers, Ryan Ver Berkmoes
and Benedict Walker

Week 2

Nuremberg to the Black Forest

❺ A short hop from Nuremberg, the quaintly medieval walled town of **Rothenburg ob der Tauber** is the highlight of Germany's most celebrated tourist route, the Romantic Road.

🚆 3hr or 🚗 3hrs

❻ No trip to Bavaria would be complete without at least a couple of days in **Munich**, Germany's 'secret capital' brimming with art and beer.

🚆 2hr or 🚗 2hrs

❼ Top trip from Munich is to dreamy **Schloss Neuschwanstein** in the foothills of the Alps.

🚆 6hr or 🚗 4½hr

❽ From the Alps it's not too far to the **Black Forest** where you can easily escape the cuckoo clocks and slabs of gateau by hitting trails into the wilds.

🚆 1¾hr or 🚗 2hr

Staying Longer

The Black Forest to Cologne

❾ **Heidelberg** is the obvious place to finish off a trip around southwest Germany, the country's oldest university still filling the pretty Altstadt with a kicking student nightlife scene.

🚆 1¾ hr or 🚗 1¼hr

❿ From Heidelberg, the beautiful **Rhine** beckons, with the stretch between Bingen and Koblenz one of Europe's prettiest river journeys.

🚆 2½hr or 🚢 1hr

⓫ Continue exploring Germany's riverways with a visit to the wineries at Traben-Trarbach on the **Moselle**.

🚆 3hr or 🚗 2¼hr

⓬ Finally, head north to **Cologne**, famous for its artwork-filled cathedral.

Contents

In Focus

Survival Guide

Berlin
p35

Potsdam ●
p85

Dresden ●
p175

● Cologne
p215

● Rhine Valley
p229

● Moselle Valley
p243

Nuremberg
p189

Heidelberg ●
p143

Rothenburg
p203

Black Forest
p155

Munich
● p97

Neuschwanstein
p133

Plan Your Trip
Germany's Top 12

TAFELZWERK / GETTY IMAGES ©

Berlin

The glamour and grit of Berlin (p35) are bound to mesmerise anyone keen on vibrant culture, edgy architecture, fabulous food, intense parties and palpable history. Over a quarter-century after the Wall's collapse, the German capital is increasingly grown up without relinquishing its indie spirit. There's haute cuisine in a former brewery, all-night parties in power stations and world-class art in a WWII bunker. Visit major historical sites – the Reichstag and Checkpoint Charlie among them – then feast on a smorgasbord of culture in myriad museums. Left: Berlin city; Right: Berliner Dom (p49)

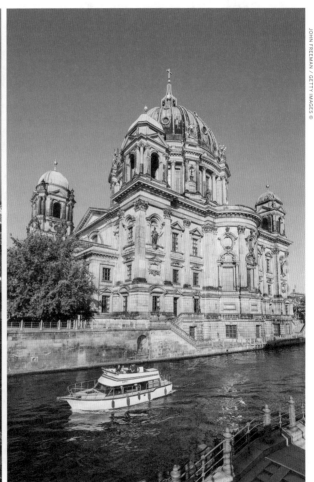

Munich

The Bavarian capital (p97) has plenty of unexpected trump cards under its often bright-blue skies. Folklore and age-old traditions exist side by side with sleek BMWs, designer boutiques and high-powered industry. The city's museums showcase everything from artistic masterpieces to technological treasures and Oktoberfest history, while its music and cultural scenes are second only to Berlin's. Top: Marienplatz (p106); Bottom: The Antiquarium, Rezidenzmuseum (p104)

2

Neuschwanstein

Commissioned by Bavaria's most celebrated (and loopiest) 19th-century monarch, King Ludwig II, Schloss Neuschwanstein (p133) rises from the mysterious Alpine forests like a bedtime-storybook illustration. Inside, the make-believe continues, with chambers and halls reflecting Ludwig's obsession with the mythical Teutonic past – and his admiration of composer Wagner – in a confection that puts even the flashiest oligarch's palazzo in the shade.

3

4

Heidelberg

The 19th-century romantics found sublime beauty and spiritual inspiration in Germany's oldest university town (p143) and so, in his way, did Mark Twain, who was beguiled by the ruins of the hillside castle. Generations of students have attended lectures, sung lustily with beer steins in hand, carved their names into tavern tables and, occasionally, been sent to the student jail. All of this has left its mark on the modern-day city, where age-old traditions endure alongside world-class research, innovative cultural events and a sometimes raucous nightlife scene. Marktplatz (p146)

5

The Black Forest

Mist, snow or shine, the deep, dark Black Forest (p155) is just beautiful. If it's back-to-nature moments you're after, this sylvan slice of southwestern Germany is the place to linger. Every valley reveals new surprises: half-timbered villages looking every inch the fairy-tale fantasy, thunderous waterfalls, cuckoo clocks the size of houses. Breathe in the cold, sappy air, drive roller-coaster roads to middle-of-nowhere lakes, have your cake, walk it off on trail after gorgeously wooded trail, then hide away in a heavy-lidded farmhouse. Hear that? Silence. What a wonderful thing. Black Forest trail

The Romantic Rhine Valley

As the mighty Rhine flows from Rüdesheim to Koblenz (p229), the landscape's unique face-off between rock and water creates a magical mix of the wild (churning whirlpools, dramatic cliffs), the agricultural (near-vertical vineyards), the medieval (hilltop castles, half-timbered hamlets) and the modern (in the 19th-century sense: barges, ferries, passenger steamers and trains). From every riverside village, trails take you through vineyards and forests.
Boppard (p238)

6

JÖRG GREUEL/GETTY IMAGES ©

Dresden

The apocalypse came on a cold February night in 1945. Hours of carpet-bombing reduced Germany's 'Florence on the Elbe' (p175) to a smouldering pile of bricks and the dead. Dresden's comeback is nothing short of a miracle. Reconstructed architectural jewels pair with stunning art collections that justify the city's place in the pantheon of European cultural capitals. Add to that a contagiously energetic pub quarter, a dramatically redesigned Militärhistorisches Museum and a tiara of villas and palaces. Frauenkirche (p178)

7

Nuremberg

Capital of Franconia, an independent region until 1806, Nuremberg (p189) may conjure visions of Nazi rallies and grisly war trials, but there's so much more to this energetic city. Dürer hailed from the Altstadt, his house now a museum. Germany's first railway trundled from here to neighbouring Fürth, leaving a trail of choo-choo heritage. And Germany's toy capital has heaps of things for kids to enjoy. When you're done with sightseeing, the local beer is as dark as the coffee and best employed to chase down Nuremberg's delicious finger-sized bratwurst. Nuremberg bratwurst

KARL-FRIEDRICH HOHL/GETTY IMAGES ©

Cologne

At unexpected moments you see it: Cologne's cathedral (p215), the city's twin-towered icon, looming over an urban vista and the timeless course of the Rhine. And why shouldn't it? This perfectly formed testament to faith and conviction was started in 1248 and consecrated six centuries later. You can feel the echoes of the passage of time as you sit in its soaring stained-glass-lit and artwork-filled interior. Climb a tower for views of the surrounding city that are like no others. Left: Hohenzollern Bridge and Kölner Dom (p218); Right: Cologne's Altstadt

Potsdam

Just across the Glienicke 'spy bridge' from Berlin, Postdam (p85), the state capital of Brandenburg, was catapulted to prominence by King Frederick the Great. His giddily rococo Sanssouci palace is the glorious crown of this Unesco-recognised cultural tapestry that synthesises 18th-century artistic trends from around Europe in one stupendous masterpiece: marvellous palaces, idyllic parks, stunning views, inspired architecture and tantalising Cold War sites. Top: Neues Palais (p89); Bottom left: Schloss Sanssouci (p88); Bottom right: Potsdam's Altstadt (p92)

10

T.W. VAN URK/SHUTTERSTOCK ©

Moselle Valley

A tributary of the Rhine, the Moselle (p243) zigzags lazily for 350km from Koblenz to northern France by way of Luxembourg. It's one of Europe's all-star waterways, hemmed in by ancient villages and miles of vineyards. Many of these cling courageously to vertiginous slopes from which a new generation of winemakers coaxes some of the most elegant, full-bodied rieslings you'll ever taste. It was the Romans that introduced grapes to this area; their legacy survives in Trier. Grevenburg (p253), Traben-Trarbach

GAVIN HELLIER/GETTY IMAGES ©

Rothenburg ob der Tauber

With its jumble of neatly restored half-timbered houses enclosed by sturdy ramparts, Rothenburg ob der Tauber (p203) lays on the medieval cuteness with a trowel. (One might even say it's too cute for its own good, if the deluges of day trippers are any indication.) The trick is to experience this historic wonderland at its most magical: early or late in the day, when the last coaches have hit the road and you can soak up the romance all by yourself on gentle strolls along moonlit cobbled lanes.

Plan Your Trip
Two-Week Itinerary

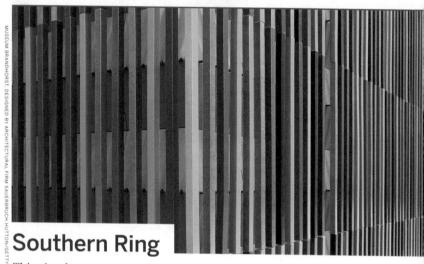

MUSEUM BRANDHORST, DESIGNED BY ARCHITECTURAL FIRM SAUERBRUCH HUTTON/GETTY IMAGES ©

Southern Ring

This circular route around the two states of Bavaria and Baden-Württemberg takes in the essence of Germany's south, a place of romantic castles, unsurpassed beer and historical city centres, all backed by the snow-dusted peaks of the German Alps.

❶ Munich (p97)

All roads in southern Germany lead to Munich and it's in the city of art and beer where we spend our first three days. The launch pad for exploring Germany's 'secret capital' is the bustling **Marienplatz** from where it's a short stroll to the **Residenz**, home to the ruling Wittelsbach dynasty for over eight centuries. The other definite highlights are the **Pinakotheken**, Munich's gathering of world-class art galleries which occupy the Kunstareal.

⮕ Munich to Füssen
🚊 2 hrs

❷ Füssen (p140)

Füssen, a gateway to the German Alps, is most famous as the location for Germany's most popular tourist attraction, fairy-tale **Schloss Neuschwanstein**. This dreamy castle, rising from the pine forest, was built by Bavaria's favourite king, Ludwig II, and is dedicated to the works of his favourite composer, Wagner.

⮕ Füssen to Triberg
🚊 6 hrs

❸ Triberg (p172)

A complicated series of train journeys across Baden-Württemberg will bring you to Triberg, birthplace of the Black Forest's two biggest exports – cuckoo clocks and black forest gateau. The latter should be sampled at **Café Schäfer** where it was first concocted in 1915.

⮕ Triberg to Baden-Baden
🚊 1¼ hrs

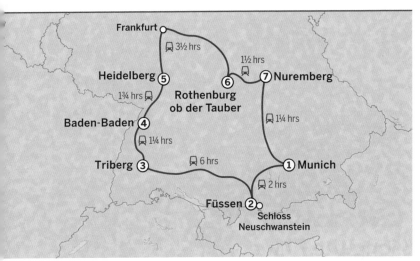

❹ Baden-Baden (p160)

In the famous spa town of Baden-Baden, you can bathe in the thermal waters in swish surroundings and enjoy wallowing in Germany's most celebrated aqua minerals.

⊙ Baden-Baden to Heidelberg

🚗 1¾ hrs

❺ Heidelberg (p143)

The university town of Heidelberg is well-known for its baroque **Altstadt**.

⊙ Heidelberg to Rothenburg ob der Tauber

🚗 3½ hrs

❻ Rothenburg ob der Tauber (p203)

Rothenburg ob der Tauber is arguably the most worthwhile stop on the Romantic Road, Germany's most popular touring route. This walled town is a relentlessly quaint affair with chocolate-box medieval architecture and winding cobbled lanes.

⊙ Rothenburg ob der Tauber to Nuremberg

🚗 1½ hrs

❼ Nuremberg (p189)

Bavaria's second city is the historically rich Nuremberg. After exploring the **Altstadt** discover more about the city's position in the Holy Roman Empire at the **Kaiserburg**, and about the city's role in the rise and fall of the Nazis at the **Reichsparteitags-gelände**, where they held their biggest pre-war rallies, and the **Memorium Nuremberg Trials**, where many prominent members of the regime were tried after WWII. From Nuremberg it's a train journey back to Munich.

⊙ Nuremberg to Munich

🚗 1¼ hrs

Above left: Museum Brandhorst (p114), designed by architectural firm Sauerbruch Hutton, Munich

Plan Your Trip
10-Day Itinerary

ALAN COPSON/GETTY IMAGES ©

Along the Rhine and Moselle

The Rhine and Moselle rivers in Germany's far west cut through mountains and valleys carpeted in vines, passing hilltop castles and quaintly historical towns and villages along the way.

❶ Cologne (p215)

This may be a bucolic tour of Germany's most famous pair of rivers, but we start with the big-city vibe of Cologne. Top sight here is the world-famous **Kölner Dom**, the city's cathedral, its twin towers dominating the cityscape. When you've negotiated the more than 509 steps to the top of the south tower and the same number down again, head for the **Römisch-Germanisches Museum**, a superb repository of the Rhine's Roman past.

⭕Cologne to Koblenz
🚌 1 hrs

❷ Koblenz (p239)

The main attractions in Koblenz are the rebuilt **Altstadt** and the confluence of the Moselle and Rhine.

⭕ Koblenz to Bacharach
🚌 30 mins

❸ Bacharach (p236)

This is one of the Rhine's quaintest villages and certainly worth a stopover.

⭕ Bacharach to Rüdesheim
🚢 50 mins

❹ Rüdesheim (p234)

This village offers spectacular river views and some of Germany's best wines. From Rüdesheim you now backtrack to Koblenz to join the Moselle on its winding way southwest towards the border with Luxembourg.

⭕ Rüdesheim to Cochem (via Koblenz)
🚌 1½ hrs

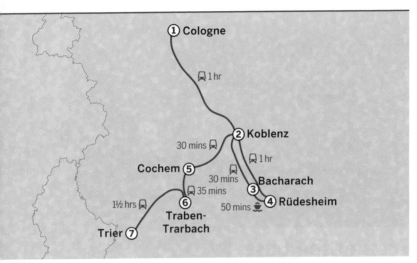

① Cologne

🚃 1 hr

② Koblenz

30 mins 🚃

🚃 1 hr

Cochem ⑤

30 mins 🚌

Bacharach

🚃 35 mins

③

1½ hrs 🚃

⑥

50 mins 🚢

④ Rüdesheim

Trier ⑦

Traben-
Trarbach

❺ Cochem (p252)

Touristy Cochem is just half an hour from Koblenz by train and is a gateway to the Moselle Valley. It's the terminus for most boat cruises and boasts an 11th-century castle, the **Reichsburg**.

➲ Cochem to Traben-Trarbach

🚃 35 mins

❻ Traben-Trarbach (p253)

The Moselle region is famous for its wines and there's no better place to indulge in a tasting session than Traben-Trarbach. The town straddles the Moselle, Traben hugging the northern shore, Trarbach the southern banks. Away from the crisp whites, a rather unexpected attraction here is the **Buddha Museum**, though it is housed in a former winery.

➲ Traben-Trarbach to Trier

🚃 1½ hrs

❼ Trier (p256)

The undisputed high point of any Moselle journey is the town of Trier. Just shy of the border with Luxembourg, Trier boasts Germany's finest gathering of **Roman monuments**, a fact recognised by Unesco in 1986. These include the Porta Nigra Roman gate, the Kaiserthermen Roman thermal baths and an amphitheatre that once held 20,000 spectators.

Above left: St Goarshausen (p237) on the Rhine

Plan Your Trip
Five-Day Itinerary

Best of the East

Despite over two decades of a reunified Germany, the former GDR (DDR in German) still maintains it's own unique character. This five-day taster including the capital Berlin and fascinating Dresden will show you the East's history and its resurrection from the bad days of Soviet dominance.

❶ Berlin (p35)

Any tour of Germany's east must kick off in Berlin, the country's capital since it was reunited in 1990. Sights to tick off here include the **Reichstag**, which was reinstated as German parliament in 1999; the **Brandenburger Tor**, once a potent symbol of a divided Europe; and the **Museumsinsel** (Museum Island), home to some world-class repositories of the past. Those with a particular interest in the Cold War should head for the **DDR Museum**, **Checkpoint Charlie** and the **East Side Gallery**, the longest stretch of the Berlin Wall to have survived and now a free, open-air gallery. Berlin has some of the best nightlife in Germany and a night out on the tiles is not to be missed.

➲ Berlin to Potsdam

S	40 mins
🚋	25 mins

❷ Potsdam (p85)

No visit to the German capital is complete without a day trip to Potsdam. The town has several palaces and parks, but the main draw here is **Schloss Sanssouci**, the private retreat of King Friedrich II (Frederick

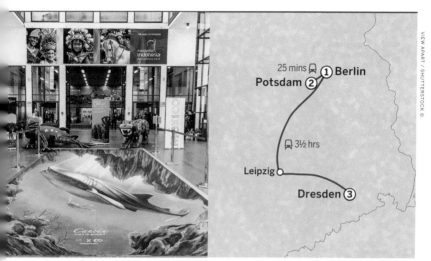

25 mins 🚆 ① **Berlin**
Potsdam ②

🚌 3½ hrs

Leipzig

Dresden ③

the Great). **Schloss Cecilienhof** is where the 1945 Potsdam Conference took place which decided Germany's postwar fate.

● Berlin to Dresden
🚆 3½ hrs

❸ Dresden (p175)

Surprisingly there are few direct trains between Berlin and the next stop Dresden, and a change in Leipzig is usually necessary. Most towns and cities across the GDR saw huge change after the fall of the Wall, but a symbol of this resurrection stands in Dresden in the shape of the **Frauenkirche**, for 50 years a pile of rubble after it was destroyed by Allied bombs in 1945. It was rebuilt between 1994 and 2005 and is now the city's top attraction.

Other unmissable sights here include the Renaissance **Residenzschloss**, home to its Saxony rulers from 1485 to 1918 and the **Zwinger**, a Versailles-inspired baroque palace housing three first-rate museums. Those on the GDR trail should head for two excellent 'nostalgia museums' – the **DDR Museum Pirna** and the **Zeitreise DDR** Museum Radebeul, both in small towns outside Dresden. Their exhibitions of junk and knick-knacks show just how Germany's other half lived in the days of the GDR.

Above left: Dresden (p175)
Above right: Street art by Edgar Müller, Berlin (p35)

Plan Your Trip
If You Like...

ERWIN PURNOMO SIDI/GETTY IMAGES ©

German Flavours

Bratwurst Nuremberg's finger-sized links are top dogs in Germany.

Pork knuckle A Munich beer hall such as the Hofbräuhaus is the perfect place for tackling this belt-stretcher.

Spätzle Noodle dish from the Stuttgart region, often smothered in cheese or topped with lentils.

Black forest gateau Enjoy this liqueur-drenched sponge-cake symphony at Café Schäfer in Triberg, where it was invented.

Beer Oktoberfest is the best time to sample Munich's famous brews.

Churches

Kölner Dom The twin spires of Germany's largest cathedral dominate Cologne's skyline. (p218)

Frauenkirche Dresden's most famous church was reopened in 2005 after six decades as a heap of WWII rubble. (p178)

Asamkirche Created by the Asam brothers, this small church has one of Germany's most impressive Baroque interiors. (p107)

Wieskirche Baroque gem is one of the highlights of the Romantic Road. (p209)

WWII Sites

Hitler's Bunker Hitler's Berlin bunker is concealed by a parking lot sporting an information panel. (p87)

Memorium Nuremberg Trials Visit the courtroom where the famous Nuremberg Trials took place. (p196)

Reichsparteitagsgelände Roam the huge site where the Nazis held their pre-WWII rallies. (p197)

KZ-Gedenkstätte Dachau Germany's first concentration camp is a disturbing experience. (p118)

GUENTER ALBERS / SHUTTERSTOCK ©

Cold War Sites

Brandenburger Tor For four decades the symbol of a divided Europe. (p40)

Berlin Wall The Gedenkstätte Berliner Mauer and the East Side Gallery are almost the only remnants of this infamous divide. (p42)

DDR Museum This museum in Berlin tells East Germany's story. (p68)

Castles & Palaces

Schloss Neuschwanstein Germany's most famous and picturesque palace was the inspiration for Disney's Sleeping Beauty castle. (p136)

Schloss Heidelberg Although destroyed repeatedly throughout the centuries, there's still a majesty surrounding this red-sandstone hilltop Gothic pile. (p148)

Schloss Sanssouci Prussian king Frederick the Great sought solace amid the splendour of his Potsdam summer palace. (p88)

Schloss Charlottenburg The only surviving Hohenzollern residence contains a number of Berlin's museums. (p52)

Residenz The Wittelsbach's main residence in central Munich is one of the city's top sights. (p102)

Above left: Black forest gateau
Above right: Cologne (p215)

Plan Your Trip
Month by Month

January

Except in the ski resorts, the Germans have the country pretty much to themselves this month. Short and cold days make this a good time to make in-depth explorations of museums and churches.

🎿 Mountain Madness

Grab your skis or snowboard and hit the slopes. No matter whether you're a black diamond daredevil or 'Sesame Street' novice, there's a piste with your name on it.

February

It's not as sweltering as Rio, but the German Carnival is still a good excuse for a party. Ski resorts are busiest thanks to school holidays, so make reservations.

☆ Berlin Film Festival

Stars, directors and critics sashay down the red carpet for two weeks of screenings and glamour parties at the Berlinale (www.berlinale.de).

🎭 Karneval/Fasching

The pre-Lenten season is celebrated with street partying, parades, satirical shows and general revelry. The biggest parties are along the Rhine, but the Black Forest and Munich also have their own traditions.

March

Days start getting longer and the first inkling of spring is in the air. Fresh herring hits the menus, and dishes prepared with *Bärlauch* (wild garlic) are all the rage.

April

No matter if you stopped believing in the Easter Bunny long ago, there's no escaping him in Germany in April. Meanwhile, nothing epitomises the arrival of spring more than the first crop of white asparagus. Germans go nuts for it.

⊙ Maifest

Villagers celebrate the end of winter on 30 April by chopping down a tree for a

Maypole (*Maibaum*), painting, carving and decorating it, and staging a merry revelry with traditional costumes, singing and dancing.

May

One of the loveliest months, often surprisingly warm and sunny. Plenty of public holidays, resulting in busy roads and lodging shortages.

♣ Karneval der Kulturen

Hundreds of thousands of revellers celebrate Berlin's multicultural tapestry with parties, exotic nosh and a fun parade of flamboyantly dressed dancers, DJs, artists and musicians shimmying through the streets of Kreuzberg.

◉ Labour Day

Throughout Germany, 1 May is a public holiday, with some cities hosting political demonstrations for workers' rights. In Berlin, protests have taken on a violent nature in the past, although now it's mostly a big street fair.

◉ Muttertag

Mothers are honoured on the second Sunday of May, much to the delight of florists and greeting-card companies. Make restaurant reservations far in advance.

June

Germany's festival pace quickens, while gourmets can rejoice in the bounty of fresh, local produce in the markets. Life moves outdoors as the summer solstice means the sun doesn't set until around 9.30pm.

◉ Vatertag

Father's Day, now also known as *Männertag* (Men's Day), is essentially an excuse for men to get liquored up with the blessing of the missus. It's always on Ascension Day.

Above left: Snowboarding in Bavaria
Above right: Dancing around the Maypole for Maifest

♣ Christopher Street Day

No matter your sexual persuasion, come out and paint the town pink at major gay-pride celebrations in Berlin, Cologne and Munich.

July

School's out for the summer and peak travelling season begins, so prebook accommodation. It won't be the Med, but swimming is now possible in lakes, rivers, and the Baltic and North Seas.

August

August tends to be Germany's hottest month but days are often cooled by afternoon thunderstorms.

✈ Shooting Festivals

More than a million Germans (mostly men) belong to shooting clubs and show off their skills at marksmen's festivals.

♥ Wine Festivals

With grapes ripening to a plump sweetness, the wine festival season starts, with tastings, folkloric parades, fireworks and the election of local and regional wine queens.

September

Often a great month weather-wise. The main travel season is over but September is still busy thanks to lots of wine and autumn festivals.

✈ Berlin Marathon

Sweat it out with the other 50,000 runners or just cheer 'em on during Germany's biggest street race (www.berlin-marathon.com), which has seen nine world records set since 1977.

♣ Erntedankfest

Rural towns celebrate the harvest with decorated church altars, *Erntedankzug* (processions) and villagers dressed in folkloric garments.

♥ Oktoberfest

Munich's legendary beer-swilling party (p100). Enough said.

October

Days get shorter, colder and wetter. Tourist offices, museums and attractions start keeping shorter hours. Some close down for the winter season.

November

This can be a dreary month mainly spent indoors. However, queues at tourist sights are short and cultural events are plentiful. Bring warm clothes and rain gear.

♣ St Martinstag

This festival held on 10–11 November honours St Martin with a lantern procession and a re-enactment of the famous scene where he cuts his coat in half to share with a beggar. This is followed by a big feast of stuffed roast goose.

December

Cold and sun-deprived days are brightened by enchanting markets, illuminated streets, Advent calendars, candle-festooned wreaths, home-baked cookies and other rituals.

◉ Nikolaustag

On the eve of 5 December, German children put their boots outside the door hoping that St Nick will fill them with sweets and small toys overnight. Ill-behaved children, though, may find only a prickly rod left behind by St Nick's helper, Knecht Ruprecht.

🔒 Christmas Markets

Mulled wine, spicy gingerbread cookies, shimmering ornaments – these and lots more are typical features of German Christmas markets, held from late November until late December. Nuremberg's Christkindlesmarkt (p199) is especially famous.

♣ Silvester

New Year's Eve is called 'Silvester' in honour of the 4th-century pope under whom the Romans adopted Christianity as their official religion. The new year is greeted with fireworks launched by thousands of amateur pyromaniacs.

Plan Your Trip
Get Inspired

Read

Grimms Märchen
(Grimms Fairy Tales;
1812) Jacob and Wilhelm
Grimm's fairy tales,
passed down orally
through generations.

**Mr Norris Changes
Trains** (1935) and
Goodbye to Berlin
(1939) Christopher
Isherwood's chronicle of
early-1930s Berlin was
the basis of the movie
Cabaret.

**The Rise & Fall of
the Third Reich**
(1960) William Shirer's
definitive tome about
Nazi Germany remains
powerful.

Watch

Das Boot (1981) Dives
into the claustrophobic
world of WWII U-boat
warfare.

Good Bye, Lenin! (2003)
Drama-comedy about a
young East Berliner pro-
tecting his ailing mother
from the knowledge that
the Wall has fallen.

Der Untergang (Downfall;
2004) Chilling account of
Hitler's last 12 days in his
Berlin bunker.

Das Leben der Anderen
(The Lives of Others;
2006) Academy Award
winner; unmasks the
pervasiveness and
destructiveness of East
Germany's secret service,
the Stasi.

Listen

Ring of the Nibelungen
(1848–74) Richard
Wagner's epic opera
cycle.

The Threepenny Opera
(1928) Runaway hit
musical by Brecht and
Weill.

Atem (1973) Ground-
breaking album by
electronic music pioneers
Tangerine Dream.

Sehnsucht (1994)
Industrial metal band
Rammstein's internation-
al breakthrough album.

Above: Performance of *The Threepenny Opera* in a Munich bar

Plan Your Trip
Family Travel

GRAHAM MONRO/GM PHOTOGRAPHICS/GETTY IMAGES ©

Germany is a safe and easy place to travel with children and most places are happy to welcome kids.

The Low-Down

Practically all hotels can provide cots (cribs), though sometimes for a small charge. Some properties allow small children to stay in their parents' room free of charge if they don't require extra bedding.

As long as they're not running wild, children are generally welcome in German restaurants, especially in informal cafes, bistros, pizzerias or *Gaststätten* (inns). Many offer a limited *Kindermenü* (children's menu) or *Kinderteller* (children's dishes).

Breastfeeding in public is common, although most women are discreet about it.

Children under 12 or smaller than 59 inches (1.5m) must ride in the back seat in cars (including taxis) and use an appropriate car seat or booster. Taxis are not equipped with car seats, and bring your own car seat or reserve one if hiring a car.

On trains children under 15 travel free if accompanied by at least one parent or grandparent as long they're registered on your ticket at the time of purchase. Children under six always travel free and without a ticket.

Kidding Around

Kids might already have seen images of things that make Germany so special: enchanting palaces and legend-shrouded castles, medieval towns and half-timbered villages, Viking ships and Roman ruins. This is the birthplace of the Brothers Grimm and their famous fairy tales. If you head to Neuschwanstein, you even get to see Sleeping Beauty's castle.

Outdoor Activities

The great outdoors yield endless variety in Germany. Tourist offices can recommend walking trails suitable for families, including stroller-friendly paths, or can

WALTER BIBIKOW/GETTY IMAGES ©

hook you up with a local guide. Also ask about kid-geared activities like geocaching, animal-spotting safaris and nature walks.

Germany's beaches and lakes are beautifully clean and usually devoid of big waves and dangerous undercurrents, although water temperatures rarely exceed 21°C (70°F). Many have a *Strandbad* (lido) with change rooms, playgrounds, splash zones, slides, restaurants and boat rentals.

All ski resorts have ski schools with English-speaking instructors that initiate kids in the art of the snow plough in group or private lessons. All of them, of course, have plenty of off-piste fun as well: snow-shoeing, sledding, walking and ice skating.

Need to Know

Baby food, formulas, milk, nappies (diapers) Buy in supermarkets and drugstores (chemists).

Best Museums for Kids

Schokoladenmuseum (Chocolate Museum; p223), Cologne

Museum für Naturkunde (p65), Berlin

Spielzeugmuseum (p257), Trier

Deutsches Technikmuseum (p70), Berlin

Cots (cribs) Available upon request in most hotels; best to reserve in advance.

Highchairs & kids' menus Standard in most restaurants.

Strollers Bring your own.

Transport Discounts widely available; bring your own car seat or reserve one early if hiring a car.

Above left: Swimming pool in the Spree River, Berlin (p35)
Above right: Schokoladenmuseum (p223), Cologne

Plan Your Trip
Need to Know

When to Go

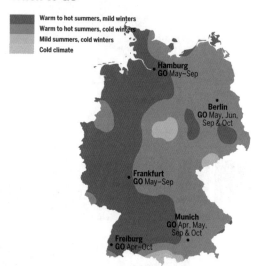

Warm to hot summers, mild winters
Warm to hot summers, cold winters
Mild summers, cold winters
Cold climate

Hamburg
GO May–Sep

Berlin
GO May, Jun, Sep & Oct

Frankfurt
GO May–Sep

Munich
GO Apr, May, Sep & Oct

Freiburg
GO Apr–Oct

High Season (Jul & Aug)
o Busy roads and long lines at key sights

o Vacancies at a premium and higher prices in seaside and mountain resorts

o Festivals celebrate everything

Shoulder Season (Apr–Jun & Sep–Oct)
o Smaller crowds and lower prices, except on public holidays

o Blooming flowers in spring; radiant foliage in autumn

o Sunny, temperate weather ideal for outdoor pursuits

Low Season (Nov–Mar)
o No queues but shorter hours at key sights; some may close for the season

o Theatre, concert and opera season in full swing

o Ski resorts busiest in January and February

Currency
Euro (€)

Language
German

Visas
Generally not required for tourist stays up to 90 days (or at all for EU nationals); some nationalities need a Schengen Visa (p303).

Money
ATMs widely available in cities and towns, rarely in villages. Cash is king almost every-where; credit cards are not widely accepted.

Mobile Phones
Mobile phones operate on GSM900/1800. If you have a European or Australian phone, save money by slipping in a German SIM card.

Time
Central European Time (GMT/UTC plus one hour)

Daily Costs

Budget: Less than €100

○ Hostel, camping or private room: €15–30

○ Up to €8 per meal or self-cater

○ Take advantage of happy hours and free or low-cost museums and entertainment

Midrange: €100–200

○ Private apartment or double room: €60–100

○ Three-course dinner at nice restaurant: €30–40

○ Couple of beers in a pub or beer garden: €8

Top End: More than €200

○ Fancy loft apartment or double in top-end hotel: from €150

○ Sit-down lunch, dinner at top-rated restaurant: €100

○ Concert or opera tickets: €50–150

Useful Websites

Lonely Planet (www.lonelyplanet.com/germany) Hotel bookings, traveller forum and more.

XE (www.xe.com) For current exchange rates.

German National Tourist Office (www.germany.travel)

Facts About Germany (www.tatsachen-ueber-deutschland.de/en) Reference tool on all aspects of German society.

Deutschland Online (www.magazine-deutschland.de) Insightful features on culture, business and politics.

Online German course (www.deutsch-lernen.com)

Opening Hours

These typical opening hours may vary seasonally and between cities and villages. Where hours vary across the year, we've provided those applicable in high season.

Banks 9am to 4pm Monday to Friday, extended hours usually on Tuesday and Thursday, some open Saturday

Bars 6pm to 1am

Cafes 8am to 8pm

Clubs 11pm to early morning hours

Post offices 9am to 6pm Monday to Friday, 9am to 1pm Saturday

Restaurants 11am to 11pm (food service often stops at 9pm in rural areas)

Major stores and supermarkets 9.30am to 8pm Monday to Saturday

Arriving in Germany

Frankfurt Airport (p303) S-Bahn train lines S8 and S9 link the airport with the city centre in 15 minutes several times hourly for €4.55. Taxis make the trip in 20 to 30 minutes and average €30.

Munich Airport (p129) The S1 and S8 trains link the airport with the city centre in 40 minutes (€10.80). The Lufthansa Airport Bus (€10.50) departs every 20 minutes and takes about the same time as the train. A taxi costs about €60.

Getting Around

Germany's public transport network is one of the best in Europe. The best ways of getting around are by car and by train.

Train Extensive network of long-distance and regional trains with frequent departures.

Car Cars can be hired in every town and city. Drive on the right.

Bus Cheaper and slower than trains. Regional bus services fill the gaps in areas not served by rail.

Air Only useful for longer distances, eg Berlin to Munich.

For more, see the Survival Guide (p292)

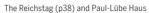

The Reichstag (p38) and Paul-Lübe Haus

BERLIN

Discover More
www.lonelyplanet.
com/germany/berlin

Berlin

Berlin's combo of glamour and grit is bound to mesmerise anyone keen to explore its vibrant culture, cutting-edge architecture, fabulous food, intense parties and tangible history.

This is a city that staged a revolution, was headquartered by Nazis, bombed to bits, divided in two and finally reunited – and that was just in the 20th century! Walk along remnants of the Berlin Wall, marvel at the splendour of a Prussian palace, visit Checkpoint Charlie or stand in the very room where the Holocaust was planned.

When it comes to creativity, the sky's the limit in Berlin. Since the fall of the Berlin Wall, the city has become a giant lab of cultural experimentation thanks to an abundance of space, cheap rent and a free-wheeling spirit that nurtures and encourages new ideas.

☑ In This Section

🎉 What's On

Berlinale (www.berlinale.de; ⏱Feb) The German capital's famous film festival.

Berlin Marathon (www.berlin-marathon.com; ⏱Sep) One of Europe's premier running events.

Jazzfest Berlin (www.jazzfest-berlin.de; ⏱Nov) One of Germany's top jazz bashes.

Christmas markets (www.visitberlin.de) Berlin gets in on the mulled wine and baubles act in the run-up to Christmas.

Clockwise from Top Left:
The Berlin Wall (p42);
a park by the Spree
River; the Reichstag (p38);
Christmas markets (p36);
Brandenburger Tor (p40)

MURAT TANER/GETTY ©

BOOK YOUR
ACOMMODATION ON
LONELYPLANET.COM/HOTELS

➡ Berlin in Two Days

Kick off day one at the **Reichstag** (p7) then stroll south to the **Brandenburger Tor** (p40), Berlin's most recognisable structure. Further south lies the famous **Holocaust Memorial** (p27) and **Potsdamer Platz**, the city's heart. **Checkpoint Charlie** (p64) is a short distance away. You could spend the entire second day at the **Museumsinsel** (p46) taking in world-class repositories of the past.

➡ Berlin in Four Days

After all the above, start day three at the **Gedenkstätte Berliner Mauer** (p43) and the **Mauerpark** (p70). Take a whirlwind tour of **Schloss Charlottenburg** (p23) before heading to the Kurfürstendamm for a spot of shopping. Day four might begin at the **Jüdisches Museum** (Jewish Museum; p69) before heading to the **East Side Gallery** (p38), the longest piece of the Wall to have survived.

From left: The Reichstag (p38); Christmas markets; Brandenburger Tor (p40); Gedenkstätte Berliner Mauer (p43)

The Reichstag

HENRYK SADURA/GETTY IMAGES ©

The Reichstag

Reinstated as the home of the German parliament in 1999, the late 19th-century Reichstag is one of Berlin's most iconic buildings.

Great For...

☑ **Don't Miss**

Free auto-activated audioguides provide info on the building, landmarks and the workings of parliament.

The Reichstag's Beginnings

It's been burned, bombed, rebuilt, buttressed by the Wall, wrapped in plastic and finally brought back from the dead by Norman Foster: 'turbulent history' just doesn't do it when describing the life that the most famous of Berlin's landmarks has endured. This neo-baroque edifice was finished in 1894 to house the German Imperial Diet and served its purpose until 1933 when it was badly damaged by fire in an arson attack carried out by Marinus van der Lubbe, a young Dutch communist. This shocking event conveniently gave Hitler a pretext to tighten his grip on the German state. In 1945 the building was a major target for the Red Army who raised the red flag from the Reichstag, an act that became a symbol of the Soviet defeat of the Nazis.

The Reichstag's dome

WESTEND61/GETTY IMAGES ©

The Cold War Years

Although in West Berlin, the Reichstag found itself very near the dividing line between East and West Berlin and from the early 1960s, the Berlin Wall. With the German government sitting safely in faraway Bonn, this grand facade lost its purpose and in the 1950s some in West Berlin thought it should be demolished. However, the wrecking balls never got their day and the Reichstag was restored, albeit without a lot of the decoration which had adorned the old building.

Reunification & Norman Foster

Almost a year after the Wall came down, the official reunification ceremony was symbolically held at the Reichstag, which, it was later decided, would become the seat of the German Bundestag (parliament) once again. Before Norman Foster began his reconstruction work, the entire Reichstag was spectacularly wrapped in plastic sheeting by the Bulgarian-American artist Christo in the summer of 1995. The following four years saw the erection of Norman Foster's now famous glittering glass cupola, the centrepiece of the visitor experience today. It is the Reichstag's most distinctive feature, serviced by lift and providing fabulous 360-degree city views and the opportunity to peer down into the parliament chamber. To reach the top, follow the ramp spiralling up around the dome's mirror-clad central cone. The cupola was a spanking new feature, but Foster's brief also stipulated that some parts of the building were to be preserved. One example is the Cyrillic graffiti left by Soviet soldiers in 1945.

OLIVER HOFFMANN/GETTY IMAGES ©

Brandenburger Tor

A symbol of division during the Cold War, the landmark Brandenburg Gate now epitomises German reunification and often serves as a picturesque backdrop for festivals and concerts.

Great For...

☑ **Don't Miss**

The north wing of the gate houses a quiet room for peaceful contemplation.

Beginnings

Commissioned by Prussian emperor Friedrich Wilhelm II, architect Carl Gotthard Langhans found inspiration in Athens' Acropolis for this elegant triumphal arch. It was completed in neoclassical sandstone in 1791 as the royal city gate and a suitably regal entrance to the grand avenue that is Unter den Linden, which once led to the palace of the Prussian royals. It is crowned by the Quadriga, Johann Gottfried Schadow's sculpture of the winged goddess of victory piloting a chariot drawn by four horses. After trouncing the Prussians in 1806, Napoleon famously kidnapped Victoria and held her hostage in Paris until she was freed by plucky Prussian general Ernst von Pfuel in 1815.

❶ Need to Know

Map p66; Pariser Platz; ⏱24hr; Ⓢ Brandenburger Tor, Ⓡ Brandenburger Tor; FREE

✕ Take a Break

You will find plenty of cafes to stop at along Unter den Linden.

★ Top Tip

Visit after dark when the gate is lit up in dramatic fashion.

Cold War Divide

The Brandenburg Gate survived the Red Army's 1945 onslaught more or less intact, though it stood in an area decimated by shelling. In a rare example of cooperation between East and West Berlin, both sides contributed to a postwar patch-up job on the structure. However, from the 1960s it became a symbol of a divided city (and continent) as it was located so close to the Berlin Wall on the western side. In the 1970s and '80s visitors could climb to the top to peer into the socialist utopia of East Berlin. On 12 June 1987, it was here that Ronald Reagan addressed his most famous Cold War words to the Soviets when he said: 'Mr Gorbachev – tear down this wall!' Two and a half years later it

wasn't the Russians who took pickaxes to the hated concrete but the East Berliners themselves.

Restoration

In the early years of the new millennium the Brandenburg Gate was restored to its former glory and reopened in 2002 on the 12th anniversary of German reunification. No longer open to traffic (which had actually caused more damage than WWII) the cobbled area around is usually busy with tourists all day long.

Pariser Platz

The Brandenburg Gate, today a symbol of German unity, stands sentinel over Pariser Platz, a harmoniously proportioned square once again framed by banks as well as the US, British and French embassies, just as it was during its 19th-century heyday.

The Berlin Wall

For 28 years the Berlin Wall was the most potent symbol of the Cold War. Surprisingly very few of its reinforced concrete slabs remain in today's reunited Berlin.

Great For...

☑ **Don't Miss**

Other hidden pieces of the Wall still stand in Berlin. Ask the tourist offices about locations.

Construction

Shortly after midnight on 13 August 1961 East German soldiers and police began rolling out miles of barbed wire that would soon be replaced with prefab concrete slabs. The wall was a desperate measure taken by the German Democratic Republic (GDR) government to stop the sustained brain and brawn drain it had experienced since its 1949 founding. Around 3.6 million people had already left for the West, putting the GDR on the verge of economic and political collapse.

Demise

The Wall's demise in 1989 came as unexpectedly as its construction. Once again the GDR was losing its people in droves, this time via Hungary, which had opened its borders with Austria. Something had to

Below: East Side Gallery

ℹ Need to Know

A double row of cobblestones guides you along 5.7km of the Wall's course. Track down remaining fragments of the Wall using Memorial Landscape Berlin Wall (www.berlin-wall-map.com).

✗ Take a Break

Not far from the Gedenkstätte Berliner Mauer is the famous Konnopke's Imbiss (p76).

★ Top Tip

There's a great view from the Documentation Centre's viewing platform.

give. It did on 9 November 1989 when a GDR spokesperson (mistakenly, it later turned out) announced during a press conference that all travel restrictions to the West would be lifted. When asked when, he said simply 'Immediately'. Amid scenes of wild partying, the two Berlins came together again.

In the course of 1990 the Wall almost disappeared from Berlin, some bits smashed up and flogged to tourists, other sections carted off to museums, parks, embassies, exhibitions and even private gardens across the globe. The longest section to survive intact is the East Side Gallery.

Gedenkstätte Berliner Mauer

The outdoor Berlin Wall Memorial extends for 1.4km along Bernauer Strasse and integrates an original section of Wall, vestiges of the border installations and escape tunnels, a chapel and a monument. Multimedia stations, panels, excavations and a Documentation Centre provide context and explain what the border fortifications looked like and how they shaped the everyday lives of people on both sides of it.

East Side Gallery

The year was 1989. After 28 years, the Berlin Wall, that grim and grey divider of humanity, finally met its maker. Most of it was quickly dismantled, but along Mühlenstrasse, paralleling the Spree, a 1.3km stretch became the **East Side Gallery** (Map p65; www.eastsidegallery-berlin.de; Mühlenstrasse, btwn Oberbaumbrücke & Ostbahnhof; ⏰24hr; Ⓢ Warschauer Strasse, ⏹Ostbahnhof, Warschauer Strasse), the world's largest open-air mural collection. In more than 100 paintings, dozens of international artists translated the era's global euphoria and optimism into a mix of political statements, drug-induced musings and truly artistic visions.

The Berlin Wall

The construction of the Berlin Wall was a unique event in human history, not only for physically bisecting a city but by becoming a dividing line between competing ideologies and political systems. It's this global impact and universal legacy that continue to fascinate people more than a quarter century after its triumphant tear-down. Fortunately, plenty of original Wall segments and other vestiges remain, along with museums and memorials, to help fathom the realities and challenges of daily life in Berlin during the Cold War.

Our illustration points out the top highlights you can visit to learn about different aspects of these often tense decades. The best place to start is at the **Gedenkstätte Berliner Mauer** ❶ for an excellent introduction to what the inner-city border actually looked liked and what it meant to live in its shadow. Reflect upon what you've learned while relaxing on the former death strip that is now the **Mauerpark** ❷ before heading to the emotionally charged exhibit at the **Tränenpalast** ❸, an actual border crossing

Brandenburg Gate

People around the world cheered as East and West Berliners partied together atop the Berlin Wall in front of the iconic city gate which today is a photogenic symbol of united Germany.

GERARD MALIE/AFP/GETTY IMAGES ©

Tränenpalast

This modernist 1962 glass-and-steel border pavilion was dubbed 'Palace of Tears' because of the many tearful farewells that took place outside the building as East Germans and their western visitors had to say goodbye.

IMAGEBROKER/ROBERT HARDING ©

JOHN FREEMAN/GETTY IMAGES ©

Potsdamer Platz

Nowhere was the death strip as wide as on the former no-man's-land around Potsdamer Platz from which sprouted a new postmodern city quarter in the 1990s. A tiny section of the Berlin Wall serves as a reminder.

Checkpoint Charlie

Only diplomats and foreigners were allowed to use this border crossing. Weeks after the Wall was built, US and Soviet tanks faced off here in one of the hottest moments of the Cold War.

LONELY PLANET/GETTY IMAGES ©

Bernauer Strasse

Chausseestr

Unter den Linden

Leipziger Str

pavilion. Relive the euphoria of the Wall's demise at the **Brandenburg Gate** ❹, then marvel at the revival of **Potsdamer Platz** ❺ that was nothing but death strip wasteland until the 1990s. The Wall's geopolitical significance is the focus at **Checkpoint Charlie** ❻, which saw some of the tensest moments of the Cold War. Wrap up with finding your favourite mural motif at the **East Side Gallery** ❼.

It's possible to explore these sights by using a combination of walking and public transport, although a bike ride is actually the best method for getting a sense of the former Wall's erratic flow through the central city.

FAST FACTS

» **Beginning of construction:** 13 August 1961
» **Total length:** 155km
» **Height:** 3.6m
» **Weight of each segment:** 2.6 tonnes
» **Number of watchtowers:** 300

remnants of the Wall →

DAVID PEEVERS/GETTY IMAGES ©

Gedenkstätte Berliner Mauer
Germany's central memorial to the Berlin Wall and its victims exposes the complexity and barbaric nature of the border installation along a 1.4km stretch of the barrier's course.

Mauerpark
Famous for its flea market and karaoke, this popular park actually occupies a converted section of death strip. A 30m segment of surviving Wall is now an official practice ground for budding graffiti artists.

JOHN FREEMAN/GETTY IMAGES ©

Alexanderplatz

Alexander Str

East Side Gallery
Paralleling the Spree for 1.3km, this is the longest Wall vestige. After its collapse, more than a hundred international artists expressed their feelings about this historic moment in a series of colourful murals.

MEIN GOTT HILF MIR. DIESE TÖDLICHE LIEBE ZU ÜBERLEBEN

DMITRY VRUBEL ©

Engelbecken

❼

Bodemuseum (p49)

RICOWDE/GETTY IMAGES ©

Museumsinsel

Berlin's Museumsinsel (Museum Island) is a treasure trove of 600,000 years of art, artefacts and architecture spread across five museums. It's a Unesco-listed highlight and essential Berlin viewing.

Great For..

☑ Don't Miss

There are fine views of the Museumsinsel from the upstairs cafe terrace at the Humboldt-Box.

Pergamonmuseum

Opening a fascinating window onto the ancient world, the palatial three-wing complex of the **Pergamonmuseum** (Map p66; ☎030-266 424 242; www.smb.museum; Bodestrasse 1-3; ⊙10am-6pm, to 8pm Thu; adult/concession €12/6; 🚌100, 🚊Hackescher Markt, Friedrichstrasse) unites a rich feast of classical sculpture and monumental architecture from Greece, Rome, Babylon and the Middle East, including the radiant-blue Ishtar Gate from Babylon, the Roman Market Gate of Miletus and the Caliph's Palace of Mshatta. Renovations put the namesake Pergamon Altar off limits until 2019. Budget at least two hours for this amazing place and be sure to pick up the free and excellent audioguide.

The Pergamon unites three major collections, the Antikensammlung (Collection

The Ishtar Gate, Pergamonmuseum

PAOLO CORDELLI/GETTY IMAGES ©

ⓘ Need to Know

If you are planning to visit all five museums the three-day pass (adult/concession €24/12) is a good deal.

✕ Take a Break

Each of the five museums has its own cafe.

★ Top Tip

Buy tickets for the Neues Museum and the Pergamonmuseum online at www.smb.museum.

of Classical Antiquities), the Museum für Islamische Kunst (Museum of Islamic Art) and the Vorderasiatisches Museum (Museum of Near Eastern Antiquities). The temporary entrance first leads you to the last of these, into the world of Babylon during the reign of King Nebuchadnezzar II. It's impossible not to be awed by the reconstructed Ishtar Gate, the Processional Way leading up to it and the facade of the king's throne hall. All are sheathed in glazed bricks glistening in radiant blue and ochre. The strutting lions, horses and dragons, which represent major Babylonian gods, are so striking that you can almost hear the roaring and fanfare.

Another key exhibit on the ground floor is the giant Market Gate of Miletus (2nd century AD). Merchants and customers once flooded through here onto the market square of this Roman trading town (in today's Turkey) that functioned as a link between Asia and Europe.

Aside from the caliph's palace, a major standout upstairs in the Islamic collection is the 17th-century Aleppo Room from the house of a Christian merchant in Syria, with its richly painted, wood-panelled walls. If you look closely, you can make out *The Last Supper* and *Mary and Child* amid all the ornamentation (straight ahead, to the right of the door).

Neues Museum

David Chipperfield's reconstruction of the bombed-out **Neues Museum** (New Museum; Map p66; ☎030-266 424 242; www.smb.muse um; Bodestrasse 1-3; ⊙10am-6pm, to 8pm Thu; adult/concession €12/6; ℝHackescher Markt; ☐100, 200) is now the residence of Queen Nefertiti, the show-stopper of the Egyptian Museum that also features mummies, sculptures and sarcophagi. Pride of place of the Museum of Pre- and Early History in the same building goes to Trojan antiquities, a

Neanderthal skull and the 3000-year-old Berliner Goldhut, a golden conical hat. Skip the queue by buying your timed ticket online.

Altes Museum

A curtain of fluted columns gives way to the Pantheon-inspired rotunda of the grand neoclassical **Altes Museum** (Old Museum; Map p66; ☎030-266 424 242; www.smb.museum; Am Lustgarten; adult/concession €10/5; ☺10am-6pm Tue, Wed & Fri-Sun, to 8pm Thu, closed Mon; 🚌100, 200, 🚊Friedrichstrasse, Hackescher Markt), which harbours a prized antiquities collection. In the downstairs galleries, sculptures, vases, tomb reliefs and jewellery shed light on various facets of life in ancient Greece, while upstairs the focus is on

the Etruscans and Romans. Top draws include the *Praying Boy* bronze sculpture, Roman silver vessels, an 'erotic cabinet' (over 18 only!) and portraits of Caesar and Cleopatra.

Alte Nationalgalerie

The Greek temple-style **Alte National-galerie** (Old National Gallery; Map p66; ☎030-266 424 242; www.smb.museum; Bodestrasse 1-3; adult/concession €10/5; ☺10am-6pm Tue, Wed & Fri-Sun, to 8pm Thu, closed Mon; 🚌100, 200, 🚊Hackescher Markt) is a three-storey showcase of 19th-century European art. To get a sense of the period's virtuosity, pay special attention to the moody landscapes by Romantic heart-throb Caspar David Friedrich, the epic canvases by Franz Krüger and Adolf Men-

Below left: Altes Museum; Below right: Berliner Dom

zel glorifying Prussia, the Gothic fantasies of Karl Friedrich Schinkel, and the sprinkling of French and German impressionists.

Bodemuseum

On the northern tip of Museumsinsel, the **Bodemuseum** (☏030-266 424 242; Map p66; www.smb.museum; cnr Am Kupfergraben & Monbijoubrücke; ⏰10am-6pm Tue, Wed & Fri-Sun, to 8pm Thu, closed Mon; adult/concession €12/6; 🚊Hackescher Markt, Friedrichstrasse) houses a comprehensive collection of European sculpture from the early Middle Ages

★ Coming Soon

British architect David Chipperfield is currently building an underground walkway called the Archaeological Promenade that will link four of the five museums.

JÖRG GREUEL/GETTY IMAGES ©

to the 18th century, including priceless masterpieces by Tilman Riemenschneider, Donatello and Giovanni Pisano. Other rooms harbour a precious coin collection and a smattering of Byzantine art, including sarcophagi and ivory carvings.

Berliner Dom

Pompous yet majestic, an Italian Renaissance–style former royal court church (1905), the **Berliner Dom** (Berlin Cathedral; Map p66; ☏030-2026 9136; www.berliner dom.de; Am Lustgarten; adult/concession/ under 18yr €7/5/free; ⏰9am-8pm Apr-Oct, to 7pm Nov-Mar; 🚌100, 200, 🚊Hackescher Markt) does triple duty as house of worship, museum and concert hall. Inside it's gilt to the hilt and outfitted with a lavish marble-and-onyx altar, a 7269-pipe Sauer organ and elaborate royal sarcophagi. Climb up the 267 steps to the gallery for glorious city views.

Humboldt-Box

A futuristic five-floor structure, the **Humboldt-Box** (Map p66; ☏0180-503 0707; www.humboldt-box.com; Schlossplatz; ⏰10am-7pm Apr-Sep, to 6pm Nov-Mar; 🚌100, 200, Ⓢ Hausvogteiplatz) 🆓 opens up a window on the Berlin City Palace, to be called 'Humboldt-Forum', whose reconstruction has been underway since 2013. On display are interactive teasers from each future resident – the Ethnological Museum, the Museum of Asian Art and the Central Library – along with a fantastically detailed model of the historic city centre.

★ Did You Know?

Museumsinsel is the product of a late 19th-century fad among European royalty to open their private collections to the public. The Louvre in Paris and the British Museum in London all date back to this period. In Berlin, King Friedrich Wilhelm III and his successors followed suit.

Museumsinsel

Navigating around this five-museum treasure repository can be a little daunting, so we've put together this itinerary to help you find the must-see highlights while maximising your time and energy. You'll need a minimum of four hours and an 'area ticket' for entry to all museums.

Start in the Altes Museum by admiring the roll call of antique gods guarded by a perky bronze statue called the **Praying Boy ❶**, the poster child of a prized collection of antiquities. Next up, head to the Neues Museum for your audience with **Queen Nefertiti ❷**, the star of the Egyptian collection atop the grand central staircase. One more floor up, don't miss the dazzling Bronze Age **Berliner Goldhut ❸** (room 305). Leaving the Neues Museum, turn left for the Pergamonmuseum. With the namesake altar off limits until 2019, the first major sight you'll see is the **Ishtar Gate ❹**. Upstairs, pick your way through the Islamic collection, past carpets, prayer niches and a caliph's palace to the intricately painted **Aleppo Room ❺**. Jump ahead to the 19th century at the Alte Nationalgalerie to zero in on paintings by **Caspar David Friedrich ❻** on the 3rd floor and precious sculptures such as Schadow's **Statue of Two Princesses ❼** on the ground floor. Wrap up your explorations at the Bodemuseum, reached in a five-minute walk. Admire the foyer with its equestrian statue of Friedrich Wilhelm, then feast your eyes on European sculpture without missing masterpieces by **Tilman Riemenschneider ❽** in room 212.

FAST FACTS

» **Oldest object:** 700,000-year-old Paleolithic hand axe at Neues Museum

» **Newest object:** piece of barbed wire from Berlin Wall at Neues Museum

» **Oldest museum:** Altes Museum, 1830

» **Most popular museum in Germany:** Pergamonmuseum (1.26 million visitors)

» **Total Museumsinsel visitors (2013):** 2.92 million

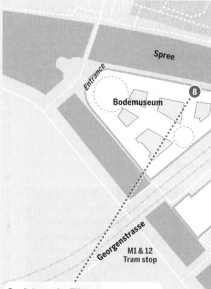

Sculptures by Tilman Riemenschneider (Room 212, Bodemuseum)

Dazzling detail and great emotional expressiveness characterise the wooden sculptures by late-Gothic master carver Tilman Riemenschneider as in this portrayal of *St Anne and Her Three Husbands* from around 1510.

Bust of Queen Nefertiti (Room 210, Neues Museum)

In the north dome, fall in love with Berlin's most beautiful woman, the 3330-year-old Egyptian queen Nefertiti, she of the long graceful neck and timeless good looks – despite the odd wrinkle and missing eye.

Aleppo Room
(Room 16, Pergamonmuseum)
A highlight of the Museum of Islamic Art, this richly painted, wood-panelled reception room from a Christian merchant's home in 17th-century Aleppo, Syria, combines Islamic floral and geometric motifs with courtly scenes and Christian themes.

Ishtar Gate
(Room 9, Pergamonmuseum)
Draw breath as you enter the 2600-year-old city gate to Babylon with soaring walls sheathed in radiant blue glazed bricks and adorned with ochre reliefs of strutting lions, bulls and dragons representing Babylonian gods.

Pergamonmuseum

Spree

Alte Nationalgalerie

Neues Museum

Bodestraße

Paintings by Caspar David Friedrich
(Top Floor, Alte Nationalgalerie)
A key artist of the romantic period, Caspar David Friedrich put his own stamp on landscape painting with his dark, moody and subtly dramatic meditations on the boundaries of human life vs the infinity of nature.

Statue of Two Princesses
(Ground Floor, Alte Nationalgalerie)
Johann Gottfried Schadow captures Prussian princesses (and sisters) Luise and Friederike in a moment of intimacy and thoughtfulness in this double marble statue created in 1795 at the height of the neoclassical period.

Altes Museum

Berliner Dom

Lustgarten

Berliner Goldhut
(Room 305, Neues Museum)
Marvel at the Bronze Age artistry of the Berlin Gold Hat, a ceremonial gold cone embossed with ornamental bands believed to have been used in predicting the best times for planting and harvesting.

Praying Boy
(Room 5, Altes Museum)
The top draw at the Old Museum is the *Praying Boy*, ancient Greece's 'Next Top Model'. The life-size bronze statue of a young male nude is the epitome of physical perfection and was cast around 300 BC in Rhodes.

Schloss Charlottenburg

This exquisite baroque pile is the finest of Berlin's nine remaining royal palaces. Inspired by Versailles, it backs up against an idyllic park, complete with carp pond, rhododendron-lined paths, two smaller palaces and a mausoleum.

Great For...

❶ Need to Know

Map p72; 📞030-320 910; www.spsg.de; Spandauer Damm 10-22; day pass to all 4 buildings adult/concession €17/13; ⏱hours vary by building; 🚌M45, 109, 309, Ⓢ Richard-Wagner-Platz, Sophie-Charlotte-Platz

★ **Top Tip**

Each palace charges separate admission but a day pass called Ticket charlottenburg+ (adult/concession €17/13) is available.

We can pretty much guarantee that your camera will have a love affair with this late-baroque jewel. The palace itself is clad in a subtle yellow typical of the royal Hohenzollern family and wonderfully adorned with slender columns and geometrically arranged windows. An ornate copper-domed tower overlooks the forecourt and the imposing equestrian statue of the Great Elector Friedrich Wilhelm. There's a lot to see here so allow at least three hours.

Altes Schloss

Also known as the Nering-Eosander Building after its two architects, the Altes Schloss is the central, and oldest, section of the palace and fronted by Andreas Schlüter's grand equestrian statue of the Great Elector (1699). Inside, the baroque living quarters of Friedrich I and Sophie-Charlotte are an

extravaganza in stucco, brocade and overall opulence. Highlights include the Oak Gallery, a wood-panelled festival hall draped in family portraits; the charming Oval Hall overlooking the park; Friedrich I's bedchamber, with the first-ever proper bathroom in a baroque palace; and the Eosander Chapel, with its *trompe l'œil* arches. The king's passion for priceless china is reflected in the dazzling Porcelain Chamber, which is weighed down with almost 3000 pieces of exquisite Chinese and Japanese blueware. Upstairs you will find paintings, vases, tapestries, weapons, porcelain, a 2600-piece silver table setting and many other items the Prussian royals found essential for their lifestyle.

Neuer Flügel

Arguably the most beautiful rooms at Charlottenburg are located in the Neuer Flügel

Schloss Charlottenburg

(New Wing). The flamboyant private chambers of King Friedrich II (Frederick the Great) were designed in 1746 by the period's star architect Georg Wenzeslaus von Knobelsdorff. Standouts include the confection-like White Hall banquet room, the mirrored Golden Gallery and paintings by Watteau, Pesne and other 18th-century French masters. In the same wing, the apartments of Queen Luise (1776–1810), wife of King Friedrich Wilhelm III, have lavish chandeliers and hand-painted silk wall coverings.

Neuer Pavilion

Returning from a trip to Italy, Friedrich Wilhelm III (r 1797–1848) commissioned Karl

Friedrich Schinkel to design this petite summer refuge modelled on a villa in Naples. Today, the minipalace is a sparkling backdrop for masterpieces by such Schinkel-era painters as Caspar David Friedrich and Eduard Gaertner as well as by the sculptor Christian Daniel Rauch. Ground-floor rooms brim with original Biedermeier furniture.

Schlossgarten

The expansive park behind Schloss Charlottenburg is part formal French, part unruly English and all idyllic playground. Hidden among the shady paths, flower beds, lawns, mature trees and carp pond are two smaller royal buildings, the sombre Mausoleum and the charming Belvedere. It's a fantastic place for strolling, jogging or lazing on a sunny afternoon. In the summer months take a picnic to enjoy on the grass.

Belvedere

This pint-size palace with the distinctive cupola got its start in 1788 as a teahouse for Friedrich Wilhelm II. Here he enjoyed reading, listening to chamber music and holding spiritual sessions with fellow members of the mystical Order of the Rosicrucians. These days, the late-rococo vision by Carl Gotthard Langhans makes an elegant backdrop for porcelain masterpieces by the royal manufacturer KPM.

Mausoleum

West of the carp pond, the neoclassical Mausoleum (1810) was conceived as the final resting place of Queen Luise but twice expanded to make room for other royals, including Luise's husband Friedrich Wilhelm III and Emperor William I and his wife Augusta. Their ornate marble sarcophagi are great works of art.

> ☑ **Don't Miss**
> Combine a visit to the palace with a spin round the local museums.

PRUSSIAN PALACES AND GARDENS FOUNDATION BERLIN-BRANDENBURG/HANS BACH/FOTOTHEK ©

> ✕ **Take a Break**
> **Kleine Orangerie** (Map p72; www.kleine-orangerie.de; mains €6-15) is located near the entrance to the palace park.

SVEIN NORDRUM/GETTY IMAGES ©

Holocaust Memorial

A short stroll from the Branden-burg Gate, this vast memorial to Europe's Jews who were murdered by the Nazis leaves few untouched. The design, hundreds of concrete columns rising from the ground, creates an unforgettable effect.

Great For...

☑ Don't Miss

Worthwhile audioguides are available from the Ort der Information.

Inaugurated in 2005, this football-field-sized memorial (the official name is the Memorial to the Murdered Jews of Europe) by American architect Peter Eisenman consists of 2711 sarcophagi-like concrete columns rising in sombre, intimidating silence from 19,000 sq metres of undulating ground. The memorial has no designated entrance or exit – you're free to access this maze at any point and make your individual journey through it. The design is purposefully disorientating, the columns meandering in slightly different heights than those around them and the walkways creating a claustrophobic effect. At busy times many can be seen sitting on the smaller blocks in contemplation of its meaning. Some have criticised the memorial for not including others murdered by the Nazis such as homosexuals and Roma, though other memorials have been built to these groups.

SVEIN NORDRUM/GETTY IMAGES ©

❶ Need to Know

Memorial to the Murdered Jews of Europe; Map p66; www.stiftung-denkmal.de; Cora-Berlin-er-Strasse 1; audioguide adult/concession €4/2; ⏱field 24hr, information centre 10am-8pm Tue-Sun Apr-Sep, to 7pm Oct-Mar, last entry 45min before closing; **S** Brandenburger Tor, **R** Brandenburger Tor; FREE

✕ Take a Break

The Roof (Map p66; www.welovecoffee.de) is a good spot to enjoy coffee and a light meal. The terrace has views over the memorial.

★ Top Tip

Visit after dark when the columns are dramatically uplit.

Conception & Construction

A holocaust memorial was a long time in the making, the idea having been put forward in the 1980s. It wasn't until 1994 that a competition for the design was launched, the winning artist to receive a budget of €25 million. The two shortlisted designs were eventually vetoed by Chancellor Kohl and a new competition was announced in 1996. The next year Peter Eisenman's design was announced as winner though the original plan had 4,000 pillars. Construction began in 2003 and was opened to the public in May 2005.

Ort der Information

For context visit the subterranean Ort der Information (Information Centre) whose exhibits are thought-provoking at the very least. The entrance is on the eastern side of the memorial, near Cora-Berliner-Strasse.

What's Nearby?

An irony that few can ignore is that Hitler's bunker (Führerbunker; Map p66) is located a short walk southeast of the Holocaust Memorial. As Berlin burnt and Soviet tanks advanced relentlessly towards the city centre, it was here that Adolf Hitler committed suicide on 30 April 1945, alongside Eva Braun, his long-time female companion, hours after their marriage. The bodies were never found. Today, a modern parking lot just off Gertrud-Kolmar-Strasse covers the site, revealing its dark history only via an information panel with a diagram of the vast bunker network, construction data and the site's post-WWII history.

Summer evening on the Spree River

MAREMAGNUM/GETTY IMAGES ©

Berlin Nightlife

With its well-deserved reputation as one of Europe's primo party capitals, Berlin offers a thousand and one scenarios for getting your cocktails and kicks (or wine or beer, for that matter).

Great For...

☑ Don't Miss

Café am Neuen See (p77) is generally regarded as Berlin's best beer garden.

Bars & Cafes

Berlin is a notoriously late city: bars stay packed from dusk to dawn and beyond, and some clubs don't hit their stride until 4am. The lack of a curfew never created a tradition of binge drinking.

Edgier, more underground venues cluster in Kreuzberg, Friedrichshain, Neukölln and up-and-coming outer boroughs like Wedding (north of Mitte) and Lichtenberg (past Friedrichshain). Places in Charlottenburg, Mitte and Prenzlauer Berg tend to be quieter and close earlier. Some proprietors have gone to extraordinary lengths to come up with special design concepts.

The line between cafe and bar is often blurred, with many changing stripes as

nuts and with cold beer and bratwurst on the menu. In 2002, Berlin also jumped on the 'sandwagon' with the opening of its first beach bar, Strandbar Mitte (p77), in a prime location on the Spree River. Many that followed have since been displaced by development, which has partly fuelled the latest trend: rooftop bars.

the hands move around the clock. Alcohol, however, is served pretty much all day. Cocktail bars are booming in Berlin and several new arrivals have measurably elevated the 'liquid art' scene. Dedicated drinking dens tend to be elegant cocoons with mellow lighting and low sound levels. A good cocktail will set you back between €10 and €15.

Beaches & Outdoor Drinking

Berliners are sun cravers and as soon as the first rays spray their way into spring, outdoor tables show up faster than you can pour a pint of beer. The most traditional places for outdoor chilling are, of course, the beer gardens with long wooden benches set up beneath leafy old chest-

Clubbing

Over the past 25 years, Berlin's club culture has put the city firmly on the map of hedonists. With more than 200 venues, finding one to match your mood isn't difficult. Electronic music in its infinite varieties continues to define Berlin's after-dark action but other sounds like hip-hop, dancehall, rock, swing and funk have also made inroads. The edgiest clubs have taken up residence in power plants, transformer stations, abandoned apartment buildings and other repurposed locations. The scene is in constant flux as experienced club owners look for new challenges and a younger generation of promoters enters the scene with new ideas and impetus.

Christmas market, Gendarmenmarkt (p64)

Walking Tour: Historical Highlights

This walk checks off Berlin's blockbuster landmarks as it cuts right through the historic city centre, Mitte (literally 'Middle'). This is the birthplace and glamorous heart of Berlin, a high-octane cocktail of culture, architecture and commerce.

Distance: 3.5km
Duration: 3 hours

Take a Break

Cafe Einstein (Map p66; www.einstein-udl.de; Unter den Linden 42; mains €9-18; 7am-10pm) **makes for an arty pit stop. Wrap up the tour at Brauhaus Georgbräu** (Map p66; 030-242 4244; www.georgbraeu.de; Spreeufer 4; mains €10-14; noon-midnight; S Klosterstrasse) **in the Nikolaiviertel.**

Start Reichstag

1 Reichstag

The 1894 **Reichstag** (p7) is the historic anchor of Berlin's federal government quarter. The sparkling glass dome, added during the building's 1990s revamp, has become a shining beacon of unified Berlin.

2 Brandenburg Gate

The only remaining gate of Berlin's 18th-century town wall, the **Brandenburger Tor** (p11) became an involuntary neighbour of the Berlin Wall during the Cold War. It's now a cheery symbol of German reunification.

3 Unter den Linden

Originally a riding path linking the city palace with the royal hunting grounds in Tiergarten, **Unter den Linden** has been Berlin's showpiece road since the 18th century but is partly torn up thanks to the construction of a new U-Bahn line.

4 Gendarmenmarkt

Berlin's most beautiful square, **Gendarmenmarkt** (p64) is bookended by domed cathedrals with the famous

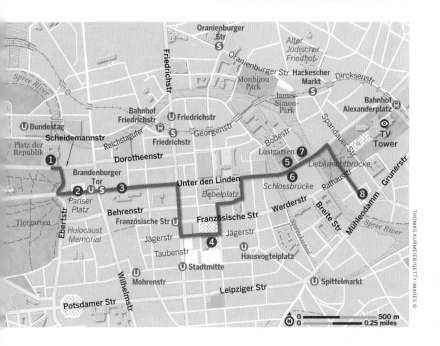

Konzerthaus (Concert Hall) in between. The surrounding streets are lined with elegant hotels, restaurants and cocktail bars.

⑤ Museum Island

The sculpture-studded Palace Bridge leads to the twee Spree island whose northern half, **Museumsinsel** (p46), is a Unesco-recognised treasure chest of art, sculpture and objects spread across five grand museums.

⑥ Humboldt-Forum

Opposite Museum Island, the massive **Humboldt-Forum** is taking shape. Its facade will mimic the old Prussian city palace; its modern interior will house museums and a library. Details at the Humboldt-Box (p49).

⑦ Berliner Dom

Pompous and majestic inside and out, the **Berlin Cathedral** (p49) is a symbol of Prussian imperial power and blessed with artistic treasures, royal sarcophagi and nice views from the gallery.

⑧ Nikolaiviertel

With its cobbled lanes and higgledy-piggledy houses, the **Nikolai Quarter** may look medieval but was actually built to celebrate Berlin's 750th birthday in 1987.

Finish Nikolai Quarter

Tiergarten

Walking Tour: A Leisurely Tiergarten Saunter

Take pleasure in getting lost amid the lawns, trees and paths of one of the world's largest city parks. A ramble around Tiergarten also delivers a relaxing respite from the sightseeing track.

Distance: 4km
Duration: 1½ to two hours

✗ Take a Break

At Café am Neuen See (p77), a lakeside beer garden in the southwest of the park, cold beers go well with bratwursts, pretzels and pizza.

Start Strasse des 17 Juni

❶ Strasse des 17 Juni

The broad boulevard bisecting Tiergarten was named **Street of 17 June** in honour of the victims of the bloodily quashed 1953 workers' uprising in East Berlin. Back in the 16th century, the road linked two royal palaces; it was doubled in width and turned into a swastika-lined triumphal road under Hitler.

❷ Sowjetisches Ehrenmal

Near the Brandenburg Gate end of the park, the **Soviet War Memorial** is flanked by two Russian T-34 tanks said to have been the first to enter the city in 1945. It was built by German workers on order of the Soviets and completed just months after the end of the war. More than 2000 Red Army soldiers are buried behind the colonnade.

❸ Schloss Bellevue

A succession of German presidents have made their home in snowy white **Bellevue Palace**. The neoclassical pile was originally a pad for the youngest brother of King Frederick the Great, then became a school under Kaiser Wilhelm II and a museum of ethnology under the Nazis. It's closed to the public.

JINX JINX/GETTY IMAGES ©

4 Siegessäule

Engulfed by roundabout traffic, the 1873 **Victory Column** was erected to celebrate Prussian military victories and is now a prominent symbol of Berlin's gay community. What would Bismarck think of that? The gilded woman on top represents the goddess of victory and is featured prominently in the Wim Wenders movie *Wings of Desire*. Climb to the top to appreciate the park's dimensions.

5 Rousseauinsel

One of Tiergarten's most idyllic spots is the **Rousseauinsel**, a teensy island in a placid pond that's a memorial to 18th-century French philosopher Jean-Jacques Rousseau. It was designed to resemble his actual burial site on an island near Paris. Just look for the stone pillar.

6 Luiseninsel

Another enchanting place, **Luiseninsel** is a tranquil gated garden brimming with statues and redolent with seasonal flower beds. It was created after Napoleon's occupying troops left town in 1808 in celebration of the return from exile of the royal couple Friedrich Wilhelm III and Queen Luise.

Finish Luiseninsel

⊙ SIGHTS

⊙ Unter den Linden

Deutsches Historisches Museum   Museum
This engaging museum covers 1500 years of German history in all its gore and glory – not in a nutshell, but on two floors of a Prussian-era armoury. Check out the Nazi globe, the pain-wrecked faces of dying warrior sculptures in the courtyard, and the temporary exhibits in the boldly modern annexe designed by IM Pei. (Map p66; 🖉030-203 040; www.dhm.de; Unter den Linden 2; adult/concession/under 18 yr €8/4/free; ⊙10am-6pm; 🚌100, 200, ⑤Hausvogteiplatz, 🚃Hackescher Markt)

Bebelplatz   Square, Memorial
In 1933, books by Brecht, Mann, Marx and other 'subversives' went up in flames on this treeless square during the first full-blown public book burning, staged by the Nazi German Student League. Named for August Bebel, the co-founder of Germany's Social Democratic Party (SPD), the square was first laid out in the 18th century under Frederick the Great. (Map p66; 🚌100, 200, TXL, ⑤Hausvogteiplatz)

⊙ Friedrichstrasse

Checkpoint Charlie   Historic Site
Checkpoint Charlie was the principal gateway for foreigners and diplomats between the two Berlins from 1961 to 1990. The only direct Cold War–era confrontation between the US and the Soviet Union took place right here when tanks faced off shortly after the Wall went up, nearly triggering a third world war. Alas, this potent symbol of the Cold War has degenerated into a tacky tourist trap, although the free open-air exhibit illustrating Cold War milestones is one redeeming aspect. (Map p71; cnr Zimmerstrasse & Friedrichstrasse; ⊙24hr; ⑤Kochstrasse, Stadtmitte)

Mauermuseum   Museum
The Cold War years, especially the history and horror of the Berlin Wall, are engagingly, if haphazardly, documented in this privately run tourist magnet. Open since 1961, the ageing exhibit is still strong when it comes to telling the stories of escape attempts to the West. Original devices used in the process, including a hot-air balloon, a one-person submarine and a BMW Isetta, are crowd favourites. (Haus am Checkpoint Charlie; Map p66; 🖉030-253 7250; www.mauermuseum.de; Friedrichstrasse 43-45; adult/concession €12.50/9.50, audioguide €3.50; ⊙9am-10pm; ⑤Kochstrasse)

Gendarmenmarkt   Square
Berlin's most graceful square is bookended by the domed 18th-century German and French cathedrals and punctuated by a grandly porticoed concert hall, the Konzerthaus. It was named for the Gens d'Armes, an 18th-century Prussian regiment consisting of French Huguenot immigrants whose story is chronicled in a museum inside the French cathedral. Climb the tower here for grand views of historic Berlin. (Map p66; ⑤Französische Strasse, Stadtmitte)

⊙ Scheunenviertel

Hackesche Höfe   Historic Site
The Hackesche Höfe is the largest and most famous of the courtyard ensembles peppered throughout the Scheunenviertel. Built in 1907, the eight interlinked Höfe reopened in 1996 with a congenial mix of cafes, galleries, boutiques and entertainment venues. The main entrance on Rosenthaler Strasse leads to Court I, prettily festooned with art nouveau tiles, while Court VII segues to the romantic Rosenhöfe with a sunken rose garden and tendril-like balustrades. (Map p66; 🖉030-2809 8010; www.hackesche-hoefe.com; enter from Rosenthaler Strasse 40/41 or Sophienstrasse 6; ⑤Weinmeisterstrasse, 🚃M1, 🚃Hackescher Markt) FREE

Neue Synagoge   Synagogue
The Neue Synagoge's gleaming gold dome is the most visible symbol of Berlin's revitalised Jewish community. The 1866 original was Germany's largest synagogue but its modern incarnation is not so much a house of worship (although prayer services do take place), as a museum and place of remem-

Friedrichshain

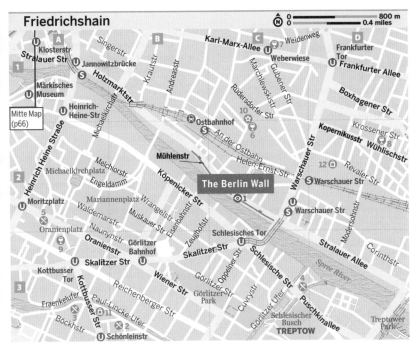

Friedrichshain

brance called Centrum Judaicum. The dome can be climbed (adult/concession €3/2.50). (Map p66; ☏030-8802 8300; www.centrumjudaicum.de; Oranienburger Strasse 28-30; adult/concession €5/4; ☉10am-6pm Mon-Fri, 10am-7pm Sun, closes 3pm Fri & 6pm Sun Oct-Mar; ⒮Oranienburger Tor, ☒Oranienburger Strasse)

Museum für Naturkunde   Museum
Fossils and minerals don't quicken your pulse? Well, how about the world's largest mounted dino skeleton? The 13m-high

Brachiosaurus branchai is joined by a dozen other Jurassic buddies, some of which are brought to virtual flesh-and-bone life with the help of clever 'Juraskopes'. Other crowd favourites include Knut, the world's most famous dead polar bear, and an ultrarare *Archaeopteryx*. (Museum of Natural History; Map p66; ☏030-2093 8591; www.naturkundemuseum-berlin.de; Invalidenstrasse 43; adult/concession incl audioguide €6/3.50; ☉9.30am-6pm Tue-Fri, 10am-6pm Sat & Sun; ⒮Naturkundemuseum)

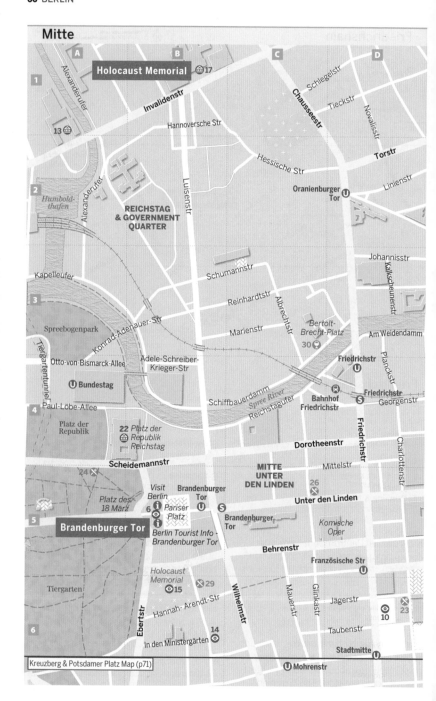

Mitte

Alexanderufer

Holocaust Memorial 🏛17

Invalidenstr

Schlegelstr

Tieckstr

Chausseestr

Novalisstr

Hannoversche Str

1

13 🏛

Hessische Str

Torstr

Humbold-thafen

Alexanderufer

Luisenstr

**REICHSTAG
& GOVERNMENT
QUARTER**

Oranienburger
Tor Ⓤ

Linienstr

2

Kapelleufer

Schumannstr

Johannisstr

Kalkscheunenstr

Reinhardtstr

Albrechtstr

Tiergartentunnel

Spreebogenpark

Konrad-Adenauer-Str

Marienstr

*Bertolt-
Brecht-Platz*

Am Weidendamm

3

Otto-von-Bismarck-Allee

Adele-Schreiber-
Krieger-Str

30 ⊘

Friedrichstr
Ⓤ

Planckstr

Ⓤ **Bundestag**

Schiffbauerdamm

Spree River

Reichstagufer

Ⓡ
**Bahnhof
Friedrichstr**

Ⓢ

Friedrichstr
Georgenstr

Paul-Löbe-Allee

Platz der
Republik

22 *Platz der
🏛 Republik
Reichstag*

Dorotheenstr

Friedrichstr

Charlottenstr

4

Scheidemannstr

**MITTE
UNTER
DEN LINDEN**

Mittelstr

24 ⊗

*Platz des
18 März*

*Visit
Berlin* ℹ

🏛
ℹ

*Pariser
Platz*

**Brandenburger
Tor**

Ⓤ Ⓢ

**Brandenburger
Tor**

26
⊗

Unter den Linden

*Komische
Oper*

5

Brandenburger Tor

*Berlin Tourist Info -
Brandenburger Tor*

Behrenstr

Französische Str
Ⓤ

*Holocaust
Memorial*
⊙15

⊗29

Mauerstr

Glinkastr

Jägerstr

⊙
10

⊗
23

Tiergarten

Ebertstr

Hannah-Arendt-Str

Wilhelmstr

Taubenstr

14 ⊙

In den Ministergärten

Stadtmitte
Ⓤ

6

Kreuzberg & Potsdamer Platz Map (p71)

Ⓤ **Mohrenstr**

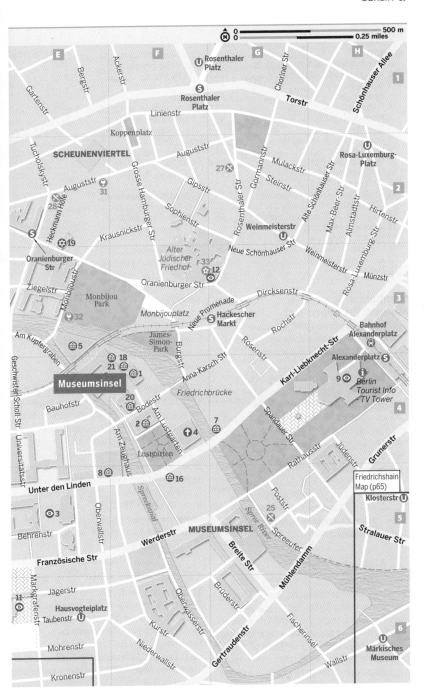

Mitte

Hamburger Bahnhof – Museum für Gegenwart Museum

Berlin's contemporary art showcase opened in 1996 in an old railway station, whose loft and grandeur are a great backdrop for this Aladdin's cave of paintings, installations, sculptures and video art. Changing exhibits span the arc of post-1950 artistic movements – from conceptual art and pop art to minimal art and Fluxus – and include seminal works by such major players as Andy Warhol, Cy Twombly, Joseph Beuys and Robert Raus-chenberg. (Map p66; ☏030-266 424 242; www.hamburgerbahnhof.de; Invalidenstrasse 50-51; adult/concession €10/5; ⊗10am-6pm Tue, Wed & Fri, 10am-8pm Thu, 11am-6pm Sat & Sun; ⑤Hauptbahnhof, Naturkundemuseum, ⑭Hauptbahnhof)

◎ Alexanderplatz

Fernsehturm Landmark

Germany's tallest structure, the TV Tower has been soaring 368m high since 1969 and is as iconic to Berlin as the Eiffel Tower is to Paris. Views are stunning on clear days from the panorama level at 203m or the upstairs restaurant, which makes one revo-lution per hour. To skip the line, buy a timed

ticket (called a 'Fast View') online. (TV Tower; Map p66; ☏030-247 575 875; www.tv-turm.de; Panoramastrasse 1a; adult/child €13/8.50, timed ticket €19.50/12; ⊗9am-midnight Mar-Oct, 10am-midnight Nov-Feb; ⑤Alexanderplatz, ⑭Alexanderplatz)

DDR Museum Museum

This interactive museum does an enter-taining job at pulling back the iron curtain on an extinct society. You'll learn how, under socialism, kids were put through collective potty training, engineers earned little more than farmers, and everyone, it seems, went on nudist holidays. A highlight is a simulated ride in a Trabi. (GDR Museum; Map p66; ☏030-847 123 731; www.ddr-museum. de; Karl-Liebknecht-Strasse 1; adult/concession €7/4; ⊗10am-8pm, to 10pm Sat; ⑭; ⑭100, 200, ⑭Hackescher Markt)

◎ Potsdamer Platz & Tiergarten

This new quarter, forged from ground once bisected by the Berlin Wall, is a showcase of fabulous contemporary architecture. Art lovers should not skip the nearby Kultur-forum museums (p75) next to the world-class Berliner Philharmonie. The leafy Tiergarten park, with its rambling paths and beer gardens, makes for a perfect sightseeing break. Catch Europe's fastest lift, **Panoramapunkt** (Map p71; www.panoramapunkt. de; Potsdamer Platz 1; adult/concession €6.50/5, without wait €10.50/8; ۞10am-8pm Apr-Oct, to 6pm Nov-Mar, last entry 30min before closing), for top views of the eastern city.

Gemäldegalerie
Gallery

The principal Kulturforum museum boasts one of the world's finest and most comprehensive collections of European art from the 13th to the 18th centuries. Wear comfy shoes when exploring the 72 galleries: a walk past masterpieces by Rembrandt, Dürer, Hals, Vermeer, Gainsborough and many more Old Masters covers almost 2km. (Gallery of Old Masters; Map p71; ✆030-266 424 242; www.smb.museum/gg; Matthäikirchplatz 8; adult/concession €10/5; ۞10am-6pm Tue, Wed & Fri, 10am-8pm Thu, 11am-6pm Sat & Sun; ▣M29, M41, 200, ⓢPotsdamer Platz, ▨Potsdamer Platz)

Topographie des Terrors
Museum

In the same spot where once stood the most feared institutions of Nazi Germany (including the Gestapo headquarters and the SS central command), this compelling exhibit chronicles the stages of terror and persecution, puts a face on the perpetrators and details the impact these brutal institutions had on all of Europe. A second exhibit outside looks at how life changed for Berlin and its people after the Nazis made it their capital. (Topography of Terror; Map p66; ✆030-2548 0950; www.topographie.de; Niederkirchner Strasse 8; ۞10am-8pm, grounds close at dusk or 8pm at latest; ♿; ⓢPotsdamer Platz, ▨Potsdamer Platz) FREE

Bauhaus Archiv
Museum

Founded in 1919, the Bauhaus was a seminal school of avant-garde architecture, design and art. This avant-garde building, designed by its founder Walter Gropius, presents paintings, drawings, sculptures, models and other objects and documents by such famous artist-teachers as Klee, Feininger and Kandinsky. There's a good cafe and gift shop. A building expansion is planned to open in 2019. (Map p71; ✆030-254 0020; www.bauhaus.de; Klingelhöferstrasse 14; adult/concession incl audioguide Wed-Fri €7/4, Sat-Mon €8/5; ۞10am-5pm Wed-Mon; ▣100, ⓢNollendorfplatz)

Tiergarten
Park

Berlin's rulers used to hunt boar and pheasants in the rambling Tiergarten until garden architect Peter Lenné landscaped the grounds in the 18th century. Today, one of the world's largest urban parks is popular for strolling, jogging, picnicking, Frisbee tossing and, yes, nude sunbathing and gay cruising (especially around the Löwenbrücke). It is bisected by a major artery, the Strasse des 17 Juni. Walking across the entire park takes about an hour, but even a shorter stroll has its rewards, or follow our walking tour (p62). (▣100, 200, ⓢBrandenburger Tor, ▨Potsdamer Platz, Brandenburger Tor) FREE

◉ Kreuzberg

Kreuzberg gets its street cred from being delightfully edgy, bipolar, wacky and, most of all, unpredictable. While the western half around Bergmannstrasse has an upmarket, genteel air, eastern Kreuzberg (still nicknamed SO36 after its pre-reunification postal code) is a multicultural mosaic, a bubbly hodgepodge of tousled students, aspiring creatives, shisha-smoking Turks and Arabs, and international life artists.

Jüdisches Museum
Museum

In a landmark building by American-Polish architect Daniel Libeskind, Berlin's Jewish Museum offers a chronicle of the trials and triumphs in 2000 years of Jewish life in Germany. The exhibit smoothly navigates all major periods, from the Middle Ages via the Enlightenment to the community's post-1990 renaissance. Find out about Jewish cultural contributions, holiday traditions, the difficult road to emancipation and outstanding individuals (eg Moses Mendelssohn, Levi Strauss) and the fates of ordinary people. (Jewish Museum; Map p71;

030-2599 3300; www.jmberlin.de; Linden-strasse 9-14; adult/concession €8/3, audioguide €3; ☉10am-8pm, to 10pm Mon, last entry 1hr before closing; ⑤Hallesches Tor, Kochstrasse)

Deutsches Technikmuseum
Museum

A roof-mounted 'candy bomber' (the plane used in the 1948 Berlin Airlift) is merely the overture to this enormous and hugely engaging shrine to technology. Standouts among the exhibits are the world's first computer, an entire hall of vintage locomotives and extensive exhibits on aerospace and navigation. At the adjacent Science Center Spectrum (enter Möckernstrasse 26, same ticket) kids can participate in hands-on experiments. (Map p71; German Museum of Technology; 030-902 540; www.sdtb.de; Trebbiner Strasse 9; adult/concession/under 18yr €8/4/free, after 3pm free, audioguide €2/1; ☉9am-5.30pm Tue-Fri, 10am-6pm Sat & Sun; ♿; ⑤Gleisdreieck, Möckernbrücke)

◉ Friedrichshain

There are few standout sights, but the web of boutique- and cafe-lined streets around Boxhagener Platz will happily repay those who simply wander and soak up the district's unique character. After dark, Friedrichshain morphs into a hugely popular bar-stumbling and high-energy party zone. There's also the East Side Gallery (p43), a 1.3km stretch of the Berlin Wall that is now the world's largest open-air mural collection.

◉ Prenzlauer Berg

Prenzlauer Berg went from rags to riches after reunification to emerge as one of Berlin's most desirable residential neighbourhoods. Its ample charms are best experienced on a leisurely meander.

Mauerpark
Park

With its wimpy trees and anaemic lawn, Mauerpark is hardly your typical leafy oasis, especially given that it was forged from a section of Cold War–era death strip (a short stretch of Berlin Wall survives).

It's this mystique combined with an unassuming vibe and a hugely popular Sunday flea market and karaoke show that has endeared the place to locals and visitors alike. (www.mauerpark.info; btwn Bernauer Strasse, Schwedter Strasse & Gleimstrasse; ⑤Eberswalder Strasse, M1)

◉ Charlottenburg

The glittering heart of West Berlin during the Cold War, Charlottenburg has been eclipsed by historic Mitte and other eastern districts since reunification, but is now trying hard to stage a comeback with major construction and redevelopment around Zoo station. Its main artery is the 3.5km-long Kurfürstendamm (Ku'damm for short), Berlin's busiest shopping strip.

Kaiser-Wilhelm-Gedächtniskirche
Church

The bombed-out tower of this landmark church, consecrated in 1895, serves as an antiwar memorial, standing quiet and dignified amid the roaring traffic. The adjacent octagonal hall of worship, added in 1961, has amazing midnight-blue glass walls and a giant 'floating' Jesus. (Kaiser Wilhelm Memorial Church; Map p72; 030-218 5023; www.gedaechtniskirche.com; Breitscheidplatz; ☉church 9am-7pm, memorial hall 10am-6pm Mon-Fri, 10am-5.30pm Sat, noon-5.30pm Sun; ⚐100, ⑤Zoologischer Garten, Kurfürstendamm, ⯬Zoologischer Garten)

Zoo Berlin
Zoo

Berlin's zoo holds a triple record as Germany's oldest, most species-rich and most popular animal park. It was established in 1844 under King Friedrich Wilhelm IV, who not only donated the land but also pheasants and other animals from the royal family's private reserve on the Pfaueninsel. The menagerie includes 20,000 critters representing 1500 species, including orangutans, koalas, rhinos, giraffes and penguins. (Map p72; 030-254 010; www.zoo-berlin.de; Hardenbergplatz 8; adult/child €13/6.50, with aquarium €20/10; ☉9am-6.30pm mid-Mar–Oct, 9am-5pm Nov–

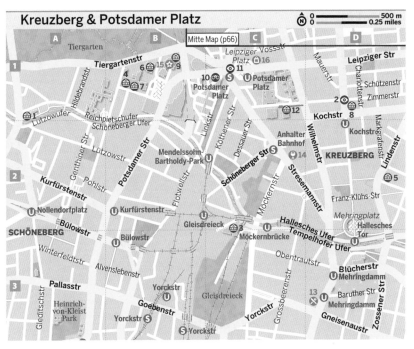

Kreuzberg & Potsdamer Platz

mid-Mar; 🚌100, 200, Ⓢ Zoologischer Garten, 🚊 Zoologischer Garten)

Story of Berlin   Museum

This multimedia museum breaks down 800 years of Berlin history into bite-size chunks that are easy to swallow but substantial enough to be satisfying. Each of the 23 rooms uses sound, light, technology and original objects to zero in on a specific theme or epoch in the city's history, from its founding in 1237 to the fall of the Berlin Wall. A creepily fascinating highlight is a tour (also in English) of a still functional atomic bunker beneath the building. (Map p72; 📞030-8872 0100; www.story-of-berlin.de; Kurfürstendamm 207-208, enter via Ku'damm Karree mall; adult/concession €12/9; ⏰10am-8pm, last admission 6pm; Ⓢ Uhlandstrasse)

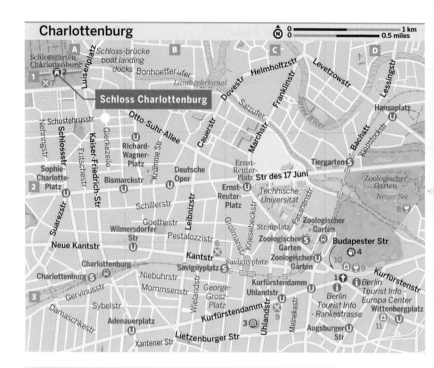

Charlottenburg

TOURS

Boat tours range from one-hour spins around the historic centre (from €11) to longer trips to Schloss Charlottenburg and beyond (from €15). Most offer live commentary in English and German.

Original Berlin Walks   Walking Tour
Berlin's longest-running English-language walking tour company does one general and various themed city tours (Third Reich, Jewish Life, Berlin Wall) as well as trips out

to Sachsenhausen concentration camp and Potsdam. (✆030-301 9194; www.berlinwalks. de; adult €12-15, concession €10-12)

Berlin on Bike   Bicycle Tour
This well-established company runs a busy schedule of general city tours (Berlin's Best) and Berlin Wall tours in English, as well as half a dozen themed tours (including Streetart Berlin, Nightseeing and Future Berlin) in German only (in English on request). Reservations recommended.

(030-4373 9999; www.berlinonbike.de; Knaackstrasse 97, Kulturbrauerei, Court 4; tours incl bike €19, concession €17; S Eberswalder Strasse)

🔒 SHOPPING

KaDeWe — Department Store
Just past the centennial mark, this venerable department store has an assortment so vast that a pirate-style campaign is the best way to plunder its bounty. If pushed for time, at least hurry up to the legendary 6th-floor gourmet food hall. The name, by the way, stands for Kaufhaus des Westens (department store of the West). (Map p72; 030-212 10; www.kadewe.de; Tauentzienstrasse 21-24; 10am-8pm Mon-Thu, 10am-9pm Fri, 9.30am-8pm Sat; S Wittenbergplatz)

Bikini Berlin — Mall
Germany's first concept mall opened in 2014 in a spectacularly rehabilitated 1950s architectural icon nicknamed 'Bikini' because of its design: a 200m-long upper and lower section separated by an open floor, now chastely covered by a glass facade. Inside are three floors of urban indie boutiques and short-lease pop-up 'boxes' that offer a platform for up-and-coming designers. (Map p72; www.bikiniberlin.de; Budapester Strasse 38-50; 10am-8pm Mon-Sat; 100, 200, S Zoologischer Garten, R Zoologischer Garten)

LP12 Mall of Berlin — Mall
This spanking new retail quarter is tailor-made for black-belt mall rats. More than 270 stores vie for your shopping euros, including flagship stores by Karl Lagerfeld, Hugo Boss, Liebeskind, Muji and other international high-end brands alongside the usual high street chains like Mango and H&M. (Map p71; www.mallofberlin.de; Leipziger Platz 12; 10am-9pm Mon-Sat; 200, S Potsdamer Platz, R Potsdamer Platz)

Friedrichstadtpassagen — Department Store
Even if you're not part of the Gucci and Prada brigade, the architectural wow factor of this trio of shopping complexes (called Quartiere) linked by a subterranean passageway is undeniable. Highlights are Jean Nouvel's shimmering glass funnel inside the Galeries Lafayette, the dazzlingly patterned art-deco-style Quartier 206 and John Chamberlain's tower made from crushed cars in Quartier 205. (Map p66; Friedrichstrasse, btwn Französische Strasse & Mohrenstrasse; 10am-8pm Mon-Sat; S Französische Strasse, Stadtmitte)

FLEA MARKETS
Berlin has some legendary flea markets selling all kinds of junk, a lot of which harks back to the days of the DDR.

Flohmarkt am Mauerpark — Market
The mother of all markets is overrun but still a good show. (www.mauerparkmarkt. de; Bernauer Strasse 63-64; 9am-6pm Sun; S Eberwalder Strasse, M1, M10)

Nowkoelln Flowmarkt — Market
This internationally flavoured hipster market is also a showcase of local creativity. (Map p65; www.nowkoelln.de; Maybachufer; 10am-6pm 2nd & 4th Sun of month; S Kottbusser Tor, Schönleinstrasse)

RAW Flohmarkt — Market
True bargains still abound at this little market on the grounds of a railway repair station turned party zone. (Map p65; www. raw-flohmarkt-berlin.de; Revaler Strasse 99, RAW Gelände; 9am-7pm Sun; S Warschauer Strasse, R Warschauer Strasse)

✖ EATING

🍽 Mitte

Augustiner am Gendarmenmarkt — German €€
Tourists, concert-goers and hearty-food lovers rub shoulders at rustic tables in this surprisingly authentic Bavarian beer hall. Soak up the down-to-earth vibe right along with a mug of full-bodied Augustiner brew. Sausages, roast pork and pretzels provide rib-sticking sustenance, but there's also plenty of lighter (even meat-free) fare as well as good-value lunch specials. (Map p66; 030-2045 4020; www.augustiner-braeu-berlin.

de; Charlottenstrasse 55; mains €6-19; ☺10am-2am; Ⓢ Französische Strasse)

Chèn Chè · Vietnamese €€

Settle down in the charming Zen garden or beneath the hexagonal chandelier of this exotic Vietnamese teahouse and pick from the small menu of steaming *pho* (soups), curries and noodle dishes served in traditional clay pots. Exquisite tea selection and small store. (Map p66; 🖉030-2888 4282; www.chenche-berlin.de; Rosenthaler Strasse 13; dishes €7-11; ☺noon-midnight; 🖋; Ⓢ Rosenthaler Platz, 🚇M1)

Katz Orange · International €€€

With its gourmet organic farm-to-table menu, stylish country flair and swift and smiling servers, the 'Orange Cat' hits a gastro grand slam. It will have you purring for Duroc pork that's been slow-roasted for 12 hours giving extra-rich flavour. The setting in a castle-like former brewery is stunning, especially in summer when the patio opens. (🖉030-983 208 430; www.katzorange.com; Bergstrasse 22; mains €18-26; ☺6-11pm; Ⓢ Rosenthaler Platz, 🚇M8)

Pauly Saal · German €€€

Regionally hunted and gathered ingredients fused with exotic flavours steer the light and contemporary menu at this Michelin-starred restaurant. Set in the high-ceilinged gym of a Bauhaus-era former Jewish girls' school, the epicurean hot spot gets 1920s glam from Murano chandeliers and such eye-catching art work as Cosima von Bonin's giant red rocket. On balmy days, sit beneath the old school yard's leafy trees. (Map p66; 🖉030-3300 6070; www.paulysaal.com; Auguststrasse 11-13; 2-/3-/4-course lunch €34/46/59, 4-/7-course dinner €68/97; ☺noon-2pm & 6-9.30pm, bar to 2.30am Tue-Sat; Ⓢ Oranienburger Tor, 🚇M1, 🚉 Oranienburger Strasse)

✖ Kreuzberg & Friedrichshain

Curry 36 · German €

Day after day, night after night, a motley crowd – cops, cabbies, queens, office jockeys, savvy tourists etc – wait their turn at this top-ranked *Currywurst* purveyor that's been frying 'em up since 1981. (Map p71; 🖉030-251 7368; www.curry36.de;

Currywurst kiosk and cafe

Mehringdamm 36; snacks €2-6; 9am-5am;
SMehringdamm)

Cafe Jacques International €€
A favourite with off-duty chefs and loyal
foodies, Jacques infallibly charms with
flattering candlelight, arty-elegant decor
and fantastic wine. It's the perfect date
spot but, quite frankly, you only have to be
in love with good food to appreciate the
French- and North African–inspired blackboard menu. Fish and meat are always
tops and the pasta is homemade. Reservations essential. (Map p65; 030-694 1048;
Maybachufer 14; mains €12-20; 6pm-late;
SSchönleinstrasse)

Freischwimmer International €€
In fine weather, few places are more idyllic
than this rustic 1930s boathouse turned
canal-side chill zone. The menu runs from
meat and fish cooked on a lava rock grill to
crisp salads, *Flammekuche* (French pizza)
and seasonal specials. It's also a popular
Sunday brunch spot (€12.90). Kayak and
boat rentals available. (Map p65; 030-6107
4309; www.freischwimmer-berlin.com; Vor dem
Schlesischen Tor 2a; mains €8.50-20; noon-
late Mon-Fri, 10am-late Sat & Sun; SSchlesis-
ches Tor, Treptower Park)

Defne Turkish €€
If you thought Turkish cuisine stopped
at the doner kebab, canal-side Defne will
teach you otherwise. The appetiser platter
alone elicits intense cravings (fabulous
walnut-chilli paste!), but inventive mains
such as *ali nacik* (sliced lamb with puréed
eggplant and yoghurt) also warrant repeat
visits. It has a lovely summer terrace. (Map
p65; 030-8179 7111; www.defne-restaurant.
de; Planufer 92c; mains €8-20; 4pm-1am
Apr-Sep, 5pm-1am Oct-Mar; SKottbusser Tor,
Schönleinstrasse)

Max und Moritz German €€
The patina of yesteryear hangs over this
ode-to-old-school brewpub named for the
cheeky Wilhelm Busch cartoon characters.
Since 1902 it has packed hungry diners and
drinkers into its rustic tile-and-stucco orna-

Museums of the Kulturforum

In addition to the Gemäldegalerie
(p69), the Kulturforum encompasses
four other top museums:

Kunstgewerbemuseum (Museum of
Decorative Arts; Map p71; 030-266 424
242; www.smb.museum; Matthäikirchplatz;
adult/concession/under 18yr €8/4/free;
10am-6pm Tue-Fri, 11am-6pm Sat & Sun;
200, SPotsdamer Platz, Potsdamer
Platz) A prized collection of European
design, fashion and decorative arts from
the Middle Ages to today.

Kupferstichkabinett (Museum of Prints
and Drawings; Map p71; 030-266 424
242; www.smb.museum/kk; Matthäikirchplatz; adult/concession €6/3; 10am-6pm
Tue-Fri, 11am-6pm Sat & Sun; 200,
M41, M29, SPotsdamer Platz, Potsdamer Platz) One of the world's finest
collections of art on paper, including
hand-illustrated books, illuminated
manuscripts, drawings and prints produced mostly in Europe from the 14th
century onward.

Musikinstrumenten-Museum (Musical
Instruments Museum; Map p71; 030-
254 810; www.mim-berlin.de; Tiergarten-
strasse 1, enter via Ben-Gurion-Strasse; adult/
concession €6/3; 9am-5pm Tue, Wed
& Fri, 9am-8pm Thu, 10am-5pm Sat & Sun;
200, SPotsdamer Platz, Potsdamer
Platz) Packed with fun, precious and rare
sound machines.

Neue Nationalgalerie Home to a fabulous collection of early 20th-century
art, it is closed for renovations which are
expected to last until at least 2018.

mented rooms for sudsy home brews and
granny-style Berlin fare. A menu favourite is
the *Kutschergulasch* (goulash cooked with
beer). (Map p65; 030-6951 5911; www.max-
undmoritzberlin.de; Oranienstrasse 162; mains
€9.50-17; 5pm-midnight; SMoritzplatz)

⚥ GLBT Berlin

Berlin's legendary liberalism has spawned one of the world's biggest, most divine and diverse GLBT playgrounds. The closest that Berlin comes to a 'gay village' is Schöneberg (Motzstrasse and Fuggerstrasse especially), where the rainbow flag has proudly flown since the 1920s. There's still plenty of (old-school) partying going on here, but anyone under 35 will likely feel more comfortable else-where. Current hipster central is Kreuz-berg, which teems with party pens along Mehringdamm and Oranienstrasse. Across the river, Friedrichshain has such key clubs as Berghain and the hard-core Lab.oratory. The weekly freebie mag *Siegessäule* is the bible for all things gay and lesbian in Berlin.

Christopher Street Day celebrations (p28)
SERGEY KOHL/SHUTTERSTOCK ©

❌ Prenzlauer Berg

Konnopke's Imbiss   German €
Brave the inevitable queue at this famous sausage kitchen, ensconced in the same spot below the elevated U-Bahn track since 1930, but now equipped with a heated pavilion and an English menu. The 'secret' sauce topping its classic *Currywurst* comes in a four-part heat scale from mild to wild. (🖉030-442 7765; www. konnopke-imbiss.de; Schönhauser Allee 44a; sausages €1.40-1.90; ⊙9am-8pm Mon-Fri, 11.30am-8pm Sat; §Eberswalder Strasse, M1, M10)

La Soupe Populaire   German €€
Helmed by local top toque Tim Raue, this industrial-chic gastro destination inside a defunct 19th-century brewery embraces the soulful goodness of German home-cooking. The star of the regular menu is Raue's riff on *Königsberger Klopse* (veal meatballs in caper sauce) but there's also a separate one inspired by changing art exhibits in the hall overlooked by the dining room. (🖉030-4431 9680; www.lasoupepopulaire.de; Prenzlauer Allee 242; mains €14-21; ⊙noon-2.30pm & 5.30-10.10pm Thu-Sat; §Senefelder Platz, 🚊M2)

❌ Charlottenburg

Good Friends   Chinese €€
Good Friends is widely considered Berlin's best Cantonese restaurant. The ducks dangling in the window are the mere overture to a menu long enough to confuse Confucius and including plenty of authentic homestyle dishes. If sea cucumber with fish belly prove too challenging, you can always fall back on sweet-and-sour pork or fried rice with shrimp. (Map p72; 🖉030-313 2659; www.goodfriends-berlin.de; Kantstrasse 30; mains €7-32; ⊙noon-1am; 🚊Savignyplatz)

Café-Restaurant Wintergarten im Literaturhaus   International €€
The hustle and bustle of Ku'damm is only a block away from this genteel art nouveau villa with attached literary salon and bookstore. Tuck into seasonal bistro cuisine amid elegant Old Berlin flair in the graceful-ly stucco-ornamented rooms or, if weather permits, in the idyllic garden. Breakfast is served until 2pm. (Map p72; 🖉030-882 5414; www.literaturhaus-berlin.de; Fasanenstrasse 23; mains €8-16; ⊙9am-midnight; §Uhlandstrasse)

🍷 DRINKING & NIGHTLIFE

Mitte

Berliner Republik   Pub
Just as in a mini–stock exchange, the price of beer (18 varieties on tap!) fluctuates

with demand after 5pm at this riverside pub. Everyone goes Pavlovian when a heavy brass bell rings, signalling rock-bottom prices. In summer, seats on the terrace are the most coveted. (Map p66; ☎030-3087 2293; www.die-berliner-republik.de; Schiffbauerdamm 8; ☉10am-6am; Ⓢ Friedrichstrasse, Ⓡ Friedrichstrasse)

Strandbar Mitte   Bar

With a full-on view of the Bodemuseum, palm trees and a relaxed ambience, Germany's first beach bar (running since 2002) is great for balancing a surfeit of sightseeing stimulus with a reviving drink and thin-crust pizza. At night, there's dancing under the stars with tango, cha cha, swing and salsa. (Map p66; ☎030-2838 5588; www.strandbar-mitte.de; Monbijoustrasse 3; ☉10am-late May-Sep; ᕫ M1, Ⓡ Oranienburger Strasse)

Clärchens Ballhaus   Club

Yesteryear is right now at this late, great 19th-century dance hall where groovers and grannies hoof it across the parquet without even a touch of irony. There's dif-ferent sounds nightly – from salsa to swing and tango to disco – as well as a live band on Saturday. (Map p66; ☎030-282 9295; www.ballhaus.de; Auguststrasse 24; ☉11am-late, dancing from 9pm or 9.30pm; ᕫ M1, Ⓡ Oranienburger Strasse)

◉ Potsdamer Platz & Tiergarten

Café am Neuen See   Beer Garden

Next to an idyllic pond in the southwestern section of Tiergarten, this restaurant gets jammed year-round for its sumptuous breakfast, pizza and seasonal fare, but really comes into its own during beer garden season. Enjoy a micro-vacation from the city bustle over a cold one or take your sweetie on a spin in a row boat. (☎030-254 4930; www.cafeamneuensee.de; Lichtensteinallee 2; ☉9am-11pm, beer garden from 11am Mon-Fri, from 10am Sat & Sun; ᕫ 200, Ⓢ Zoologischer Garten, Tiergarten, Ⓡ Zoologischer Garten)

fabulous 360-degree views

Rooftop restaurant at the Reichstag (p38)

MICHAEL TAYLOR/GETTY IMAGES ©

Solar Bar

Watch the city light up from this 17th-floor glass-walled sky lounge above a posh restaurant (mains €17 to €34). With its dim lighting, soft black leather couches and breathtaking views, Solar is a great spot for a date or sunset drinks. Even getting there aboard an exterior glass lift is half the fun. The entrance is behind the Pit Stop auto shop. (Map p71; ☎0163 765 2700; www.solar-berlin.de; Stresemannstrasse 76; ⏰6pm-2am Sun-Thu, to 4am Fri & Sat; Ⓡ Anhalter Bahnhof)

🅤 Kreuzberg & Friedrichshain

Würgeengel Bar

For a swish night out, point the compass to Würgeengel, a stylish art-deco-style bar with lots of chandeliers and shiny black surfaces. It's always busy but especially so after the final credits roll at the adjacent Babylon cinema. (Map p65; ☎030-615 5560; www.wuergeengel.de; Dresdener Strasse 122; ⏰7pm-late; Ⓢ Kottbusser Tor)

Briefmarken Weine Wine Bar

For *dolce vita* right on socialist Karl-Marx-Allee, head to this charmingly nostalgic Italian wine bar ensconced in a former stamp shop. The original wooden cabinetry now holds a handpicked selection of bottles from Italy while old black-and-white movies are projected onto walls with faded wallpaper. For eats, there's a daily pasta and quality cheeses, prosciutto and salami. (Map p65; ☎030-4202 5292; www.briefmarkenweine.de; Karl-Marx-Allee 99; ⏰7pm-midnight; Ⓢ Weberwiese)

Monkey Bar Bar

On the 10th floor of the 25hours Hotel Bikini Berlin, this 'urban jungle' hot spot delivers fabulous views of the city and the Berlin Zoo – in summer from a sweeping terrace. Drinks-wise, the list gives prominent nods to tiki concoctions and gin-based cocktail sorcery. (Map p72; ☎030-120 221 210; www.25hours-hotel.com; Budapester Strasse 40; ⏰noon-1am Sun-Thu, to 2am Fri & Sat; 🚕; 🚌100, 200, Ⓢ Bahnhof Zoologischer Garten, Ⓡ Bahnhof Zoologischer Garten)

ENTERTAINMENT **79**

Hops & Barley Pub
Conversation flows as freely as the
unfiltered Pilsner, malty *Dunkel* (dark)
and fruity *Weizen* (wheat) produced right
at one of Berlin's oldest craft breweries
inside a former butcher's shop. For variety,
the brewmeisters also produce weekly
blackboard specials and potent cider. Two
beamers project soccer games. (Map p65;
☎030-2936 7534; www.hopsandbarley-berlin.
de; Wühlischstrasse 22/23; ⏰from 5pm Mon-
Fri, from 3pm Sat & Sun; ⓢWarschauer Strasse,
Samariterstrasse, ⓡWarschauer Strasse,
Ostkreuz)

Berghain/Panorama Bar Club
Only world-class spinmasters heat up this
hedonistic bass junkie hellhole inside a
labyrinthine ex-power plant. Hard-edged
minimal techno dominates the ex-turbine
hall (Berghain) while house dominates at
Panorama Bar one floor up. Strict door, no
cameras. Check the website for midweek
concerts and record-release parties at
the main venue and the adjacent Kantine
am Berghain (Map p65; www.berghain.de;
Am Wriezener Bahnhof; ⏰midnight Fri to Mon
morning; ⓡOstbahnhof)

🍺 Prenzlauer Berg
Prater Biergarten Beer Garden
Berlin's oldest beer garden has seen beer-
soaked nights since 1837 and is still a charismatic spot for guzzling a custom-brewed
Prater Pilsner beneath the ancient chestnut
trees (self-service). Kids can romp around
the small play area. (☎030-448 5688; www.
pratergarten.de; Kastanienallee 7-9; ⏰noon-late
Apr-Sep, weather permitting; ⓢEberswalder
Strasse)

✪ ENTERTAINMENT
Chamäleon Varieté Cabaret
A marriage of art nouveau charms and
high-tech theatre trappings, this intimate
1920s-style venue in an old ballroom hosts
classy variety shows – comedy, juggling
acts and singing – often in sassy, sexy and
unconventional fashion. (Map p66; ☎030-400
0590; www.chamaeleonberlin.com; Rosenthaler
Strasse 40/41; 🚋M1, ⓡHackescher Markt)

ADAM BERRY / STRINGER/GETTY IMAGES ©

★ Top Five for Architecture
Reichstag (p38)
Jüdisches Museum (p69)
Bauhaus Archiv (p69)
Humboldt-Box (p49)
Fernsehturm (p68)

From left: Würgeengel; beer; Fernsehturm (p68) and the
Rotes Rathaus (Red Town Hall)

DAVE G KELLY/GETTY IMAGES ©

 Sachsenhausen Concentration Camp

Located about 35km north of central Berlin, **Sachsenhausen** (☏03301-200 200; www.stiftung-bg.de; Strasse der Nationen 22; ◷8.30am-6pm mid-Mar–mid-Oct, to 4.30pm mid-Oct–mid-Mar; museums closed Mon; ⒮S1 to Oranienburg) FREE was built by prisoners brought here from another concentration camp and opened in 1936 as a model for other camps. By 1945, some 200,000 people passed through its sinister gates, most of them political opponents, Roma, Jews and POWs. Tens of thousands died here from hunger, exhaustion, illness, exposure, medical experiments and executions. Thousands more succumbed during the death march of April 1945, when the Nazis evacuated the camp in advance of the Red Army.

Updated many times since, today's memorial delivers a predictably sobering experience. A tour of the memorial site with its remaining buildings and exhibits will leave no one untouched.

The S1 makes the trip thrice hourly from central Berlin (eg Friedrichstrasse station) to Oranienburg (€3.30, 45 minutes). Hourly regional RE5 and RB12 trains leaving from Hauptbahnhof are faster (€3.30, 25 minutes). From the station it's a 2km signposted walk to the camp entrance.

Berliner Philharmonie   Classical Music
This world-famous concert hall has supreme acoustics and, thanks to Hans Scharoun's clever terraced vineyard design, not a bad seat in the house. It's the home turf of the Berliner Philharmoniker, who will be led by Sir Simon Rattle until 2018 when Russia-born Kirill Petrenko will pick up the baton as music director. Chamber music concerts take place at the adjacent Kammermusiksaal. (Map p66; ☏tickets 030-254 888 999; www.berliner-philharmoniker.de; Herbert-von-Karajan-Strasse 1; ⒭200, ⒮Potsdamer Platz, ⒭Potsdamer Platz)

❶ INFORMATION

The city tourist board, **Visit Berlin** (www.visitberlin.de) has info desks at both airports, five walk-in offices and a **call centre** (☏030-2500 2333; ◷9am-7pm Mon-Fri, 10am-6pm Sat, 10am-2pm Sun) with multilingual staff who field general questions and make hotel and ticket bookings.

Brandenburger Tor (Map p66; south wing, Pariser Platz; ◷9.30am-7pm Apr-Oct, to 6pm Nov-Mar; ⒮Brandenburger Tor, ⒭Brandenburger Tor)

Rankestrasse (Map p72; cnr Rankestrasse & Kurfürstendamm; ◷10am-6pm Apr-Oct, to 4pm Nov-Mar; ⒮Kurfürstendamm)

Hauptbahnhof (Europaplatz entrance, ground fl; ◷8am-10pm; ⒮Hauptbahnhof, ⒭Hauptbahnhof)

Europa Center (Map p72; Tauentzienstrasse 9, ground fl; ◷10am-8pm Mon-Sat; ⒮Kurfürstendamm)

TV Tower (Map p66; Panoramastrasse 1a, ground fl; ◷10am-6pm Apr-Oct, to 4pm Nov-Mar; ⒭100, 200, ⒮Alexanderplatz, ⒭Alexanderplatz)

Berliner Philharmonie

🛈 GETTING THERE & AWAY

AIR

Until the completion of the Berlin Brandenburg Airport, flights continue to land at the city's **Tegel Airport**, about 8km northwest of the city centre, and at **Schönefeld Airport**, about 24km southeast.

BUS

Berlin is served by a large number of long-haul bus companies, including Berlinlinienbus, Postbus and Mein Fernbus, from throughout Germany. Check www.busliniensuche.de (also in English) for details. Most buses arrive at the **Zentraler Omnibusbahnhof** (ZOB; www.iob-berlin.de; Masurenallee 4-6; Ⓢ Kaiserdamm, Ⓡ Messe/ICC Nord) near the trade fair grounds in far western Berlin. The U2 U-Bahn line links to the city centre. Some bus operators also stop at Alexanderplatz and other points around town.

TRAIN

Berlin is well connected by train to other German cities, as well as to popular European destina-

tions, including Prague, Warsaw and Amsterdam. While all long-distance trains converge at the Hauptbahnhof, some also stop at other stations such as Spandau, Ostbahnhof, Gesundbrunnen and Südkreuz.

🛈 GETTING AROUND

TO/FROM THE AIRPORTS

TEGEL

The TXL bus connects Tegel with Alexanderplatz (40 minutes) every 10 minutes. For Kurfürstendamm and Zoo Station, take bus X9 (20 minutes). Each of these trips costs €2.70. Taxi rides cost about €20 to Zoologischer Garten and €23 to Alexanderplatz and should take between 30 and 45 minutes.

SCHÖNEFELD

Airport-Express trains make the 30-minute trip to central Berlin twice hourly. Note: these are regular Regional trains, identified as RE7 and RB14 in timetables. You need a transport ticket covering zones ABC (€3.30). Taxi rides average €40 and take 35 minutes to an hour.

PUBLIC TRANSPORT

One ticket is good on all forms of public transport. Most trips within Berlin require an AB ticket (€2.70), valid for two hours (interruptions and transfers allowed, round trips not).

One-day travel passes (*Tageskarte*) are valid for unlimited travel on all forms of public transport until 3am the following day. The cost for the AB zone is €6.90. Group day passes (*Kleingruppenkarte)* are valid for up to five people travelling together and cost €16.90.

Buy tickets from vending machines in U-Bahn or S-Bahn stations and aboard trams, from bus drivers and at station offices and news kiosks sporting the yellow BVG logo.

All tickets, except those bought from bus drivers and on trams, must be stamped before boarding. Anyone caught without a validated ticket escapes only with a red face and a €40 fine, payable on the spot.

U-BAHN

U-Bahn lines (underground, subway) are best for getting around Berlin quickly. Trains operate from 4am until about 12.30am and throughout the night on Friday, Saturday and public holidays (all lines except U4 and U55).

S-BAHN

The S-Bahn (suburban trains) don't run as frequently as U-Bahns but make fewer stops and thus are useful for covering longer distances.

BUS & TRAM

Buses are slow but useful for city sightseeing on the cheap. They run frequently between 4.30am and 12.30am. Trams only operate in the eastern districts.

TAXI

You can order a **taxi** (📞 44 33 11, 030-20 20 20) by phone, flag one down or pick one up at a rank. Flag fall is €3.20, then it's €1.65 per kilometre up to 7km and €1.28 for each kilometre after that.

Berlin train

CANADASTOCK/SHUTTERSTOCK ©

Where to Stay

Berlin offers the gamut of places to unpack your suitcase. Just about every international chain now has a flagship in the German capital, but more interesting options that better reflect the city's verve and spirit abound.

Neighbourhood	Atmosphere
Historic Mitte	Close to major sights; great transport; top restaurants; handy for the city's best classical venues; can be touristy and expensive.
Museumsinsel & Alexanderplatz	Supercentral sightseeing quarter; easy transport access; large and new hotels; noisy and busy; hardly any nightlife.
Potsdamer Platz & Tiergarten	Cutting-edge architecture; high-end international hotels; next to huge Tiergarten city park; limited eating options; no nightlife.
Scheunenviertel	Trendy, historic, central; indie shopping; international eats and strong cafe scene; top galleries and street art; pricey and busy.
City West & Charlottenburg	Great shopping; stylish lounges, 'Old Berlin' bars and top restaurants; best range of good-value lodging; historic B&Bs; far from key sights and happening nightlife.
Kreuzberg & Neukölln	Vibrant arty, underground and multicultural party quarter; cheap; excellent street art; gritty, noisy and busy; away from main sights.
Friedrichshain	Student and young-family quarter; bubbling nightlife; inexpensive; not so central for sightseeing; transport difficult in some areas.
Prenzlauer Berg	Well-heeled, charming residential area; lively cafe and restaurant scene; indie boutiques; limited late-night action, no essential sights.

Park Sanssouci (p88)

POTSDAM

Potsdam

Potsdam, on the Havel River just 25km southwest of central Berlin, is the capital and crown jewel of the federal state of Brandenburg. Easily reached by S-Bahn, the former Prussian royal seat is the most popular day trip from Berlin, luring visitors with its splendid gardens and palaces that garnered Unesco World Heritage status in 1990.

Headlining the roll call of royal pads is Schloss Sanssouci, the private retreat of King Friedrich II (Frederick the Great), who was also the mastermind behind many of Potsdam's other fabulous parks and palaces, which miraculously survived WWII with nary a shrapnel wound. When the shooting stopped, the Allies chose Schloss Cecilienhof for the Potsdam Conference of August 1945 to lay the groundwork for Germany's postwar fate.

☑ In This Section

➡ Arriving in Potsdam

Potsdam-Charlottenhof and Potsdam-Sanssouci are served by Regional trains (30 min) from Berlin Hauptbahnhof and Zoologischer Garten. Potsdam Hauptbahnhof is served by the S7 from central Berlin (40 minutes, €3.30). You need a ticket covering zones A, B and C (€3.30) for either service.

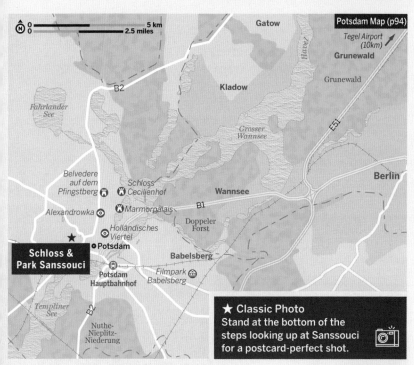

Potsdam Map (p94)

Tegel Airport (10km)

Gatow

Grunewald

Grunewald

Havel

E51

Berlin

Kladow

B2

Fahrlander See

Grosser Wannsee

Belvedere auf dem Pfingstberg

Schloss Cecilienhof

Wannsee

Marmorpalais

B1

Alexandrowka

Hollandisches Viertel

Doppeler Forst

★

Potsdam

Babelsberg

Schloss & Park Sanssouci

Potsdam Hauptbahnhof

Filmpark Babelsberg

Templiner See

B2

Nuthe-Nieplitz-Niederung

★ **Classic Photo**
Stand at the bottom of the steps looking up at Sanssouci for a postcard-perfect shot.

From left: Park Charlottenhof (p91); Park Sanssouci (p88); Römische Bäder (p91)

Neues Palais

PRUSSIAN PALACES AND GARDENS FOUNDATION BERLIN-BRANDENBURG/HANS BACH/FOTOTHEK ©

Schloss & Park Sanssouci

Potsdam's chief draw are the summer palaces and parks of Sanssouci, built and laid out in the 18th and 19th centuries. The park is huge and the sights numerous so choose what you want to see carefully.

Great For...

☑ Don't Miss

One of the joys of visiting Potsdam's palaces are the walks through exquisite parkland in-between.

Schloss Sanssouci

Frederick the Great's famous summer palace, **Schloss Sanssouci** (🕐10am-6pm Tue-Sun Apr-Oct, to 5pm Nov-Mar; adult/concession incl audioguide €12/8; 🚌650, 695), was designed by Georg Wenzeslaus von Knobelsdorff in 1747; the rococo jewel sits daintily above vine-draped terraces with the king's grave nearby. Admission is limited and by timed ticket only; book online to avoid wait times and/or disappointment. Otherwise, only city tours booked through the tourist office guarantee entry to the palace.

Standouts on the audioguided tours include the Konzertsaal (Concert Hall), whimsically decorated with vines, grapes and even a cobweb where sculpted spiders frolic. The king himself gave flute recitals

Sculpture, Park Sanssouci

BACHPRUSSIAN PALACES AND GARDENS FOUNDATION BERLIN-BRANDENBURG HANS CHRISTIAN KRASS/FOTOTHEK ©

❶ Need to Know

📞 0331-969 4200; www.spsg.de; Maulbeer-allee; ⏱ varies by palace; day pass to all palaces adult/concession €19/14; 🚌 650, 695 from Potsdam Hauptbahnhof

✕ Take a Break

Vast **Potsdam Zur Historischen Mühle** (📞 0331-281 493; www.moevenpick-restaurants.com; Zur Historischen Mühle 2; mains €10-18; ⏱ 8am-10pm), part of the Mövenpick chain, serves international favourites, and has a beer garden and a children's playground.

★ Top Tip

The palaces are fairly well spaced – it's almost 2km between the Neues Palais and Schloss Sanssouci. Take your sweet time wandering along the park's meandering paths to discover your personal favourite spot.

here. Also note the intimate Bibliothek (library), lidded by a gilded sunburst ceiling, where the king would seek solace amid 2000 leather-bound tomes ranging from Greek poetry to the latest releases by his friend Voltaire. Another highlight is the Marmorsaal (Marble Room), an elegant white Carrara marble symphony modelled after the Pantheon in Rome.

As you exit the palace, don't be fooled by the Ruinenberg, a pile of classical 'ruins' looming in the distance: they're merely a folly conceived by Frederick the Great.

Neues Palais

The final palace commissioned by Frederick the Great, the **Neues Palais** (New Palace; Am Neuen Palais; adult/concession incl tour or audioguide €8/6; ⏱ 10am-6pm Wed-Mon Apr-Oct, to 5pm Nov-Mar; 🚌 605 or 695 to Neues Palais, 🚉 Potsdam Charlottenhof) has made-to-impress dimensions, a central dome and a lavish exterior capped with a parade of sandstone figures. The interior attests to the high level of artistry and craftsmanship of the 18th century. The palace is an opulent symphony of ceiling frescos, gilded stucco ornamentation, ornately carved wainscoting and fanciful wall coverings alongside paintings (by Antoine Pesne, for example) and richly crafted furniture.

The palace was built in only six years, largely to demonstrate the undiminished power of the Prussian state following the bloody Seven Years War (1756–63). The king himself rarely camped out here, preferring the intimacy of Schloss Sanssouci and using it for representational purposes only. Only the last German Kaiser, Wilhelm II, used it as a residence until 1918.

Chinesisches Haus

The 18th-century fad for the Far East is poignantly reflected in the **Chinese House** (Am Grünen Gitter; adult/concession €3/2; ⊙10am-6pm Tue-Sun May-Oct; 🚌605, 606 to Schloss Charlottenhof, 🚋91 to Schloss Charlottenhof). The cloverleaf-shaped shutterbug favourite sports an enchanting exterior of exotically dressed gilded figures shown sipping tea, dancing and playing musical instruments amid palm-shaped pillars.

Inside is a precious collection of Chinese and Meissen porcelain.

Bildergalerie

The **Bildergalerie** (Gallery of Old Masters; Im Park Sanssouci 4; adult/concession €6/5; ⊙10am-6pm Tue-Sun May-Oct; 🚌650, 695) is the oldest royal museum in Germany and shelters a prized collection of Old Masters, including works by Peter Paul Rubens and Caravaggio's *Doubting Thomas*.

The interior of the elongated hall with its gilded barrel-vaulted ceiling and patterned marble floors is perhaps just as impressive as the mostly large-scale paintings that cover practically every inch of wall space.

Park Sanssouci

Neue Kammern

The **Neue Kammern** (New Chambers; adult/concession incl tour or audioguide €4/3; 10am-6pm Tue-Sun Apr-Oct; 650, 696) were originally an orangery and later a guesthouse. The rococo interior drips in opulence, most notably in the Ovidsaal, a grand ballroom with a gilded relief, and in the Jasper Hall, drenched in precious stones and lidded by a Venus fresco.

★ Top Tip

Park Sanssouci is open from dawn till dusk year-round. Admission is free, but there are machines by the entrance where you can make a voluntary donation of €2. Picnicking is permitted throughout the park.

PRUSSIAN PALACES AND GARDENS FOUNDATION BERLIN-BRANDENBURG/HANS BACH/FOTOTHEK ©

Frederick's Postmortem Odyssey

Frederick the Great so loved Sanssouci, he gave specific instructions to be buried – next to his beloved dogs – on the highest terrace of the vineyards in front of the palace. Alas, his nephew and successor Friedrich Wilhem II blithely ignored his request, putting him instead next to his father, the 'Soldier King' Friedrich Wilhelm I, in a nearby church. In WWII, the sarcophagi of both father and son were moved by German soldiers for safekeeping and, after the war, ended up in the ancestral Hohenzollern castle in southern Germany. Only after reunification, in 1991, did Frederick the Great get his final wish, being reburied in the exact spot he'd personally picked out more than 250 years before. It's marked by a simple gravestone.

What's Nearby?

Laid out by Peter Lenné for Friedrich Wilhelm IV, **Park Charlottenhof** segues imperceptibly from Park Sanssouci but gets a lot fewer visitors. Buildings here reflect the king's passion for Italy. The small neoclassical **Schloss Charlottenhof** (Geschwister-Scholl-Strasse 34a; tours 10am-6pm Tue-Sun May-Oct; tours adult/concession €4/3), for instance, was modelled after a Roman villa. It was designed by Karl Friedrich Schinkel who, aided by his student Ludwig Persius, also dreamed up the nearby **Römische Bäder** (10am-6pm Tue-Sun May–Oct; adult/concession €5/4), a picturesque cluster of Italian country villas. A same-day combination ticket is €8 (concession €6).

✕ Take a Break

Right in Park Sanssouci, the exotic 1770 **Drachenhaus** (www.drachenhaus.de; Maulbeerallee 4; mains €8-23; 11am-8pm or later Apr-Oct, to 6pm Tue-Sun Nov, Dec & Mar, 11am-6pm Sat & Sun Jan & Feb) is a Chinese miniature palace. It now houses a pleasant cafe-restaurant.

⊙ SIGHTS

⊙ Altstadt

Although Potsdam's historic town centre fell victim to WWII bombing and socialist town planning, it's still worth a leisurely stroll. Coming from Park Sanssouci, you'll pass by the baroque Brandenburger Tor (Brandenburg Gate), a triumphal arch built to commemorate Frederick the Great's 1770 victory in the Seven Years War. It's the gateway to pedestrianised Brandenburger Strasse, the main commercial drag, which takes you straight to the Holländisches Viertel (Dutch Quarter).

Holländisches Viertel   Neighbourhood

This picturesque cluster of 134 gabled red-brick houses was built around 1730 for Dutch workers invited to Potsdam by Friedrich Wilhelm I. The entire district has been done up beautifully and brims with galleries, boutiques, cafes and restaurants; Mittelstrasse is especially scenic.
(Dutch Quarter; www.hollaendisches-viertel.net; Mittelstrasse)

Potsdamer Stadtschloss (Landtag Brandenburg)   Palace

Potsdam's newest landmark is the replica of the 18th-century Prussian City Palace that was partly destroyed in WWII and completely removed by East German town planners in 1960. It reopened in October 2013 as the new home of the Brandenburg state parliament. Of the original building, only the ornate Fortuna Portal remains and now forms the main entrance to the compound, sections of which are open to the public.
(Potsdam City Palace; ☎0331-966 1253; www.stadtschloss-potsdam.org; Alter Markt; ⊙usually 10am-5pm Mon-Fri) FREE

Nikolaikirche   Church

In Potsdam's historic centre, around the Alter Markt (old market), the great green dome of Karl Friedrich Schinkel's neoclassical Nikolaikirche (1850) is complemented by a 16m-high obelisk festooned with imagery of famous local architects, including Schinkel. The tower can be climbed. (☎0331-270 8602; www.nikolai-potsdam.de; Alter Markt 1; tower €5; ⊙9am-7pm Mon-Sat, 11.30am-7pm Sun Apr-Oct, to 5pm Nov-Mar)

Obelisk in Park Sanssouci (p88)

◎ Neuer Garten & Around

North of the Potsdam old town, the winding lakeside Neuer Garten (New Garden), laid out in natural English style on the western shore of the Heiliger See, is another fine park in which to relax.

Marmorpalais · Palace

The neoclassical Marble Palace was built in 1792 as a summer residence for Friedrich Wilhelm II by Carl Gotthard Langhans (of Berlin's Brandenburg Gate fame) and has a stunning interior marked by a grand central staircase, marble fireplaces, stucco ceilings and lots of precious Wedgwood porcelain. The most fanciful room is the Turkish-tent-style Orientalisches Kabinett (Oriental Cabinet). (Marble Palace; ☑0331-969 4550; www.spsg.de; Im Neuen Garten 10; tours adult/concession €5/4; ☺10am-6pm Tue-Sun May-Oct, 10am-4pm Sat & Sun Nov-Mar; 🚃603)

Schloss Cecilienhof · Palace

This English-style country palace was completed in 1917 for crown prince Wilhelm and his wife Cecilie, but is most famous for hosting the 1945 Potsdam Conference where Stalin, Truman and Churchill (replaced by his successor Clement Atlee) hammered out Germany's postwar fate. The conference room, with its giant round table, looks as though the delegates just left. (☑0331-969 4520; www.spsg.de; Im Neuen Garten 11; tours adult/concession €6/5; ☺10am-6pm Tue-Sun Apr-Oct, to 5pm Nov-Mar; 🚃603)

◎ Alexandrowka & Pfingstberg

North of the Altstadt, Potsdam slopes up to the Pfingstberg past a Russian colony, a Russian Orthodox church and a Jewish cemetery.

Alexandrowka · Neighbourhood

One of Potsdam's most unusual neighbourhoods, Alexandrowka is a Russian colony that was a gift from Friedrich Wilhelm III to his close friend Tsar Alexander in 1820. The first residents were the singers of a Russian military choir who had much delighted the king. Descendants of the original settlers

 ## Potsdam & the Silver Screen

Film buffs will know that Potsdam is famous not merely for its palaces but also for being the birthplace of European film production. For it was here, in the suburb of Babelsberg, about 4km west of the city centre, that the venerable UFA Studio was founded in 1912. A few years later, it was already producing such seminal flicks as *Metropolis* and *Blue Angel*. Continuing as DEFA in GDR times, the dream factory was resurrected as Studio Babelsberg after reunification and has since produced or co-produced such international blockbusters as *Inglorious Basterds*, *The Grand Budapest Hotel* and *The Hunger Games*.

There are two ways to plug into the Potsdam film experience. In town, the handsome baroque royal stables now house the **Filmmuseum Potsdam** (www.filmmuseum-potsdam.de; Breite Strasse 1a; adult/concession €4.50/3.50; ☺10am-6pm Tue-Sun), which presents an engaging romp through German movie history with an emphasis on the DEFA period. In Babelsberg, next to the actual film studios, **Filmpark Babelsberg** (www.filmpark-babelsberg.de; Grossbeerenstrasse 200; adult/concession/child €21/17/14; ☺10am-6pm Apr-Oct; 🚃601, 690, 🚋Medienstadt Babelsberg) is a movie-themed amusement park with stunt shows, movie sets and a studio tour with stops at the prop room, costume department and workshops.

still live in the chalet-like wooden houses surrounded by gardens and orchards. Learn more at the pretty little museum with nearby garden cafe.

Karl Friedrich Schinkel designed the Russian Orthodox church, called Alexander-Newski-Gedächtniskirche, just north of the colony. (www.alexandrowka.de; Russische Kolonie 1; museum adult/concession/under 14 €3.50/3/free; ☺museum 10am-6pm Tue-Sun; 🚃92 or 96 from Hauptbahnhof)

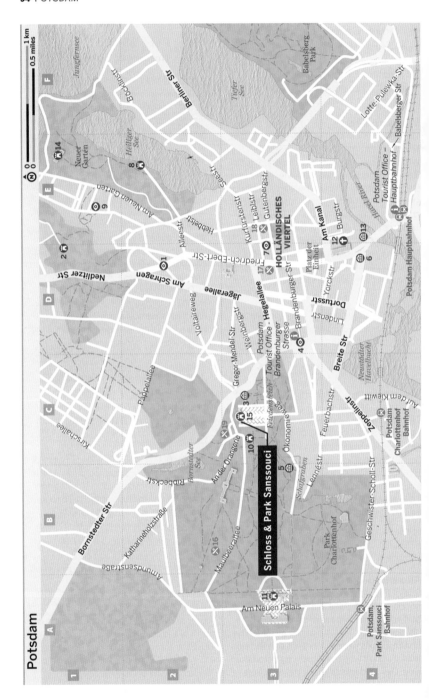

Potsdam

Schloss & Park Sanssouci

Potsdam

Belvedere auf dem Pfingstberg
Palace

For splendid views over Potsdam and surrounds, ascend the spiralling wrought-iron staircases of the twin-towered Belvedere palace commissioned by Friedrich Wilhelm IV and modelled on an Italian Renaissance–style villa. The 1801 Pomonatempel just below it was Karl Friedrich Schinkel's very first architectural commission. (☑0331-2005 7930; www.pfingstberg.de; Pfingstberg; adult/concession €4/3; ⊙10am-6pm Apr-Oct, 10am-4pm Sat & Sun Mar & Nov; ☐92 or 96 from Hauptbahnhof) FREE

Memorial Leistikowstrasse (KGB Prison)
Memorial

Now a memorial site, Potsdam's central remand prison for Soviet Counter Intelligence – colloquially known as KGB prison – is a particularly sinister Cold War relic. All sorts of (real or alleged) crimes could land you here, including espionage, desertion, insubordination or Nazi complicity. Using letters, documents, photographs, personal items and taped interviews, exhibits outline the fate of individuals. Prisoners were often abused and tortured until they confessed, then tried in closed sessions without legal representation and usually sent straight to the Gulag or the executioner. (☑0331-201 1540; www.gedenkstaette-leistikowstrasse.de; Leistikowstrasse 1; ⊙2-6pm Tue-Sun) FREE

◉ EATING

Hafthorn
Gastropub €

Check your pretensions in at the door of this cheerily charming pub, the home of quirky metal lamps, big burgers and sudsy Bohemian beer. An all-ages crowd shares laughter inside this former bakery and, in summer, along candlelit benches in the beer garden. (☑0331-280 0820; www.hafthorn.de; Friedrich-Ebert-Strasse 90; dishes €5-9; ⊙from 6pm; ☐695)

Maison Charlotte
French €€

There's a rustic lyricism to the French country cuisine in this darling Dutch Quarter bistro, no matter whether your appetite runs towards a simple *Flammkuchen* (Alsatian pizza), Breton fish soup or a multicourse menu. Budget bon vivants come for the daily lunch special: €7.50, including a glass of wine. (☑0331-280 5450; www.maison-charlotte.de; Mittelstrasse 20; Flammkuchen €8-12.50, 3-/4-course menu €39-47; ⊙noon-11pm)

❶ INFORMATION

The **Potsdam Tourist Office – Hauptbahnhof** (☑0331-2755 8899; www.potsdam-tourism.com; ⊙9.30am-8pm Mon-Sat May-Oct, to 6pm Mon-Sat Nov-Apr, 10am-4pm Sun year-round) is located inside the main train station. There's another office at **Brandenburger Tor** (Brandenburger Strasse 3; ⊙10am-6pm Mon-Sat, 10am-4pm Sun Apr-Oct, shorter hours Sat & Sun Nov-Mar; ☐605, 631, 650). Most people visit Potsdam on a day trip from Berlin. At night, the town gets very quiet. The tourist office can book rooms.

Schloss Nymphenburg (p107)

MUNICH

Munich

The natural habitat of well-heeled power dressers and Lederhosen-clad thigh-slappers, Mediterranean-style street cafes and Mitteleuropa beer halls, highbrow art and high-tech industry, Germany's unofficial southern capital is a flourishing success story that revels in its own contradictions. If you're looking for Alpine clichés, they're all here, but the Bavarian metropolis has many an unexpected card down its dirndl.

Munich's walkable centre retains a small-town air but holds some world-class sights, especially art galleries and museums. Throw in royal Bavarian heritage, an entire suburb of Olympic legacy and a kitbag of dark tourism, and it's clear why southern Germany's metropolis is such a favourite among those who seek out the past but like to hit the town once they're done.

➡ Arriving in Munich

Munich Airport Located about 30km northeast of the city; handles flights from all major destinations.

Hauptbahnhof Western end of the city centre; a major terminus in Germany.

Central Bus Station On the Stammstrecke; easy access to the rest of the city.

Allgäu Airport Some services touting themselves as flights to Munich actually land here, over 100km away.

From left: Oktoberfest (p100); Munich Airport; Antiquarium, Residenzmuseum (p104); BMW Welt (p116)
MICHAEL TAYLOR/GETTY IMAGES © KVIKTOR/SHUTTERSTOCK © GARY YIM/SHUTTERSTOCK © MICHAEL THALER/SHUTTERSTOCK ©

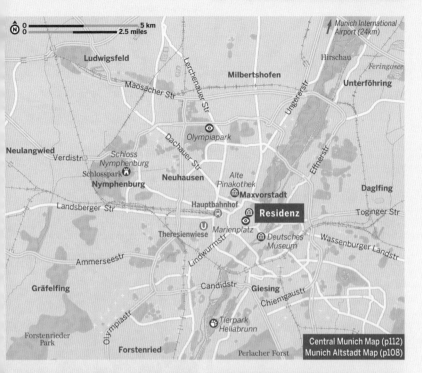

➡ Munich in Two Days

Start your day with breakfast at the **Viktualienmarkt** (p110) then cross **Marienplatz** (p106) for a tour of the royal splendour of the **Residenz** (p102). Take a break in the **Englischer Garten** (p115), then spend the afternoon admiring technical achievements at the **Deutsches Museum** (p115). Finish the day at a typical Munich **beer hall**. Your second day can be devoted entirely to the top-notch museums and galleries in the Kunstareal (Arts Quarter).

➡ Munich in Four Days

Start day three at **BMW Welt** (p117) and the **BMW Museum** (p116) followed by a clamber up the **Olympiaturm** (p116) at the **Olympiapark** (p116). In the afternoon head to **Nymphenburg** (p107) to see one of Bavaria's finest palaces. Finish off at one of the city's superb beer gardens. Board the S-Bahn on day four for trips to **Starnberg** (p128) and **Dachau** (p118).

Beer tent, Oktoberfest

MAREMAGNUM/GETTY IMAGES ©

Oktoberfest

The world's most famous beer festival is an event only ever described in superlatives – biggest, most visited, longest-running... the list goes on. Come and join six million beer lovers for Munich's most raucous party of the year.

Great For...

☑ Don't Miss

Dress for the part by buying or hiring some Bavarian national garb: lederhosen for men, dirndl for women.

Oktoberfest's Beginnings

It all started as an elaborate wedding toast – and turned into the world's biggest collective booze-up. In October 1810 the future king, Bavarian Crown Prince Ludwig I, married Princess Therese and the newlyweds threw an enormous party at the city gates, complete with a horse race. The next year Ludwig's fun-loving subjects came back for more. The festival was extended and, to fend off autumn, was moved forward to September. As the years rolled on, the racehorses were dropped and sometimes the party had to be cancelled, but the institution called Oktoberfest was here to stay.

Oktoberfest parade

EURASIA PRESS/GETTY IMAGES ©

Dirndl, Lederhosen & Wies'nbier

Nearly two centuries later, this 16-day extravaganza draws more than six million visitors a year to celebrate a marriage of good cheer and outright debauchery. A special dark, strong beer (Wies'nbier) is brewed for the occasion, and Müncheners spend the day at the office in lederhosen and dirndl in order to hit the festival right after work. No admission fee is charged, but most of the fun costs something.

Oktoberfest Traditions

On the meadow called Theresienwiese (Wies'n for short) 15 minutes' walk from the Hauptbahnhof, a temporary city is erected, consisting of beer tents, amusements and rides – just what drinkers need after several frothy ones! The action kicks off with the Brewer's Parade at 11am on the first day of the festival. The parade begins at Sonnenstrasse and winds its way to the fairgrounds via Schwanthalerstrasse. At noon, the lord mayor stands before the thirsty crowds at Theresienwiese and, with due pomp, slams a wooden tap into a cask of beer. As the beer gushes out, the mayor exclaims, '*O'zapft ist's!*' (It's tapped!). The next day resembles the opening of the Olympics, as a young woman on horseback leads a parade of costumed participants from all over the world.

Head to the popular **Bier & Oktoberfestmuseum** (Beer & Oktoberfest Museum; Map p108; www.bier-und-oktoberfestmuseum.de; Sterneckerstrasse 2; adult/concession €4/2.50; ☺1-6pm Tue-Sat; 🚊Isartor, Ⓢ Isartor) to learn all about Bavarian suds and the world's most famous booze-up. The four floors heave with old brewing vats, historical photos and some of the earliest Oktoberfest regalia. The 14th-century building has some fine medieval features, including painted ceilings and a kitchen with an open fire.

Tapestry in the Residenz

Residenz

Home to Bavaria's Wittelsbach rulers from 1508 until WWI, the Residenz is Munich's number-one attraction. The Residenzmuseum takes up around half of the palace – allow around two hours to do it justice.

Great For...

ℹ Need to Know

Map p108; www.residenz-muenchen. de; ☉ vary between individual attractions; Ⓤ Odeonsplatz

★ **Top Tip**

Outside the summer months, visit the Residenz in the afternoon when the Cuvilliés-Theater is open.

Residenzmuseum

Tours of the **Residenzmuseum** (Map p108; ☎089-290 671; www.residenz-muenchen.de; Residenzstrasse 1; adult/concession/under 18yr €7/6/free; ⏰9am-6pm Apr–mid-Oct, 10am-5pm mid-Oct–Mar, last entry 1hr before closing; Ⓤ Odeonsplatz) kick off at the Grottenhof (Grotto Court), home of the wonderful Perseusbrunnen (Perseus Fountain), with its namesake holding the dripping head of Medusa. Next door is the famous Antiquarium, a barrel-vaulted hall smothered in frescos and built to house the Wittelsbach's enormous antique collection. It's widely regarded as the finest Renaissance interior north of the Alps.

Upstairs are the Kurfürstenzimmer (Electors Rooms), with some stunning Italian portraits and a passage lined with two dozen views of Italy, painted by local romantic artist Carl Rottmann. Also up here are François Cuvilliés' Reiche Zimmer (Ornate Rooms), a six-room extravaganza of exuberant rococo carried out by the top stucco and fresco artists of the day. They're a definite museum highlight. More rococo magic awaits in the Ahnengallery (Ancestors Gallery), with 121 portraits of the rulers of Bavaria in chronological order.

The Hofkapelle, reserved for the ruler and his family, is stunning but not as memorable as the exquisite Reiche Kapelle (Ornate Chapel) with its blue and gilt ceiling, inlaid marble and 16th-century organ. This chapel was reserved for court residents in the reign of the Wittelsbachs – the Bavarian rulers who lived in the Residenz from 1385 to 1918s. Considered

Aerial view of the Theatinerkirche (p111), Residenz and Hofgarten

the finest rococo interiors in southern Germany, another spot to linger longer is the Steinzimmer (Stone Rooms), the emperor's quarters awash in intricately patterned and coloured marble.

Schatzkammer der Residenz

The palace's **treasury** (Residence Treasury; Map p108; Residenzstrasse 1; adult/concession/under 18yr €7/6/free; ☺9am-6pm Apr–mid-Oct, 10am-5pm mid-Oct–Mar, last entry 1hr before closing; ⓤOdeonsplatz) is a veritable banker's bonus worth of jewel-encrusted

bling of yesteryear, from golden tooth-picks to finely crafted swords, miniatures in ivory to gold entombed cosmetics trunks. The 1250 incredibly intricate and attractive items on display come in every precious material you could imagine, including rhino horn, lapis lazuli, crystal, coral and amber.

Cuvilliés-Theater

Commissioned by Maximilian III in the mid-18th century, François Cuvilliés fashioned one of Europe's finest rococo **theatres** (Map p108; Residenzstrasse 1; adult/concession/under 18yr €3.50/2.50/free; ☺2-6pm Mon-Sat, 9am-6pm Sun Apr-Jul & Sep–mid-Oct, 9am-6pm daily Aug, 2-5pm Mon-Sat, 10am-5pm Sun Nov-Mar; 🚇Nationaltheater), famous for hosting the premiere of Mozart's opera *Idomeneo*. Restoration work between 2004 and 2008 revived the theatre's former glory and its stage once again hosts high-brow musical and operatic performances. Access is limited to the auditorium, where you can take a seat and admire the four tiers of loggia (galleries), dripping with rococo embellishment, at your leisure.

Hofgarten

Office workers catching some rays during their lunch break, stylish mothers pushing prams, seniors on bikes, a gaggle of chatty nuns – everybody comes to the **Hofgarten** (Map p108; ⓤOdeonsplatz). The formal court gardens, with fountains, radiant flower beds, lime-tree-lined gravel paths and benches galore, sit just north of the Residenz. Paths converge at the Dianatempel, a striking octagonal pavilion honouring the Roman goddess of the hunt. Enter the gardens from Odeonsplatz.

> ### ❶ Did You Know?
> The four giant bronze lion statues guarding the entrance to the Residenz have remarkably shiny noses: scores of people walk by and casually rub them for wealth and good luck.

WESTEND61/GETTY IMAGES ©

> ### ✗ Take a Break
> Light, airy, vaguely Portuguese Stereo Cafe (p125) is right opposite the Residenz entrance.

◉ SIGHTS

Munich's major sights cluster around the Altstadt, with the main museum district just north of the Residenz. However, it will take another day or two to explore bohemian Schwabing, the sprawling Englischer Garten, and trendy Haidhausen to the east. Northwest of the Altstadt you'll find cosmopolitan Neuhausen, the Olympiapark, and another of Munich's royal highlights – Schloss Nymphenburg.

◎ Altstadt

Marienplatz   Square

The epicentral heart and soul of the Altstadt, Marienplatz is a popular gathering spot and packs a lot of personality into a compact frame. It's anchored by the Mariensäule (Mary's Column), built in 1638 to celebrate victory over Swedish forces during the Thirty Years' War. This is the busiest spot in all Munich, throngs of tourists swarming across its expanse from early morning till late at night. (Map p108; S̲Marienplatz, U̲Marienplatz)

Neues Rathaus   Historic Building

The soot-blackened facade of the neo-Gothic Neues Rathaus is festooned with gargoyles, statues and a dragon scaling the turrets; the tourist office is on the ground floor. For pinpointing Munich's landmarks without losing your breath, catch the lift up the 85m-tall **tower** (adult/concession €2.50/1; ◷10am-7pm).

The **Glockenspiel** (◷11am, noon, 5pm & 9pm) has 43 bells and 32 figures that perform two historical events. The top half tells the story of a tournament held in 1568 to celebrate the marriage of Duke Wilhelm V to Renata of Lothringen, while the bottom half portrays the **Schäfflertanz** (cooper's dance). (New Town Hall; Map p108; Marienplatz; U̲Marienplatz, S̲Marienplatz)

Altes Rathaus   Historic Building

The eastern side of Marienplatz is dominated by the Altes Rathaus. Lightning got the better of the medieval original in 1460 and WWII bombs levelled its successor, so what you see is really the third incarnation of the building designed by Jörg von

Neues Rathaus

Halspach of Frauenkirche fame. On 9 November 1938 Joseph Goebbels gave a hate-filled speech here that launched the nationwide Kristallnacht pogroms. (Old Town Hall; Map p108; Marienplatz; [U]Marienplatz, [S]Marienplatz)

Frauenkirche   Church
The landmark Frauenkirche, built between 1468 and 1488, is Munich's spiritual heart and the Mt Everest among its churches. No other building in the central city may stand taller than its onion-domed twin towers, which reach a skyscraping 99m. The south tower can be climbed but was under urgent renovation at the time of writing.

The church sustained severe bomb damage in WWII; its reconstruction is a soaring passage of light but otherwise fairly spartan. Of note are the epic cenotaph (empty tomb) of Ludwig the Bavarian, just past the entrance, and the bronze plaques of Pope Benedict XVI and his predecessor John Paul II, affixed to nearby pillars. (Church of Our Lady; Map p108; www.muenchner-dom.de; Frauenplatz 1; ⊙7am-7pm Sat-Wed, to 8.30pm Thu, to 6pm Fri; [S]Marienplatz)

Asamkirche   Church
Though pocket sized, the late-baroque Asamkirche, built in 1746, is as rich and epic as a giant's treasure chest. Its creators, the brothers Cosmas Damian Asam and Egid Quirin Asam, dug deep into their considerable talent box to swathe every inch of wall space with gilt garlands and docile cherubs, false marble and oversized barley twist columns. (Map p108; Sendlinger Strasse 32; ⊙9am-6pm Sat-Thu, 1-6pm Fri; 🚇Sendlinger Tor, [U]Sendlinger Tor) FREE

St Peterskirche   Church
Some 306 steps divide you from the best view of central Munich from the 92m tower of St Peterskirche, Munich's oldest church (1150). Inside awaits a virtual textbook of art through the centuries. Worth a closer peek are the Gothic St-Martin-Altar, the baroque ceiling fresco by Johann Baptist

Schloss Nymphenburg

This commanding **palace** (Map p112; www.schloss-nymphenburg.de; adult/concession €6/5; ⊙9am-6pm Apr–mid-Oct, 10am-4pm mid-Oct–Mar; 🚇Schloss Nymphenburg) and its lavish gardens sprawl around 5km northwest of the Altstadt. Begun in 1664 as a villa for Electress Adelaide of Savoy, the stately pile was extended over the next century to create the royal family's summer residence.

The main palace building consists of a large villa and two wings of creaking parquet floors and sumptuous period rooms. Right at the beginning of the self-guided tour comes the high point of the entire Schloss, the **Schönheitengalerie** (Gallery of Beauties), housed in the former apartments of Queen Caroline. Some 38 portraits of attractive females chosen by an admiring King Ludwig I peer prettily from the walls.

Further along the tour route comes the Queen's Bedroom, which still contains the sleigh bed on which Ludwig II was born, and the King's Chamber, resplendent with three-dimensional ceiling frescos.

Also in the main building is the **Marstallmuseum** (adult/concession/under 18yr €4.50/3.50/free), displaying royal coaches and riding gear. This includes Ludwig II's fairy-tale-like rococo sleigh, ingeniously fitted with oil lamps for his crazed nocturnal outings. The sprawling park behind Schloss Nymphenburg is a favourite spot with Müncheners and visitors for strolling, jogging or whiling away a lazy afternoon.

Zimmermann and rococo sculptures by Ignaz Günther. (Map p108; Church of St Peter; Rindermarkt 1; church free, tower adult/concession €2/1; ⊙tower 9am-6pm Mon-Fri, from 10am Sat & Sun; [U]Marienplatz, [S]Marienplatz)

Munich Altstadt

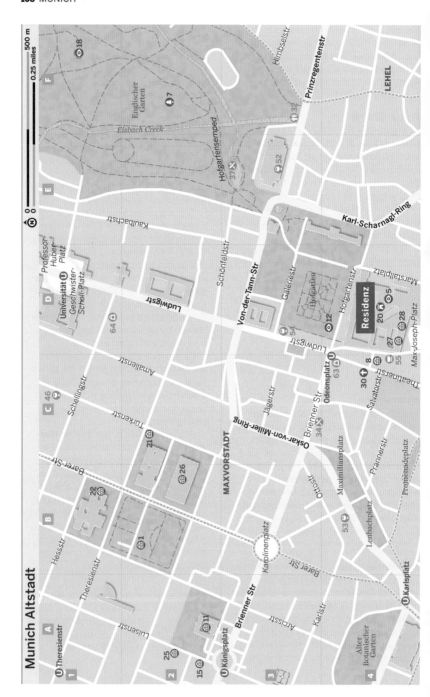

500 m
0.25 miles

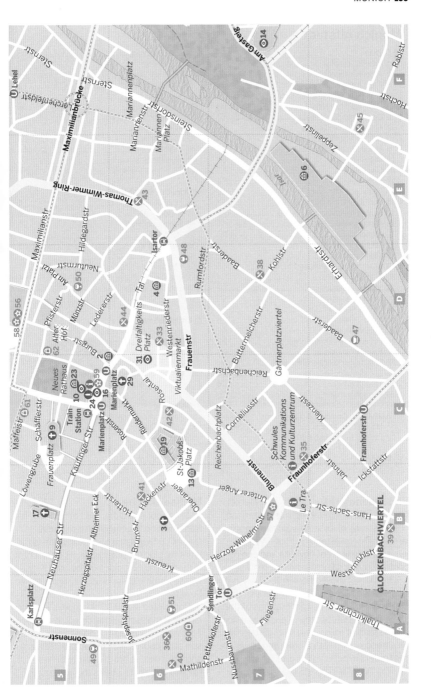

Munich Altstadt

Viktualienmarkt   Market

Fresh fruit and vegetables, piles of artisan cheeses, tubs of exotic olives, hams and jams, chanterelles and truffles – Viktual-ienmarkt is a feast of flavours and one of central Europe's finest gourmet markets.

The market moved here in 1807 when it outgrew the Marienplatz and many of the stalls have been run by generations of the same family. Put together a picnic and head for the market's very own beer garden for an alfresco lunch with a brew and to watch the traders in action. (Map p108; ⊗ Mon-Fri & morning Sat; Ⓤ Marienplatz, Ⓢ Marienplatz)

Michaelskirche   Church

It stands quiet and dignified amid the retail frenzy out on Kaufingerstrasse, but to fans of Ludwig II, the Michaelskirche is the ultimate place of pilgrimage. Its dank crypt is the final resting place of the Mad King, whose humble tomb is usually drowned in flowers.

Completed in 1597, St Michael's was the largest Renaissance church north of the Alps when it was built. It boasts an impressive unsupported barrel-vaulted ceiling, and the massive bronze statue between the two entrances shows the archangel finishing off a dragon-like creature, a classic Counter-Reformation-era symbol of Catholicism triumphing over Protestantism. The building has been fully renovated in recent years and has never looked more impressive. (Map p108; Church of St Michael; Kaufingerstrasse 52; crypt admission €2; ☉crypt 9.30am-4.30pm Mon-Fri, to 2.30pm Sat & Sun; 🚊Karlsplatz, **S**Karlsplatz, **U**Karlsplatz)

Münchner Stadtmuseum Museum
Installed for the city's 850th birthday (2008), the Münchner Stadtmuseum's *Typisch München* (Typical Munich) exhibition – taking up the whole of a rambling building – tells Munich's story in an imaginative, uncluttered and engaging way. Exhibits in each section represent something quintessential about the city; a booklet/audioguide relates the tale behind them, thus condensing a long and tangled history into easily digestible themes. (Map p108; City Museum; www.muenchner-stadt museum.de; St-Jakobs-Platz 1; adult/concession/child €6/3.50/free, audioguide free; ☉10am-6pm Tue-Sun; **U**Marienplatz, **S**Marienplatz)

Jüdisches Museum Museum
Coming to terms with its Nazi past has not historically been a priority in Munich, which is why the opening of the Jewish Museum in 2007 was hailed as a milestone. The permanent exhibition offers an insight into Jewish history, life and culture in the city. The Holocaust is dealt with, but the focus is clearly on contemporary Jewish culture. (Jewish Museum; Map p108; www.juedisches-museum-muenchen.de; St-Jakobs-Platz 16; adult/child €6/3; ☉10am-6pm Tue-Sun; 🚊Sendlinger Tor, **U**Sendlinger Tor)

Feldherrnhalle Historic Building
Corking up Odeonsplatz' southern side is Friedrich von Gärnter's Feldherrnhalle, modelled on the Loggia dei Lanzi in Florence. The structure pays homage to the Bavarian army and positively drips with testosterone; check out the statues of General Johann Tilly, who kicked the Swedes out of Munich during the Thirty

Years' War; and Karl Philipp von Wrede, an ally turned foe of Napoleon.

It was here on 9 November 1923 that police stopped the so-called Beer Hall Putsch, Hitler's attempt to bring down the Weimar Republic (Germany's government after WWI). A fierce skirmish left 20 people, including 16 Nazis, dead. A plaque in the pavement of the square's eastern side commemorates the police officers who perished in the incident. Hitler was subsequently tried and sentenced to five years in jail, but he ended up serving a mere nine months in Landsberg am Lech prison, where he penned his hate-filled manifesto, *Mein Kampf*. (Field Marshalls Hall; Map p108; Residenzstrasse 1; **U**Odeonsplatz)

Theatinerkirche Church
The mustard-yellow Theatinerkirche, built to commemorate the 1662 birth of Prince Max Emanuel, is the work of Swiss architect Enrico Zuccalli. Also known as St Kajetan's, it's a voluptuous design with two massive twin towers flanking a giant cupola. Inside, an ornate dome lords over the *Fürstengruft* (royal crypt), the final destination of several Wittelsbach rulers, including King Maximilian II (1811–64). The building was receiving much-needed renovation at the time of research but was still open to the public. (Map p108; Theatinerstrasse 22; **S**Odeonsplatz)

◉ Maxvorstadt & the Englischer Garten

Alte Pinakothek Museum
Munich's main repository of Old European Masters is crammed with all the major players that decorated canvases between the 14th and 18th centuries. This neoclassical temple was masterminded by Leo von Klenze and is a delicacy even if you can't tell your Rembrandt from your Rubens. The collection is world famous for its exceptional quality and depth, especially when it comes to German masters. (Map p108; ☎089-238 0526; www.pinakothek.de; Barer Strasse 27; adult/child €4/2, Sun €1, audioguide €4.50; ☉10am-8pm Tue, to 6pm Wed-Sun; 🚊Pinakotheken, 🚊Pinakotheken)

Central Munich

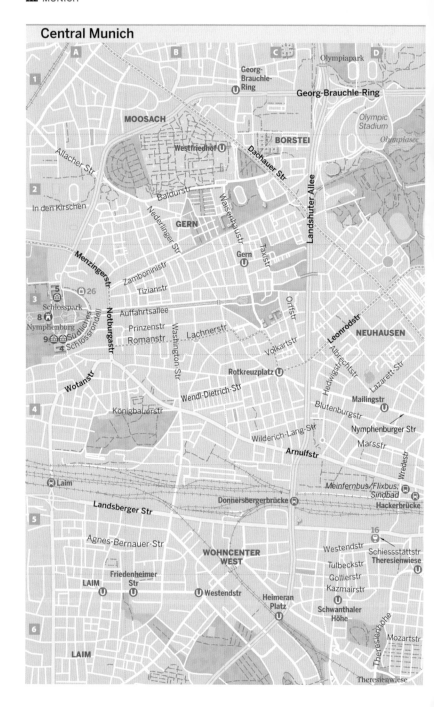

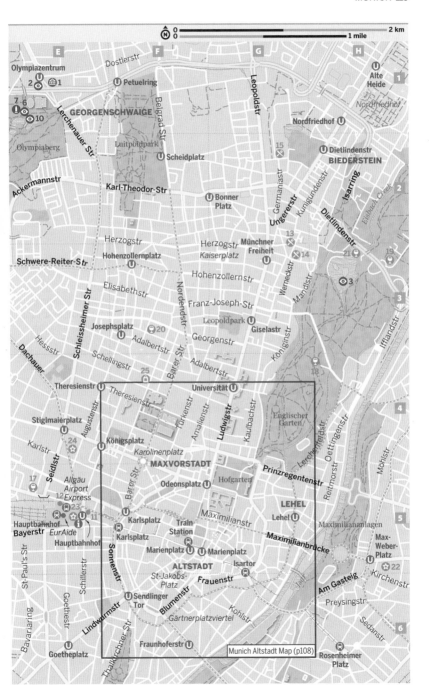

Central Munich

Neue Pinakothek   Museum
The Neue Pinakothek harbours a
well-respected collection of 19th- and
early-20th-century paintings and sculpture,
from rococo to *Jugendstil* (art nouveau).
All the world-famous household names get
wall space here, including crowd-pleasing
French impressionists such as Monet,
Cézanne and Degas as well as Van Gogh,
whose boldly pigmented *Sunflowers* (1888)
radiates cheer. (Map p108; ☑089-2380 5195;
www.pinakothek.de; Barer Strasse 29; adult/child
€7/5, Sun €1; ⊙10am-6pm Thu-Mon, to 8pm
Wed; ☐Pinakotheken, ☐Pinakotheken)

Pinakothek der Moderne   Museum
Germany's largest modern-art museum
unites four significant collections under
a single roof: 20th-century art, applied
design from the 19th century to today, a
graphics collection and an architecture museum. It's housed in a spectacular building
by Stephan Braunfels, whose four-storey
interior centres on a vast eye-like dome
through which soft natural light filters
throughout the blanched white galleries.
(Map p108; ☑089-2380 5360; www.pinakothek.
de; Barer Strasse 40; adult/child €10/7, Sun €1;
⊙10am-6pm Tue, Wed & Fri-Sun, to 8pm Thu;
☐Pinakotheken, ☐Pinakotheken)

Museum Brandhorst   Gallery
A big, bold and aptly abstract building, clad
entirely in vividly multihued ceramic tubes,
the Brandhorst jostled its way into the
Munich Kunstareal (Arts Quarter) in a punk
blaze of colour mid-2009. Its walls, its floor
and occasionally its ceiling provide space
for some of the most challenging art in the
city, among it some instantly recognisable
20th-century images by Andy Warhol,
whose work dominates the collection. (Map
p108; www.museum-brandhorst.de; Theresien-
strasse 35a; adult/child €7/5, Sun €1; ⊙10am-
6pm Tue, Wed & Fri-Sun, to 8pm Thu; ☐Maxvor-
stadt/Sammlung Brandhorst, ☐Pinakotheken)

Glyptothek   Museum
If you're a fan of classical art or simply enjoy
the sight of naked guys without noses (or
other pertinent body parts), make a beeline
for the Glyptothek. One of Munich's oldest
museums, it's a feast of art and sculpture
from ancient Greece and Rome amassed
by Ludwig I between 1806 and 1830, and it
opens a surprisingly naughty window onto
the ancient world. Tickets for the museum
are also valid for the Antikensammlungen.
(Map p108; www.antike-am-koenigsplatz.mwn.de;
Königsplatz 3; adult/concession €6/4, Sun €1;
⊙10am-5pm Fri-Sun, Tue & Wed, to 8pm Thu;
☐Königsplatz, ☐Königsplatz)

Lenbachhaus   Museum

Reopened in 2013 to rave reviews after a four-year renovation that saw the addition of a new wing by noted architect Norman Foster, this glorious gallery is once again the go-to place to admire the vibrant canvases of Kandinsky, Franz Marc, Paul Klee and other members of ground-breaking modernist group Der Blaue Reiter (The Blue Rider), founded in Munich in 1911.

Contemporary art is another focal point. An eye-catcher is a glass-and-steel sculpture by Olafur Eliasson in the soaring new atrium. Many other big names are also represented, including Gerhard Richter, Sigmar Polke, Anselm Kiefer, Andy Warhol, Dan Flavin, Richard Serra and Jenny Holzer. Tickets are also valid for special exhibits at the nearby Kunstbau, a 120m-long tunnel above the Königsplatz U-Bahn station. (Municipal Gallery; Map p108; ☑089-2333 2000; www.lenbachhaus.de; Luisenstrasse 33; adult/concession incl audioguide €10/5; �---10am-9pm Tue, to 6pm Wed-Sun; ⚑Königsplatz, ⓊKönigsplatz)

Englischer Garten   Park

The sprawling English Garden is among Europe's biggest city parks – it even rivals London's Hyde Park and New York's Central Park for size – and is a popular playground for locals and visitors alike. Stretching north from Prinzregentenstrasse for about 5km, it was commissioned by Elector Karl Theodor in 1789 and designed by Benjamin Thompson, an American-born scientist working as an adviser to the Bavarian government.

Paths piddle around in dark stands of mature oak and maple before emerging into sunlit meadows of lush grass. Locals are mindful of the park's popularity and tolerate the close quarters of cyclists, walkers and joggers. Street musicians dodge balls kicked by children and students sprawl on the grass to chat about missed lectures. Sooner or later you'll find your way to the **Kleinhesseloher See**, a lovely lake at the centre of the park. Work up a sweat while taking a spin around three little islands, then quaff a well-earned foamy one at the

Seehaus beer garden (Kleinhesselohe 3; 🚼; ⓈMünchner Freiheit). Several historic follies lend the park a playful charm. The wholly unexpected **Chinesischer Turm** (Chinese Tower; p124), now at the heart of Munich's oldest beer garden, was built in the 18th century during a pan-European craze for all things oriental. Further south, at the top of a gentle hill, stands the heavily photographed **Monopteros** (1838), a small Greek temple whose ledges are often knee-to-knee with dangling legs belonging to people admiring the view of the Munich skyline. Another hint of Asia awaits further south by an idyllic pond at the Japanisches Teehaus (Japanese Teahouse), built for the 1972 Olympics. The best time to come is for an authentic tea ceremony celebrated by a Japanese tea master. (Map p108; ⓊUniversität)

◎ South of the Altstadt

Deutsches Museum   Museum

If you're one of those people for whom science is an unfathomable turn-off, a visit to the Deutsches Museum might just show you that physics and engineering are more fun than you thought. This temple to technology is an eye-opening place of discovery and the exhibitions and demonstrations will certainly be a hit with young, sponge-like minds.

There are tons of interactive displays (including glass blowing and paper making), live demonstrations and experiments, model coal and salt mines, and engaging sections on cave paintings, geodesy, microelectronics and astronomy. In fact, it can be pretty overwhelming after a while, so it's best to prioritise what you want to see. The place to entertain children aged three to eight is the fabulous KinderReich, where 1000 activities, from a kid-size mouse wheel to interactive water fun, await. Get the littlies to climb all over a fire engine, build things with giant Lego, construct a waterway with canals and locks, or bang on a drum all day in a – thankfully – soundproof instrument room. Note that KinderReich closes at 4.30pm. (Map p108; ☑089-217 9333; www.deutsches-museum.de;

Museumsinsel 1; adult/child €11/4; ☺9am-5pm; 🚇Deutsches Museum)

⊚ Olympiapark & Around

Olympiapark   Stadium

The area to the north of the city where soldiers once paraded and the world's first Zeppelin landed in 1909 found a new role in the 1960s as the Olympiapark. Built for the 1972 Olympic Summer Games, it has quite a small-scale feel and some may be amazed that the games could once have been held at such a petite venue.

The complex draws people year-round with concerts, festivals and sporting events, and its swimming hall and ice-skating rink are open to the public. A good first stop is the Info-Pavilion, which has information, maps, tour tickets and a model of the complex. Staff also rent out MP3 players for a self-guided audio tour. Olympiapark has two famous eye-catchers: the 290m **Olympiaturm** (Olympic Tower; adult/child €5.50/3.50; ☺9am-midnight) and the warped Olympiastadion. Germans have a soft spot for the latter because it was on this hallowed turf in 1974

that the national soccer team – led by 'the Kaiser' Franz Beckenbauer – won the FIFA World Cup. When the sky is clear, you'll quite literally have Munich at your feet against the breathtaking backdrop of the Alps from the top of the Olympiaturm. (Olympic Park; Map p112; www.olympiapark.de; stadium adult/child €3/2, stadium tour adult/concession €7.50/5; ☺stadium tours 11am, 1pm & 4pm Apr-Oct; 🇺Olympiazenturm)

BMW Museum   Museum

This silver bowl-shaped museum comprises seven themed 'houses' that examine the development of BMW's product line and include sections on motorcycles and motor racing. Even if you can't tell a head gasket from a crankshaft, the interior design, with its curvy retro feel, futuristic bridges, squares and huge backlit wall screens, is reason enough to visit.

The museum is linked to two architecturally stunning buildings: the BMW headquarters (closed to the public) and the BMW Welt showroom. (Map p112; www.bmw-welt. de; Am Olympiapark 2; adult/concession €10/7; ☺10am-6pm Tue-Sun; 🇺Olympiazentrum)

Olympiapark

DANIEL SCHOENEN/GETTY IMAGES ©

BMW Welt   Notable Building
Next to the Olympiapark, the glass-and-steel, double-cone tornado spiralling down from a dark cloud the size of an aircraft carrier holds BMW Welt, truly a petrolhead's dream. Apart from its role as a prestigious car pick-up centre, this king of showrooms acts as a shop window for BMW's latest models and a show space for the company as a whole.

Straddle a powerful motorbike, marvel at technology-packed saloons and estates (no tyre kicking, please), browse the 'lifestyle' shop or take the 80-minute guided tour. On the Junior Campus, kids learn about mobility, fancy themselves car engineers and even get to design their own vehicle in workshops. Hang around long enough and you're sure to see motorbike stunts on the staircases and other petroleum-fuelled antics. (BMW World; Map p112; ☑089-125 016 001; www.bmw-welt. de; Am Olympiapark 1; tours adult/child €7/5; ☺7.30am-midnight; ⓊOlympiazentrum) FREE

BMW Plant Tours   Tour
If you like cars, be sure not to miss a tour of BMW's state-of-the-art plant. The tours in English and German last 2½ hours and take in the entire production process. Booking well ahead is essential, especially in summer. (☑089-125 016 001; www.bmw-welt.com; adult/concession €8/5; ☺9am-6.15pm Mon-Fri; ⓊPetuelring)

TOURS

City Bus 100   Bus Tour
Ordinary city bus that runs from the Hauptbahnhof to the Ostbahnhof via 21 sights, including the Residenz and the Pinakothek museums.

Radius Tours & Bike Rental   Tour
Entertaining and informative English-language tours include the two-hour Discover Munich walk (€13), the fascinating 2½-hour Hitler and the Third Reich tour (€15), and the three-hour Bavarian Beer tour (€29.50). The company also runs popular excursions to Neuschwanstein, Salzburg and Dachau, and has bikes for hire (€14.50

Munich for Children

There are plenty of parks for romping around, swimming pools and lakes for cooling off in, and family-friendly beer gardens with children's playgrounds for making new friends. Many museums have special kid-oriented programs, but the highly interactive Deutsches Museum (p115) specifically lures the single-digit set. Other attractions:

Tierpark Hellabrunn (Hellabrunn Zoo; ☑089-625 080; www.tierpark-hellabrunn. de; Tierparkstrasse 30; adult/child €14/5; ☺9am-6pm Apr-Sep, to 5pm Oct-Mar; ⬚52 from Marienplatz, ⬚Tiroler Platz, ⓊThalkirchen) Pet baby goats, feed pelicans, watch falcons and hawks perform, or even ride a camel.

SeaLife München (Map p112; www.visitsealife.com; Willi-Daume-Platz 1; adult/child gate prices €16.95/13.50; ☺10am-7pm; ⓈOlympiazentrum) For a fishy immersion head to this aquarium in the Olympiapark.

Paläontologisches Museum (Palaeontological Museum; Map p108; www.palmuc. de; Richard-Wagner-Strasse 10; ☺8am-4pm Mon-Thu, to 2pm Fri; ⬚Königsplatz, ⓊKönigsplatz) FREE For Dino fans.

Museum Mensch und Natur (Museum of Humankind & Nature; Map p112; www.mmn-muenchen.de; Schloss Nymphenburg; adult/child €3/2; ☺9am-5pm Tue, Wed & Fri, to 8pm Thu, 10am-6pm Sat & Sun; ⬚Schloss Nymphenburg) Budding scientists will find plenty to marvel.

Münchner Marionettentheater (Map p108; ☑089-265 712; www.muema-theater. de; Blumenstrasse 32; ☺3pm Wed-Sun, 8pm Sat) The adorable singing and dancing marionettes have enthralled generations of wee ones.

Münchner Theater für Kinder (Map p112; ☑089-594 545; www.mtfk.de; Dachauer Strasse 46) Fairy tales and children's classics.

Dachau Concentration Camp

Dachau was the Nazis' first concentration camp, built by Heinrich Himmler in March 1933 to house political prisoners. All in all it 'processed' more than 200,000 inmates, killing between 30,000 and 43,000, and is now a haunting memorial. Expect to spend two to three hours here to fully absorb the exhibits. Note that children under 12 may find the experience too disturbing.

Officially called the **KZ-Gedenkstätte Dachau** (Dachau Concentration Camp Memorial Site; 08131-669 970; www. kz-gedenkstaette-dachau.de; Peter-Roth-Strasse 2a, Dachau; 9am-5pm Tue-Sun; admission free), the place to start is the visitors centre, which houses a bookshop, cafe and tour booking desk where you can pick up an audioguide (€3). Tours (€3; 2½ hours) also run from here from Tuesday to Sunday at 11am and 1pm (extra tours run at 12.15pm on Sundays between August and September).

You pass into the compound itself through the Jourhaus, originally the only entrance. Set in wrought iron, the chilling slogan *'Arbeit Macht Frei'* (Work Sets You Free) hits you at the gate.

The museum is at the southern end of the camp. Here an English-language documentary runs at 10am, 11.30am, 12.30pm, 2pm and 3pm and uses mostly post-liberation footage. Either side of the small cinema extends an exhibition relating the camp's harrowing story.

Dachau is about 16km northwest of central Munich. The S2 makes the trip from Munich Hauptbahnhof to the station in Dachau in 21 minutes. You'll need a two-zone ticket (€5.20). Here change to bus 726 (direction Saubachsiedlung) to get to the camp. Show your stamped ticket to the driver. By car, follow Dachauer Strasse straight out to Dachau and follow the KZ-Gedenkstätte signs.

per day). (Map p112; 089-543 487 7720; www. radiustours.com; Arnulfstrasse 3; Hauptbahnhof, Hauptbahnhof, Hauptbahnhof)

Mike's Bike Tours   Bicycle Tour
This outfit runs various guided bike tours of the city as well as a couple of other themed excursions. The standard tour is around four hours long (with a one-hour beer-garden break; lunch is not included); the deluxe tour goes for seven hours and covers 16km. (Map p108; 089-2554 3987; www.mikesbiketours.com; Bräuhaus Strasse 10; tours from €30; Marienplatz, Marienplatz)

Grayline Hop-On-Hop-Off Tours   Bus Tour
This tour-bus company offers a choice of three tours, from one-hour highlights to the 2½-hour grand tour, as well as excursions to Ludwig II's castles, the Romantic Road, Dachau, Berchtesgaden, Zugspitze and Salzburg. All tours can be booked online and the buses are new. The **main departure point** (Map p112; Hauptbahnhof, Hauptbahnhof) is outside the Karstadt department store opposite the Hauptbahnhof. (www.grayline.com/Munich; adult/child €15/10; hourly)

New Europe Munich   Walking Tour
Departing from Marienplatz, these free English-language walking tours tick off all of Munich's central landmarks in three hours. Guides are well informed and fun, though they are under pressure at the end of the tour to get as much as they can in tips. The company also runs (paid) tours to Dachau (€22) and Neuschwanstein (€37). (www.newmunichtours.com; tours 10am, 10.45am & 2pm; Marienplatz, Marienplatz)

🛍 SHOPPING

Holareidulijö   Clothing
Munich's only secondhand traditional-clothing store (the name is a phonetic yodel) is worth a look even if you don't intend buying. Apparently, wearing hand-me-down Lederhosen greatly reduces the risk of chafing. (Map p112; www.holareidulijoe.

com; Schellingstrasse 81; ⏰noon-6.30pm Tue-Fri, 10am-1pm Sat; 🚇Schellingstrasse)

Porzellan Manufaktur
Nymphenburg   Ceramics
Traditional and contemporary porcelain masterpieces by the royal manufacturer. There's another **branch** (Map p108; 📞089-282 428; Odeonsplatz 1; ⏰10am-6.30pm Mon-Fri, to 4pm Sat; 🅄Odeonsplatz) in the Altstadt. (Map p112, www.nymphenburg.com; Nördliches Schlossrondell 8; ⏰10am-5pm Mon-Fri; 🚇Schloss Nymphenburg)

Loden-Frey   Clothing
The famous cloth producer stocks a wide range of Bavarian wear and other top-end clothes. The lederhosen and dirndl outfits are a cut above the discount night-out versions and prices are accordingly high. (Map p108; www.lodenfrey.com; Maffeistrasse 5-7; ⏰10am-8pm Mon-Sat; 🚇Theatinerstrasse)

Words' Worth Books   Books
You'll find tons of English-language books, from secondhand novels to the latest bestsellers, at this excellent and long-established bookstore. (Map p108; www.

wordsworth.de; Schellingstrasse 3; ⏰9am-8pm Mon-Fri, 10am-4pm Sat; 🚇Schellingstrasse)

Manufactum   Homewares
Anyone with an admiration for top-quality design from Germany and further afield should make a beeline for this store. Last-a-lifetime household items compete for shelf space with retro toys, Bauhaus lamps and times-gone-by stationery. The stock changes according to the season. (Map p108; www.manufactum.de; Dienerstrasse 12; ⏰9.30am-7pm Mon-Sat; 🅂Marienplatz, 🚇Marienplatz)

🍴 EATING

Munich's food was once described by Viennese actor Helmut Qualtinger as 'garnish for the beer', and while that may still ring true in traditional beer halls and restaurants, where the menu rarely ventures beyond the roast pork and sausage routine, elsewhere Munich can claim to have southern Germany's most exciting cuisine scene. There's lots of exciting innovation going on in Munich's kitchens, where the best dishes make use of fresh regional, seasonal and organic ingredients. The Bavarian capital

Bavarian sausages

Schmalznudel at Schmalznudel cafe

is also the best place between Vienna and Paris for a spot of internationally flavoured dining, especially when it comes to Italian and Afghan food, and even vegetarians can look forward to something other than noodles and salads.

Schmalznudel   Cafe €

This incredibly popular institution serves just four traditional pastries, one of which, the *Schmalznudel* (an oily type of dough-nut), gives the place its local nickname. Every baked goodie you munch here is crisp and fragrant, as they're always fresh off the hotplate. They're best eaten with a steaming pot of coffee on a winter's day. (Map p108; Cafe Frischhut; Prälat-Zistl-Strasse 8; pastries €1.70; ☺8am-6pm; Ⓤ Marienplatz, Ⓢ Marienplatz)

Hans im Glück   Burgers €

Plugging into Munich's current obsession with the burger, this new joint in the old post-office building serves a juicy selection of meat in buns amid a forest of real birch trunks that grow straight out of the floor. Takeaway and vegie versions available. (Map p108; Sonnenstrasse 24; burgers €8;

☺11am-midnight Mon-Thu, to 2am Fri & Sat; 🚇Karlsplatz, Ⓢ Karlsplatz, Ⓤ Karlsplatz)

Bratwurstherzl   Franconian €€

Cosy panelling and an ancient vaulted brick ceiling set the tone of this Old Munich tavern with a Franconian focus. Homemade organic sausages are grilled to perfection on an open beechwood fire and served on heart-shaped pewter plates. They're best enjoyed with a cold one from the Hacker-Pschorr brewery. (Map p108; Dreifaltigkeit-splatz 1; mains €7-16; ☺10am-11pm Mon-Sat; Ⓤ Marienplatz, Ⓢ Marienplatz)

Fraunhofer   Bavarian €€

With its screechy parquet floors, stuccoed ceilings, wood panelling and virtually no trace that the last century even happened, this wonderfully characterful inn is perfect for exploring the region with a fork. The menu is a seasonally adapted checklist of southern German favourites but also fea-tures at least a dozen vegetarian dishes and the odd exotic ingredient. (☏089-266 460; www.fraunhofertheater.de; Fraunhoferstrasse 9; mains €7-25; ☺4.30pm-1am Mon-Fri, 10am-1am Sat; 🎨; 🚇Müllerstrasse)

Königsquelle European €€

This Munich institution is well loved for its attentive service, expertly prepared food and dark, well-stocked hardwood bar containing what must be the Bavarian capital's best selection of malt whiskies. The hardly decipherable handwritten menu hovers somewhere mid-Alps, with anything from schnitzel to linguine and goat's cheese to cannelloni to choose from. (Map p108; 089-220 071; www.koenigsquelle.com; Baaderplatz 2; mains €9-21; 5pm-1am Sun-Fri, from 7pm Sat; Isartor, Isartor)

Weisses Brauhaus Bavarian €€

One of Munich's classic beer halls, in the evenings this place is charged with red-faced, ale-infused hilarity, with Alpine whoops accompanying the rabble-rousing oompah band. The *Weisswurst* (veal sausage) sets the standard; sluice down a pair with the unsurpassed Schneider *Weissbier* (wheat beer). It's understandably very popular and reservations are recommended after 7pm. (Map p108; 089-290 1380; www.weisses-brauhaus.de; Tal 7; mains €7-20; Marienplatz, Marienplatz)

Wirtshaus in der Au Bavarian €€

This Bavarian tavern's simple slogan is 'Beer and dumplings since 1901', and it's that time-honoured staple (the dumpling) that's the speciality here (the tavern even runs a dumpling-making course in English). Once a brewery, the space-rich dining area has chunky tiled floors, a lofty ceiling and a crackling fireplace in winter. (Map p108; 089-448 1400; Lilienstrasse 51; mains €10-16; 5pm-midnight Mon-Fri, from 10am Sat & Sun; Deutsches Museum)

Prinz Myshkin Vegetarian €€

This place is proof, if any were needed, that the vegetarian experience has left the sandals, beards and lentils era. Occupying a former brewery, Munich's premier meat-free dining spot is an vaulted and open-plan but intimate space. Health-conscious eaters come to savour imaginative dishes such as curry-orange-carrot soup, unexpectedly good curries and 'wellness desserts'. (Map

 Gay & Lesbian Munich

Munich's gay and lesbian scene is the liveliest in Bavaria but tame if compared to Berlin, Cologne or Amsterdam. The rainbow flag flies especially proudly along Müllerstrasse and the adjoining Glockenbachviertel and Gärtnerplatzviertel. To plug into the scene, keep an eye out for the freebie mags *Our Munich* and *Sergej*, which contain up-to-date listings and news about the community and gay-friendly establishments around town. Another source of info is www.gaytouristoffice.com.

Sub (Map p108; 089-856 346 400; www.subonline.org; Müllerstrasse 14; 7-11pm Sun-Thu, to midnight Fri & Sat; Müllerstrasse) is a one-stop service and information agency; lesbians can also turn to **Le Tra** (Map p108; 089-725 4272; www.letra.de; Angertorstrasse 3; 2.30-5pm Mon & Wed, 10.30am-1pm Tue; Müllerstrasse).

The main street parties of the year are **Christopher Street Day** (www.csd-munich.de; Jul) and the **Schwules Strassenfest** (www.schwules-strassenfest.de; mid-Aug) along Hans-Sachs-Strasse in the Glockenbachviertel. During Oktoberfest, lesbigay folks invade the Bräurosl beer tent on the first Sunday and Fischer-Vroni on the second Monday.

p108; 089-265 596; www.prinzmyshkin.com; Hackenstrasse 2; mains €10-19; 11am-12.30am; ; Marienplatz, Marienplatz)

★ Top Five Munich Beer Spots

Augustiner Bräustuben (p124)

Hofbräuhaus (p124)

Weisses Brauhaus (p121)

Fraunhofer (p120)

Chinesischer Turm (p124)

From left: Hofbräuhaus; *Weissbier* (wheat beer); inside the Hofbräuhaus

Vegelangelo   Vegetarian €€

Reservations are compulsory at this petite vegie spot, where Indian odds and ends, a piano and a small Victorian fireplace distract little from the superb meat-free cooking, all of which can be converted to suit vegans. There's a set-menu-only policy Friday and Saturday. No prams allowed. (Map p108; ☎089-2880 6836; www.vegelangelo. de; Thomas-Wimmer-Ring 16; mains €10-19, set menu €24-30; ☺noon-2pm Tue-Thu, 6pm-late Mon-Sat; ☑; ☐Isartor, ⑤Isartor)

La Vecchia Masseria   Italian €€

One of Munich's longest-established Italian *osterie*, this earthy, rurally themed place has chunky wood tables, baskets and clothing irons, all conjuring up the ambience of an Apennine farmhouse. There's a small beer garden out the front, but this only operates until 9.30pm. (Map p108; Mathildenstrasse 3; mains €9-18, pizzas €7-8.50; ☺11.30am-12.30am; ☐Sendlinger Tor, ⑤Sendlinger Tor)

Potting Shed   Burgers €€

This relaxed hang-out serves tapas, gourmet burgers and cocktails to an easy-going crowd. The burger menu whisks you round the globe, but it's the house speciality, the 'Potting Shed Special', involving an organic beef burger flambéed in whisky, that catches the eye on the simple but well-concocted menu. (Map p112; Occamstrasse 11; mains €6-17; ☺from 6pm; ☑Münchner Freiheit)

Ruff's Burger   Burgers €€

Munich's obsession with putting a fried bit of meat between two buns continues at this Schwabing joint, where the burgers are 100% Bavarian beef. Erdinger and Tegern-seer beer and mostly outdoor seating. (Map p112; Occamstrasse 4; burgers €7-15; ☺11.30am-11pm Mon-Wed, to midnight Thu-Sat, to 10pm Sun; ☑Münchner Freiheit)

Cafe Luitpold   Cafe €€

A cluster of pillarbox-red street-side tables and chairs announces you've arrived at this stylish retreat. It offers a choice of three spaces: a lively bar, a less boisterous col-umned cafe and a cool palm-leaved atrium. Good for a daytime coffee-and-cake halt or a full evening blowout with all the trim-mings. (Map p108; www.cafe-luitpold.de; Brien-nerstrasse 11; mains €11-20; ☺8am-7pm Mon, to 11pm Tue-Sat, 9am-7pm Sun; ☑Odeonsplatz)

La Bouche — French €€€

Expect good Gallic goings-on at this French-inspired port of call, where tables are squished as tight as lovers and the accent is on imaginative but gimmick-free fare, such as truffle ravioli, veal liver with caramelised apple, and plenty of fish. It's much bigger than first meets the eye: there's a second room at the back. (☏089-265 626; www. restaurant-la-bouche.de; Jahnstrasse 30; mains €14.50-30; ☺noon-3pm Mon-Fri, 6pm-midnight Mon-Sat; ⓤFraunhoferstrasse)

Tantris — International €€€

Tantris means 'the search for perfection' and here, at one of Germany's most famous restaurants, they're not far off it. The interior design is full-bodied '70s – all postbox reds, truffle blacks and illuminated yellows – the food gourmet sublimity and the service sometimes as unobtrusive as it is efficient. The wine cellar is probably Germany's best. Reservations essential. (Map p112; ☏089-361 9590; www.tantris.de; Johann-Fichte-Strasse 7; menu from €80; ☺noon-3pm & 6.30pm-1am Tue-Sat; ☎; ⓤDietlindenstrasse)

Esszimmer — Mediterranean €€€

It took Bobby Bräuer, head chef at the gourmet restaurant at BMW World, just two years to gain his first Michelin star. Munich's top dining spot is the place to sample high-octane French and Mediterranean morsels, served in a dining room above the i8s and 7 Series. (Map p112; ☏089-358 991 814; www.bmw-welt.com; BMW Welt, Am Olympiapark 1; 4/5 courses €90/110; ☺from 4pm Tue-Sat; ✲☎; ⓤOlympiazentrum)

🍷 DRINKING & NIGHTLIFE

Munich is a great place for boozers. Raucous beer halls, snazzy hotel lounges, chestnut-canopied beer gardens, hipster DJ bars, designer cocktail temples – the variety is so huge that finding a party pen to match your mood is not exactly a tall order. Generally speaking, student-flavoured places abound in Maxvorstadt and Schwabing, while traditional beer halls and taverns cluster in the Altstadt; Haidhausen goes for trendy types and the Gärtnerplatzviertel and Glockenbachviertel is a haven for gays and hipsters.

No Wave Goodbye

Possibly the last sport you might expect to see being practised in Munich is surfing, but go to the southern tip of the English Garden at Prinzregentenstrasse and you'll see scores of people leaning over a bridge to cheer on wetsuit-clad daredevils as they hang on an artificially created wave in the **Eisbach** (Map p108; Prinzregentenstrasse; 🚇Nationalmuseum/Haus der Kunst). It's only a single wave, but it's a damn fine one.

Surfing on the Eisbach
DPA PICTURE ALLIANCE/ALAMY ©

No matter where you are, you won't be far from an enticing cafe to get a Java-infused pick-me-up. Many also serve light fare and delicious cakes (often homemade) and are great places to linger, chat, write postcards or simply watch people on parade.

Bavaria's brews are best sampled in a venerable old *Bierkeller* (beer hall) and *Biergarten* (beer garden). People come here primarily to drink, although food is usually served. In beer gardens you are usually allowed to bring your own picnic as long as you sit at tables without tablecloths and order something to drink. Sometimes there's a resident brass band pumping oompah music. And don't even think about sitting at a *Stammtisch*, a table reserved for regulars (look for a brass plaque or some other sign)! Beer gardens are, for the most part, very family friendly.

Augustiner Bräustuben
Beer Hall

Depending on the wind, an aroma of hops envelops you as you approach this traditional beer hall inside the Augustiner brewery. The Bavarian fare is superb, especially the *Schweinshaxe* (pork knuckle). Due to the location the atmosphere in the evenings is slightly more authentic than that of its city-centre cousins, with fewer tourists at the long tables. (Map p112; 📞089-507 047; www.braeustuben. de; Landsberger Strasse 19; ⏱10am-midnight; 🚇Holzapfelstrasse)

Hofbräuhaus
Beer Hall

Every visitor to Munich should make a pilgrimage to this mothership of all beer halls, if only once. There is a range of spaces in which to do your mass lifting: the horse-chestnut-shaded garden, the main hall next to the oompah band, tables opposite the industrial-scale kitchen and quieter corners. (Map p108; 📞089-290 136 100; www. hofbraeuhaus.de; Am Platzl 9; 1L beer €8, mains €10-20; ⏱9am-11.30pm; 🚇Kammerspiele, Ⓢ Marienplatz, Ⓤ Marienplatz)

Chinesischer Turm
Beer Garden

This one's hard to ignore because of its English Garden location and pedigree as Munich's oldest beer garden (open since 1791). Camera-toting tourists and laid-back locals, picnicking families and businessmen sneaking a sly brew clomp around the wooden pagoda, showered by the strained sounds of possibly the world's drunkest oompah band. (Map p112; 📞089-383 8730; www.chinaturm.de; Englischer Garten 3; ⏱10am-11pm; 🚇Chinesischer Turm, 🚇Tivolistrasse)

Augustiner Keller
Beer Garden

Every year this leafy 5000-seat beer garden, about 500m west of the Hauptbahnhof, buzzes with fairy-lit thirst-quenching activity from the first sign that spring may have *gesprungen*. The ancient chestnuts are thick enough to seek refuge under when it rains, or else lug your mug to the actual

Königssee

beer cellar. Small playground. (Map p112; Arnulfstrasse 52; ⏰10am-1am Apr-Oct; 👶; 🚋Hopfenstrasse)

Hirschau   Beer Garden
This monster beer garden can seat 1700 quaffers and hosts live music almost every day in the summer months. Dispatch the kids to the excellent playground and adjacent minigolf course while you indulge in some tankard caressing. (Map p112; Gysslingstrasse 15; ⏰11.30am-11pm Mon-Fri, from 10am Sat & Sun; Ⓤ Dietlindenstrasse)

Salon Иркутск   Bar
Escape the sugary cocktails and belly-inflating suds one of Munich's more cultured watering holes, which touts itself as a Franco-Slavic evening bistro. You'll soon see this is no place to get slammed on Russian ethanol or cheap Gallic plonk – Monday is piano night, Wednesday is French evening and the green-painted, wood-panelled interior hosts exhibitions of local art. (Map p112; www.salonirkutsk.de; Isabellastrasse 4; ⏰5pm-late; Ⓤ Josephsplatz)

Schumann's Bar   Bar
Urbane and sophisticated, Schumann's shakes up Munich's nightlife with libational flights of fancy in an impressive range of concoctions. It's also good for weekday breakfasts. (Map p108; ☎089-229 060; www.schumanns.de; Odeonsplatz 6-7; ⏰8am-3am Mon-Fri, 6pm-3am Sat & Sun; Ⓢ Odeonsplatz)

Stereo Cafe   Cafe
Right opposite the Residenz, with bar stools looking out of huge windows at its western flank, this light, airy, vaguely Portuguese place (port, *pastel de nata*, Atlantic fish dishes) is a real gem and a nice spot for a pre-theatre aperitif or mid-sightseeing/shopping time out. It's accessed through the downstairs men's-accessory emporium. (Map p108; www.stereocafe.de; Residenzstrasse 25; ⏰10am-8pm Mon-Sat; 🚋Theatinerstrasse)

Baader Café   Cafe
Around since the mid-'80s, this literary think-and-drink place lures all sorts, from short skirts to tweed jackets, who linger

over daytime coffees and night-time cocktails. It's normally packed, even on winter Wednesday mornings, and is popular for Sunday brunch. (Map p108; Baaderstrasse 47; ☉9.30am-1am; 🛜; 🚊Fraunhoferstrasse)

Alter Simpl — Pub

Thomas Mann and Hermann Hesse used to knock 'em back at this well-scuffed and wood-panelled thirst parlour. A bookish ambience still pervades, making this an apt spot to curl up with a weighty tome over a few Irish ales. The curious name is an abbreviation of the satirical magazine *Simplicissimus*. (Map p108; www.eggerlokale. de; Türkenstrasse 57; ☉11am-3am Mon-Fri, to 4am Sat & Sun; 🚊Schellingstrasse)

Braunauer Hof — Pub

Near the Isartor, drinkers can choose between the traditional Bavarian interior or the beer garden out the back that enjoys a surprisingly tranquil setting

This monster beer garden hosts live music almost every day in the summer months

Hirschau (p125)

despite its city-centre location. Most come for the Paulaner beer of an eve, but the €8.50 lunch menu is commendable value for money. (Map p108; Frauenstrasse 42; ☉11.30am-11pm Mon-Sat; 🚊Isartor, Ⓢ Isartor)

Rote Sonne — Club

Named for a 1969 Munich cult movie starring It-Girl Uschi Obermaier, the Red Sun is a fiery nirvana for fans of electronic sounds. A global roster of DJs keeps the wooden dance floor packed and sweaty until the sun rises. (Map p108; www.rote-sonne. com; Maximiliansplatz 5; ☉from 11pm Thu-Sun; 🚊Lenbachplatz)

Harry Klein — Club

Follow the gold-lined passageway off Sonnenstrasse to what some regard as one of the best *elektro-clubs* in the world. Nights here are an amazing alchemy of electro sound and visuals, with live video art projected onto the walls Kraftwerk style blending to awe-inspiring effect with the music. (Map p108; www.harrykleinclub.de; Sonnenstrasse 8; ☉from 11pm; 🚊Karlsplatz, Ⓢ Karlsplatz, Ⓤ Karlsplatz)

MilchundBar   Club

This relative newcomer is one of the hottest addresses in the city centre for those who like to spend the hours between supper and breakfast boogieing to an eclectic mix of nostalgia hits during the week and top DJs at the weekends. (Map p108; www. milchundbar.de; Sonnenstrasse 27; Ⓢ Sendlinger Tor, Ⓤ Sendlinger Tor)

P1   Club

If you make it past the notorious face control at Munich's premier late spot, you'll encounter a crowd of Bundesliga reserve players, Q-list celebs and quite a few Russian speakers too busy seeing and being seen to actually have a good time. But it's all part of the fun, and the decor and summer terrace have their appeal. (Map p108; www.p1-club.de; Prinzregentenstrasse 1; Ⓢ Nationalmuseum/Haus der Kunst)

⭐ ENTERTAINMENT

Tickets to cultural and sporting events are available at venue box offices and official ticket outlets, such as **Zentraler Kartenvorverkauf** (Map p108; ☏ 089-5450 6060; www.zkv-muenchen.de; Marienplatz; ⊙9am-8pm Mon-Sat; Ⓤ Marienplatz) which has a kiosk within the Marienplatz U-Bahn station. It's also good for online bookings, as is **München Ticket** (Map p112; ☏ 089-5481 8181; www.muenchenticket.de; Bahnhofplatz 2; ⊙10am-8pm Mon-Sat; Ⓤ Hauptbahnhof), which shares premises with the tourist office at the Hauptbahnhof.

Münchner Philharmoniker   Classical Music

Munich's premier orchestra regularly performs at the **Gasteig Cultural Centre** (Map p108; ☏ 089-480 980; www.gasteig. de; Rosenheimer Strasse 5; ⊙8am-11pm; Ⓢ Am Gasteig). Be sure to book tickets early, as performances usually sell out. (☏ 089-480 985 500; www.mphil.de; Rosenheimer Strasse 5; ⊙mid-Sep–Jun; Ⓢ Am Gasteig)

🎉 What's On in Munich

Tollwood Festival (www.tollwood. de; ⊙late Jun-late Jul & Dec) Major world-culture festival held from late June to late July and in December.

Filmfest München (www.film-fest-muenchen.de; ⊙late Jun) This festival presents intriguing and often high-calibre fare by newbies and masters from around the world.

Oktoberfest (p100) World-famous beer festival in late September and early October attracting around six million visitors.

Christkindlmarkt (www.christkindlmarkt. de; ⊙late Nov-Christmas Eve) Traditional Christmas market on Marienplatz.

Gingerbread Oktoberfest souvenirs

KATJEN/SHUTTERSTOCK ©

Bayerische Staatsoper   Opera

One of the world's best opera companies, the Bavarian State Opera performs to sell-out crowds at the **Nationaltheater** (Map p108; www.staatstheater.bayern.de; Max-Joseph-Platz 2; Ⓢ Nationaltheater) in the Residenz and puts the emphasis on Mozart, Strauss and Wagner. In summer it hosts the prestigious **Opernfestspiele** (Opera Festival; www.muenchner-opern-festspiele.de). The opera's house band is the Bayerisches Staatsorchester, in business since 1523 and thus Munich's oldest orchestra. (Map p108; Bavarian State Opera; ☏ 089-218 501; www.staatsoper.de; Max-Joseph-Platz 2; Ⓢ Nationaltheater)

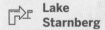

Lake Starnberg

Around 25km southwest of Munich, glittering Lake Starnberg (Starnberger See) was once the haunt of Bavaria's royal family, but now provides a bit of easily accessible R&R for anyone looking to escape the hustle of the Bavarian capital.

At the northern end of the lake, the affluent, century-old town of Starnberg is the heart of the Fünf-Seen-Land (Five-Lakes-Area). Besides Lake Starnberg the area comprises the Ammersee and the much smaller Pilsensee, Wörthsee and Wesslinger See. Naturally the region attracts water-sports enthusiasts, but also has enough history to keep fans of the past happy.

King Ludwig II famously (and mysteriously) drowned along with his doctor in Lake Starnberg. The spot where his body was found, in the village of Berg on the eastern shore, is marked with a large cross backed by a *Votivkapelle* (Memorial Chapel). Berg is 5km from Starnberg and can be reached on foot in around an hour.

From early May to mid-October Bayerische-Seen-Schifffahrt (www.seenschifffahrt.de) runs boat services from Starnberg to other lakeside towns as well as offering longer cruises. Boats dock behind the S-Bahn station in Starnberg.

If you'd rather get around the lake under your own steam, **Bike It** (✆08151-746 430; Bahnhofstrasse 1) hires out two-wheelers. **Paul Dechant** (✆08151 121 06; Hauptstrasse 20) near the S-Bahn station hires out rowing, pedal and electric-powered boats from €15 per hour.

Starnberg is a half-hour ride on the S6 train from Munich Hauptbahnhof (€5.20).

Jazzclub Unterfahrt im Einstein   Live Music

Join a diverse crowd at this long-established, intimate club for a mixed bag of acts ranging from old bebop to edgy experimental. The Sunday open-jam session is legendary. (Map p112; ✆089-448 2794; www.unterfahrt.de; Einsteinstrasse 42; Ⓤ Max-Weber-Platz)

FC Bayern München   Football

Germany's most successful team both nationally and on a European level plays home games at the impressive Allianz Arena, built for the 2006 World Cup. Tickets can be ordered online. (✆089-6993 1333; www.fcbayern.de; Allianz Arena, Werner-Heisenberg-Allee 25, Fröttmaning; Ⓤ Fröttmaning)

ⓘ INFORMATION

Tourist Office – Hauptbahnhof (Map p112; ✆089-2339 6500; www.muenchen.de; Bahnhofplatz 2; ⏱9am-8pm Mon-Sat, 10am-6pm Sun; Ⓡ Hauptbahnhof, Ⓤ Hauptbahnhof, Ⓢ Hauptbahnhof)

Tourist Office – Marienplatz (Map p108; ✆089-2339 6500; www.muenchen.de; Marienplatz 2; ⏱10am-8pm Mon-Fri, to 4pm Sat, to 2pm Sun Apr-Dec, closed Sun Jan-Mar; Ⓤ Marienplatz, Ⓢ Marienplatz)

CITY TOUR CARD

The Munich City Tour Card (www.citytourcard-muenchen.com; one/three days €10.90/20.90) includes all public transport in the Innenraum (Munich city – zones 1 to 4; marked white on transport maps) and discounts of between 10% and 50% for over 50 attractions, tours, eateries and theatres. These include the Residenz, the BMW Museum and the Bier und Oktoberfestmuseum. It's available at some hotels, tourist offices, Munich public transport authority (MVV) offices and U-Bahn, S-Bahn and DB vending machines.

Lake Starnberg

ℹ GETTING THERE & AWAY

AIR

Munich Airport, aka Flughafen Franz-Josef Strauss, is second in importance only to Frankfurt for international and domestic connections. The main carrier is Lufthansa (Terminal 2), but over 80 other companies operate from the airport's two runways, from major carriers such as British Airways and Emirates to minor operations such as Luxair and AirMalta.

Only one major airline from the UK doesn't use Munich's main airport – Ryanair flies into Memmingen's **Allgäu Airport** (FMM; ☎08331-984 2000; www.allgaeu-airport.de), 125km to the west. It is served by the **Allgäu Airport Express** (Map p112; www.aaexpress.de; single €17, €12 if prebooked online), which makes the trip between airport and Munich Hauptbahnhof up to seven times a day.

BUS

The Romantic Road Coach links Munich to the Romantic Road. For times and fares for this service and all other national and international coaches contact **Sindbad** (Map p112; ☎089-5454 8989; www.sindbad-gmbh.de; Hackerbrücke 4-6 ZOB; ⑤Hackerbrücke) near the Hauptbahnhof.

The bold new Zentraler Omnibusbahnhof next to the Hackerbrücke S-Bahn station handles the vast majority of international and domestic coach services. The main operator is low-cost coach company **Meinfernbus/Flixbus** (Map p112; ☎0180 515 9915; www.meinfernbus. de; Zentraler Omnibusbahnhof, Arnulfstrasse 21) which links Munich to countless destinations across Germany and Europe.

CAR & MOTORCYCLE

Munich has autobahns radiating in all directions. Take the A9 to Nuremberg, the A8 to Salzburg, the A95 to Garmisch-Partenkirchen and the A8 to Ulm or Stuttgart.

TRAIN

Train connections from Munich to destinations in Bavaria are excellent and there are also numerous services to more distant cities within

Germany and around Europe. All services leave from the Hauptbahnhof (Central Station).

Staffed by native English speakers, EurAide (p308) is a friendly agency based at the Hauptbahnhof that sells all DB products, makes reservations and can create personalised rail tours of Germany and beyond.

Train connections from Munich:

Frankfurt €101, 3¼ hours hourly

Nuremberg €19 to €55, one hour to 1¼ hours, twice hourly

Würzburg €71, two hours, twice hourly

 GETTING AROUND

Central Munich is compact enough to explore on foot. To get to the outlying suburbs, make use of the public transport network, which is extensive and efficient, if showing its age slightly.

TO/FROM THE AIRPORT

Munich's airport is about 30km northeast of the city and linked by S-Bahn (S1 and S8) to the Hauptbahnhof. The trip costs €10.80, takes about 40 minutes and runs every 20 minutes almost 24 hours a day.

The Lufthansa Airport Bus shuttles at 20-minute intervals between the airport and Arnulfstrasse at the Hauptbahnhof between 5am and 8pm. The trip takes about 45 minutes and costs €10.50 (return €17).

A taxi from Munich Airport to the Altstadt costs in the region of €50 to €70.

CAR & MOTORCYCLE

Driving in central Munich can be a nightmare; many streets are one-way or pedestrian only, ticket enforcement is Orwellian and parking is a nightmare. Car parks (indicated on the tourist office map) charge about €1.70 to €2.20 per hour.

PUBLIC TRANSPORT

Munich's efficient public transport system is composed of buses, trams, the U-Bahn and the S-Bahn. It's operated by MVV (www.mvv-muenchen.de), which maintains offices in the U-Bahn stations at Marienplatz, Hauptbahnhof, Sendlinger Tor, Ostbahnhof and Poccistrasse. Staff hand out free network maps and timetables, sell tickets and answer questions.

Munich

WESTEND61/GETTY IMAGES ©

Automated trip planning in English is best done online. The U-Bahn and S-Bahn run almost 24 hours a day, with perhaps a short gap between 2am and 4am. Night buses and trams operate in the city centre.

TICKETS & FARES

The City of Munich region is divided into four zones with most places of visitor interest (except Dachau and the airport) conveniently clustering within the white *Innenraum* (inner zone).

Short rides (*Kurzstrecke*; four bus or tram stops; or two U-Bahn or S-Bahn stops) cost €1.40; longer trips cost €2.70. Children aged between six and 14 pay a flat €1.30 regardless of the length of the trip. Day passes are €6.20 for individuals and €11.70 for up to five people travelling together. There's also a weekly pass called IsarCard, which costs €14.10. Bikes cost €2.60 to take aboard and may only be taken on U-Bahn and S-Bahn trains, but not during the 6am to 9am and 4pm to 6pm rush hours.

Bus drivers sell single tickets and day passes, but tickets for the U-/S-Bahn and other passes must be purchased from vending machines at stations or MVV (www.mvv-muenchen.de)

Where to Stay

Room rates in Munich tend to be high, and they skyrocket during Oktoberfest (late September to early October). Booking accommodation during Oktoberfest can be almost impossible, and expensive. Book well ahead.

Budget travellers are spoilt for choice around the Hauptbahnhof, where the majority of hostels congregate, but the Altstadt has the most top-end hotels. Hostels are widespread but tend to be big, professionally run affairs that lack atmosphere.

If you're staying in Munich for a week or longer, it usually works out cheaper to rent a room, flat or apartment.

offices. Tram tickets are available from vending machines aboard. Most tickets must be stamped (validated) at station platform entrances and aboard buses and trams before use. The fine for getting caught without a valid ticket is €40.

Schloss Neuschwanstein (p136)

NEUSCHWANSTEIN

Neuschwanstein

At the southern end of the Romantic Road, the castle of Neuschwanstein commissioned by King Ludwig II, and his less well-known ancestral home, Schloss Hohenschwangau, are a highlight of any trip to Germany. The country's most popular tourist attraction lures tourists in droves all year long, many on day trips from Munich. In the summer months the place is overrun so try to arrive early or come outside of July and August to avoid the biggest crowds.

Having toured Ludwig II's fantasy palaces, the nearest town to the castles is tourist-busy Füssen, worth half a day's exploration. And don't forget, you are now in the Alps where you can easily escape from the crowds into a landscape of gentle hiking trails and dramatic mountain vistas.

☑ **In this Section**

ℹ **Arriving in Neuschwanstein**

Füssen train station The nearest train station. It handles services to/from Munich. First train leaves Munich at 5.53am (€26.20, change in Buchloe), reaching Füssen at 7.52am. Otherwise, direct trains leave once every two hours. The Romantic Road Coach (p307) leaves from outside Füssen train station at 8am.

Hohenschwangau bus station The bus station for Neuschwanstein; served from Füssen train station by RVO buses 78 and 73 hourly.

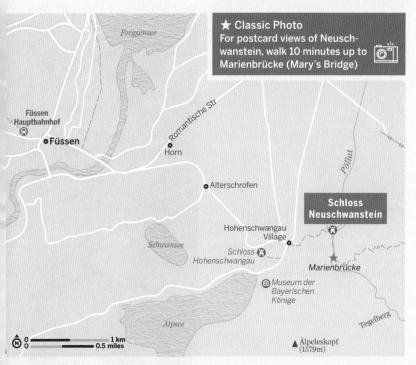

★ **Classic Photo**
For postcard views of Neuschwanstein, walk 10 minutes up to Marienbrücke (Mary's Bridge)

Forggensee

Füssen
Hauptbahnhof

Füssen

Horn

Romantische Str

Alterschrofen

Pöllat

Schloss Neuschwanstein

Hohenschwangau Village

Schloss Hohenschwangau

Marienbrücke

Schwansee

Museum der Bayerischen Könige

Alpsee

Tegelberg

0   1 km
0   0.5 miles

Älpeleskopf
(1579m)

From left: Interior of Schloss Neuschwanstein (p136); Train to Füssen; Schloss Neuschwanstein (p136)
PATRYK KOSMIDER/SHUTTERSTOCK © IMAGEBROKER/ALAMY © BRIAN LAWRENCE/GETTY IMAGES ©

The Thronsaal (p138), Schloss Neuschwanstein

Schloss Neuschwanstein

Appearing through the mountainous forest like a mirage, Schloss Neuschwanstein was the model for Disney's Sleeping Beauty castle.

Great For...

ⓘ Need to Know

www.neuschwanstein.de; Neuschwanstein-strasse 20; ⊘9am-6pm Apr–mid-Oct, 10am-4pm mid-Oct–Mar; adult/concession €12/11, incl Hohenschwangau €23/21

Construction

Built as a romantic medieval castle, work on the grey-white granite pile started in 1869 but was an anachronism from the start: at the time of Ludwig's death in 1886, the first high-rises had pierced New York's skyline. However, despite his love for the old-fashioned look, the palace had plenty of high-tech features, including a hot-air heating system and running water. Like so many of the king's grand schemes, Neuschwanstein was never finished. For all the coffer-depleting sums spent on it, the king spent just over 170 days in residence.

The Interior

Completed sections include Ludwig's Tristan and Isolde–themed **bedroom**, dominated by a huge Gothic-style bed crowned with

intricately carved cathedral-like spires; a gaudy artificial grotto (an allusion to the opera *Tannhäuser*); and the Byzantine-style **Thronsaal** (Throne Room) with an incredible mosaic floor containing over two million stones. The painting opposite the (throneless) throne platform depicts another castle dreamed up by Ludwig that was never built. The most impressive room is the **Sängersaal** (Minstrels' Hall), whose frescos depict scenes from *Tannhäuser*.

Schloss Hohenschwangau

King Ludwig II grew up at the sun-yellow **Schloss Hohenschwangau** (☎08362-930 830; www.hohenschwangau.de; Alpseestrasse 30; adult/concession €12/11, incl Neuschwanstein €23/21; ⏰8am-5.30pm Apr–mid-Oct, 9am-3.30pm mid-Oct–Mar) and later enjoyed summers here until his death in 1886. His

Schloss Hohenschwangau

father, Maximilian II, built this palace in a neo-Gothic style atop 12th-century ruins left by Schwangau knights. Far less showy than Neuschwanstein, Hohenschwangau has a distinctly lived-in feel where every piece of furniture is a used original. After his father died, Ludwig's main alteration was having stars, illuminated with hidden oil lamps, painted on the ceiling of his bedroom.

It was at Hohenschwangau where Ludwig first met Richard Wagner. The **Hohen-staufensaal** features a square piano where the hard-up composer would entertain Ludwig with excerpts from his latest oeuvre.

Castle Tickets & Tours

Strictly timed tickets are available from the **Ticket Centre** (www.hohenschwangau.de; Alpenseestrasse 12; ☺8am-5.30pm Apr–mid-Oct, 9am-3.30pm mid-Oct–Mar) at the foot of the castles. Enough time is left between tours for the steep 30- to 40-minute walk between the castles. All Munich's tour companies run day excursions out to the castles.

Ludwig II: The Fairy-Tale King

King Ludwig II drew the blueprints for this fairy-tale pile himself. He envisioned it as a giant stage on which to re-create the world of Germanic mythology, inspired by the operatic works of Wagner. His obsession with French culture and the Sun King, Louis XIV, further inspired the fantastical design.

Ludwig was an enthusiastic leader initially, but Bavaria's days as a sovereign state were numbered, and he became a puppet king after the creation of the German Reich in 1871. Ludwig withdrew completely to drink, draw up castle plans and view concerts and operas in private.

In January 1886, several ministers and relatives arranged a hasty psychiatric test that diagnosed Ludwig as mentally unfit to rule. That June, he was removed to Schloss Berg on Lake Starnberg. A few days later the dejected bachelor and his doctor took a Sunday-evening lakeside walk and were found several hours later, drowned in just a few feet of water. No one knows with certainty what happened that night, and conspiracy theories abound. That summer the authorities opened Neuschwanstein to the public to help pay off Ludwig's huge debts. King Ludwig II was dead, but the myth was just being born.

★ Top Tip

Schloss Neuschwanstein and Hohenschwangau can only be visited on guided tours (in German or English), which last about 35 minutes each (Hohenschwangau is first).

[GENESIS] - KORAWEE RATCHAPAKDEE/GETTY IMAGES ©

✗ Take a Break

Several restaurants line the road that runs from the ticket office to the castles.

Füssen

Nestled at the foot of the Alps, tourist-busy Füssen is the southern climax of the Romantic Road, with the nearby castles of Neuschwanstein and Hohenschwangau the highlight of many a southern Germany trip. But having 'done' the country's most popular tourist route and seen Ludwig II's fantasy palaces, there are other reasons to linger longer in the area. The town of Füssen is worth half a day's exploration and, from here, you can easily escape from the crowds into a landscape of gentle hiking trails and Alpine vistas.

 SIGHTS

Museum der Bayerischen Könige   Museum

Palace-fatigued visitors often head straight for the bus stop, coach park or nearest beer after a tour of the castles, most overlooking this worthwhile museum, installed in a former lakeside hotel 400m from the castle ticket office (heading towards Alpsee Lake). The architecturally stunning museum is packed with historical background on Bavaria's first family and well worth the extra legwork. (Museum of the Bavarian Kings; www.museumderbayerischenkoenige.de; Alpseestrasse 27; adult/concession €9.50/8; ⏲10am-6pm)

Hohes Schloss   Castle, Gallery

The Hohes Schloss, a late-Gothic confection and one-time retreat of the bishops of Augsburg, lords it over Füssen's compact historical centre. The north wing of the palace contains the **Staatsgalerie** (State Gallery), with regional paintings and sculpture from the 15th and 16th centuries. The **Städtische Gemäldegalerie** (City Paintings Gallery) below is a showcase of 19th-century artists. (Magnusplatz 10; adult/concession €6/4; ⏲galleries 11am-5pm Tue-Sun Apr-Oct, 1-4pm Fri-Sun Nov-Mar)

 EATING

Beim Olivenbauer   Austrian, Italian €€

The Tyrol meets the Allgäu at this fun eatery, its interior a jumble of Doric columns, mismatched tables and chairs, multihued paint and assorted rural knick-knackery.

Maultaschen (pork and spinach ravioli)

Treat yourself to a wheel of pizza and a glass of Austrian wine, or go local with a plate of *Maultaschen* (pork and spinach ravioli) and a mug of local beer. (Ottostrasse 7; mains €6.50-16; ⊘11.30am-11.30pm)

Zum Hechten   Bavarian €€

Füssen's best hotel restaurant keeps things regional with a menu of Allgäu staples like schnitzel and noodles, Bavarian pork-themed favourites, and local specialities such as venison goulash from the Ammertal. Post-meal, relax in the wood-panelled dining room caressing a König Ludwig Dunkel, one of Germany's best dark beers brewed by the current head of the Wittelsbach family. (Ritterstrasse 6; mains €8-19; ⊘10am-10pm)

Zum Franziskaner   Bavarian €€

This revamped restaurant specialises in *Schweinshaxe* (pork knuckle) and schnitzel, prepared in more varieties than you can shake a haunch at. There's some choice for non-carnivores such as *Käsespätzle* (rolled cheese noodles) and salads, and when the sun shines the out-

Where to Stay

Accommodation in the area is surprisingly good value and the tourist office can help track down private rooms from as low as €30 per person.

door seating shares the pavement with the 'foot-washing' statue. (Kemptener Strasse 1; mains €6-19.50; ⊘noon-11pm)

 INFORMATION

Tourist Office (☏08362-938 50; www.fuessen. de; Kaiser-Maximilian-Platz; ⊘9am-6pm Mon-Fri, 10am-2pm Sat, 10am-noon Sun) Can help find rooms.

 GETTING AROUND

RVO buses 78 and 73 serve the castles from Füssen Bahnhof (€4.40 return, eight minutes, at least hourly). Taxis are about €10 each way.

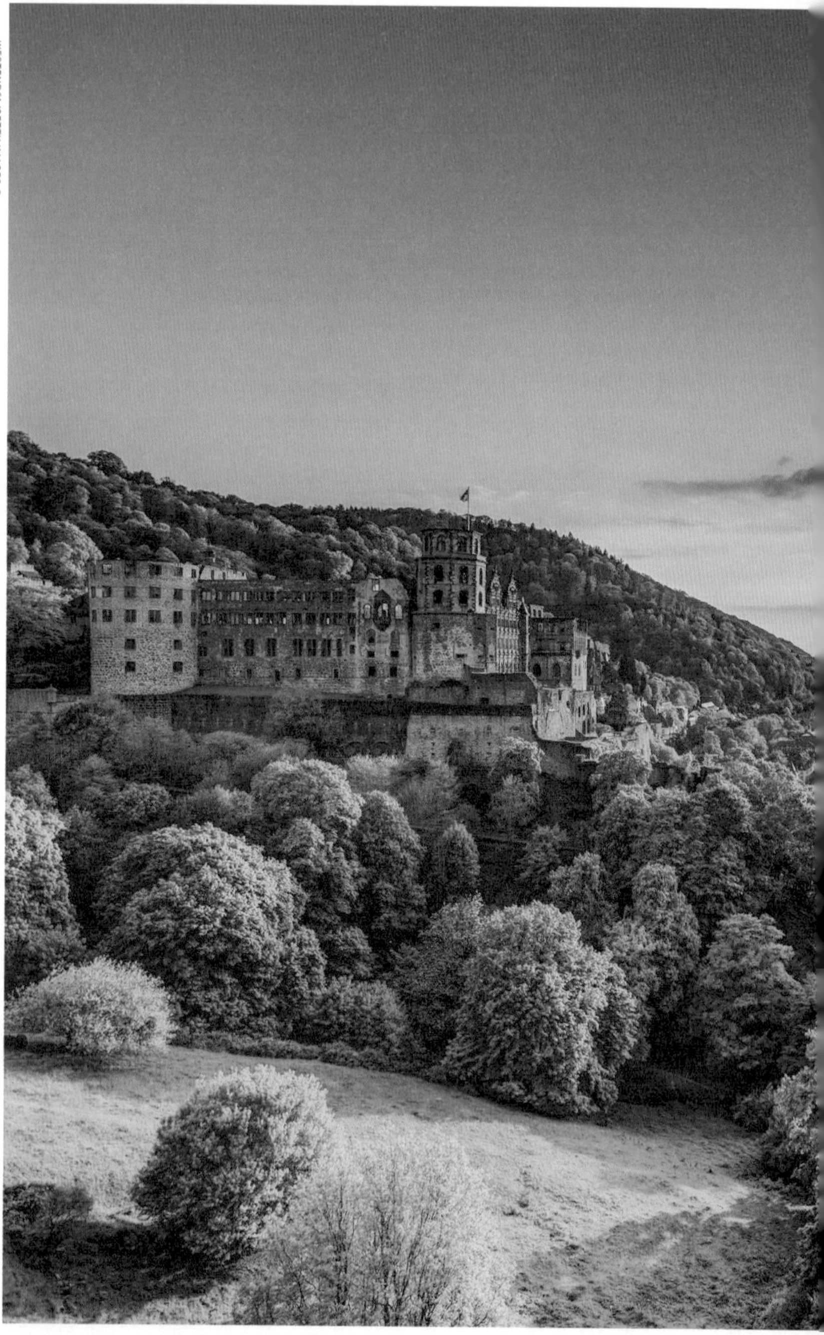

HEIDELBERG

Heidelberg

Surrounded by forest 93km south of Frankfurt, Germany's oldest and most famous university town is renowned for its baroque Altstadt, spirited student atmosphere, beautiful riverside setting and evocative half-ruined hilltop castle, which draw 12 million visitors a year. They follow in the footsteps of the late 18th- and early 19th-century romantics, most notably the poet Goethe. Britain's William Turner also loved Heidelberg, which inspired him to paint some of his greatest landscapes.

In 1878, Mark Twain began his European travels with a three-month stay in Heidelberg, recounting his observations in A Tramp Abroad *(1880). Heidelberg's rich literary history, along with its thriving contemporary scene involving authors, translators, publishing houses, bookshops, libraries, festivals and events, saw it named a Unesco City of Literature in 2014.*

☑ In this Section

➡ Arriving in Heidelberg

Hauptbahnhof Handles all local and national train services.

Frankfurt airport The nearest airport is at Frankfurt, reached by regular Lufthansa bus.

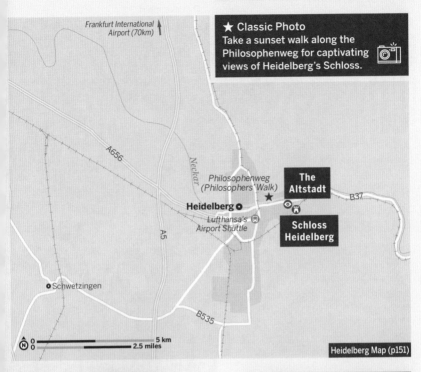

Frankfurt International
Airport (70km)

★ **Classic Photo**
Take a sunset walk along the
Philosophenweg for captivating
views of Heidelberg's Schloss.

A656

Neckar

*Philosophenweg
(Philosophers' Walk)*

Heidelberg ○

*Lufthansa's
Airport Shuttle*

**The
Altstadt**

B37

**Schloss
Heidelberg**

A5

○ Schwetzingen

B535

N
0 —— 5 km
0 —— 2.5 miles

Heidelberg Map (p151)

From left: Heiliggeistkirche (p146); Heidelberg on the Neckar River; Haspelgasse
G215/SHUTTERSTOCK © SMILEUS/SHUTTERSTOCK © WWW.VICTORIAWLAKA.COM/GETTY IMAGES ©

Christmas market

SHANTI HESSE/SHUTTERSTOCK ©

The Altstadt

The highlight of any visit to Heidelberg is a stroll through its well-preserved Altstadt, a red-roofed townscape of remarkable architectural unity. Built pretty much from scratch during the 18th century it emerged from WWII almost unscathed.

Great For...

☑ Don't Miss

Next to the Universitätsmuseum, the Alte Aula is a neo-Renaissance hall whose rich decoration dates from 1886.

Marktplatz

The Marktplatz is the focal point of Altstadt street life. The trickling Hercules fountain – that's him up on top of the pillar – in the middle is where petty criminals were chained and left to face the mob in the Middle Ages.

Heiliggeistkirche

For bird's-eye views, climb 208 stairs to the top of the tower of Heidelberg's famous **church** (☎06221-980 30; www.ekihd.de; Marktplatz; tower adult/child €2/1; ⏲church 11am-5pm daily, tower 11am-5pm Mon-Sat, 12.30-5pm Sun Apr-Oct, 11am-3pm Fri & Sat, 12.30-3pm Sun Nov-Mar), constructed between 1344 and 1441, which was shared by Catholics and Protestants from 1706 until 1936 (it's now Protestant).

Hercules fountain in the Marktplatz

OLEG SENKOV/SHUTTERSTOCK ©

Marktplatz ⊙ *Altstadt*

❶ Need to Know

The Altstadt is served by its own S-Bahn station (Altstadt).

✕ Take a Break

The Zum Roten Ochsen (p152) tavern is located at the eastern end of the Altstadt.

★ Top Tip

The Heidelberg Card (1/2/4 days €13/15/17) is worth buying if you intend visiting most of Heidelberg's museums.

Studentenkarzer

From 1823 to 1914, students convicted of misdeeds such as public inebriation, loud nocturnal singing, freeing the local pigs or duelling were sent to the **Studenten-karzer** (Student Jail; 📞06221-543 554; www. uni-heidelberg.de; Augustinergasse 2; adult/child incl Universitätsmuseum €3/2.50; ⊗10am-6pm Tue-Sun Apr-Sep, 10am-4pm Tue-Sat Oct-Mar) for at least 24 hours. Judging by the inventive wall graffiti, some found their stay highly amusing. Delinquents were let out to attend lectures or take exams. In certain circles, a stint in the Karzer was considered a rite of passage.

Universitätsmuseum

The three-room **University Museum** (www. uni-heidelberg.de; Grabengasse 1; adult/child incl Studentenkarzer €3/2.50; ⊗10am-6pm Tue-Sun Apr-Sep, 10am-4pm Tue-Sat Oct-Mar), inside the Alte Universität building, has paintings, por-traits, documents and photos chronicling the university's mostly illustrious history. Only the signs on the Third Reich period are in English but the admission fee includes an English audioguide.

Alte Brücke

Heidelberg's 200m-long **Alte Brücke** (Old Bridge; Karl-Theodor-Brücke), built in 1786, connects the Altstadt with the river's right bank and the Schlangenweg (Snake Path), whose switchbacks lead to the Philoso-phenweg (Philosophers' Walk). Next to the tower gate on the Altstadt side of the bridge, look for the brass sculpture of a monkey holding a mirror. It's the 1979 replacement of the 17th-century original sculpture.

The view from Schloss Heidelberg

SERGEY NOVIKOV/SHUTTERSTOCK ©

Schloss Heidelberg

Towering over the Altstadt, Heidelberg's ruined Renaissance castle cuts a romantic figure, especially from across the Neckar River when illuminated at night. It's one of the most idyllic spots in Germany, but also one with a tumultuous past.

Great For...

☑ **Don't Miss**

The cafe next to the Grosses Fass is a good place to sample German wine.

Palatinate princes, stampeding Swedes, rampaging French, Protestant reformers and lightning strikes – this Renaissance pile has seen the lot. Its turbulent history, lonely beauty and changing moods helped inspire the German Romantic movement two centuries ago. Goethe and Mark Twain are its most illustrious visitors to date.

Attractions

The **Schlosshof**, the castle's central courtyard, is hemmed by Gothic and Renaissance buildings so elaborate they often elicit visitor oohs and aahs. The most eye-catching facade belongs to the **Friedrichsbau**, which is festooned with life-size sculptures of kings and emperors. Psalm 118 is inscribed on the front in Hebrew. Another breathtaking feature are the

The Grosses Fass

PETER SCHICKERT/ALAMY ©

❶ Need to Know

www.schloss-heidelberg.de; ⊙grounds 24hr, castle 8am-6pm, English tours hourly 11.15am-4.15pm Mon-Fri, 10.15am-4.15pm Sat & Sun Apr-Oct, reduced tours Nov-Mar; adult/child incl Bergbahn €6/4, tours €4/2, audioguide €4

✕ Take a Break

There's a cafe next to the Grosses Fass or pack a picnic to enjoy in the Schlossgarten.

★ Top Tip

In summer visit in the evening when admission charges don't apply.

far-reaching **views** over the Neckar River and the Altstadt rooftops.

With a capacity of 228,000L, the **Grosses Fass** is the world's largest wine cask. It was fashioned from 130 oak trees. Describing it as being 'as big as a cottage' Mark Twain bemoaned its emptiness and mused on its possible functions as a dance floor and a gigantic cream churn.

The surprisingly interesting **Deutsches Apotheken-Museum** off the Schlosshof traces the history of Western pharmacology, in which Germany played a central role. Exhibits include pharmacies from the early 1700s and the Napoleonic era.

The grassy and flower-filled **Schloss-garten** on the hillside south and east of the castle is a lovely spot for a stroll.

Visiting

Tickets are only required between 8am and 5.30pm – after this you can stroll the grounds for free. The only way to see the less-than-scintillating interior is by tour – multilingual audioguides that cite Goethe's poems and Mark Twain's stories can be hired at the ticket office to the right as you enter the gardens from the Bergbahn. Except for the museum the entire Schloss is wheelchair accessible though the cobblestones make for rough going.

Getting There

To reach the red sandstone hulk perched about 80m above the Altstadt you can either make the long slog up the steep, cobbled Burgweg in around 10 minutes, or take the Bergbahn (funicular railway). This was opened in 1890 and services run every 10 minutes from the Kornmarkt stop. Schloss tickets include the ride on the Bergbahn.

◎ SIGHTS

At 10.15pm on the first Saturday in June and September and the second Saturday in July the Schloss, the Alte Brücke and the Altstadt are lit up by fantastic fireworks that commemorate the French assault on the Schloss in 1693. The best views are from both banks of the Neckar, west of the Alte Brücke.

Kurpfälzisches Museum   Museum

The city-run Palatinate Museum has well-presented exhibits on Heidelberg's eventful history and is especially strong on the Roman period – exhibits include original wood beams from a 3rd-century bridge. To learn about really ancient local life, check out the replica of the 600,000-year-old jaw-bone of *Homo heidelbergensis* (Heidelberg Man), unearthed about 18km southeast of here in 1907 (the original is stored across the river at the university's palaeontology institute). (www.museum-heidelberg.de; Haupt-strasse 97; adult/child €3/free; ☺10am-6pm Tue-Sun)

Jesuitenkirche   Church

Rising above an attractive square just east of Universitätsplatz, the red-sandstone Jesuits' church is a fine example of 18th-century baroque. This part of town was once the focal point of Heidelberg's Jewish quarter. The Schatzkammer (Treasury; admission €3; ☺10am-5pm Tue-Sat & 1-5pm Sun Jun-Oct, 1-5pm Sat & Sun Nov-May) displays precious religious artefacts. (☺9.30am-6pm May-Sep, to 5pm Oct-Apr)

Alte Universität   University

The most historic facilities of Ruprecht-Karls-Universität are around Universitätsplatz, dominated by the Alte Universität (1712–28; on the south side) and the Neue Universität (1931; on the north side), the 'old' and 'new' university buildings respectively. Nearby stands the Löwenbrunnen (Lions Fountain). (Heidelberg University; www.uni-heidelberg.de)

Philosophenweg   Trail

Winding past monuments, towers, ruins, a beer garden and an enormous *Thingstätte* (amphitheatre; built by the Nazis in 1935), the 2.5km-long Philosophers' Walk, on the south bank of the Neckar River, has captivating views of Heidelberg's Schloss, especially at sunset when the city is bathed in a reddish glow. Access is easiest via the steep Schlangenweg from Alte Brücke. Don't attempt to drive up as the road is narrow and there's nowhere to turn around up the top.

☺ ACTIVITIES

Solarschiff   River Cruise

One of the most peaceful ways to appreci-ate Heidelberg's charms is to get out on the river on the Solarschiff. This solar-panelled boat's engine is silent – all you hear during a 50-minute cruise, apart from onboard commentary in English and German, is the water and the distant sounds of the city. (www.hdsolarschiff.com; Alte Brücke; adult/child €8/3.50; ☺every 90min 10am-6pm Tue-Sun Mar-Oct) 🖼

☻ TOURS

Tourist Office Walking Tours   Walking Tour

One-and-a-half-hour English-language tours taking in the Altstadt's highlights de-part from the Marktplatz (Rathaus) tourist office (p153). (www.heidelberg-marketing.de; adult/child €7/5; ☺English tours 10.30am Thu-Sat Apr-Oct)

☻ EATING

Joe Molese   Diner €

Amazing sandwiches like pastrami, tomato and honey-mustard vinaigrette; brie, rocket and truffle oil; or wild smoked salmon with lemon juice and olive oil are the standout at Joe's, but it also has fantastic salads, chicken drumsticks, burgers and buffalo

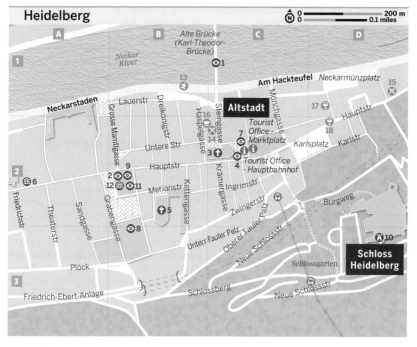

Heidelberg

wings. Black-and-white chequerboard tiling and fire-engine-red walls give it a souped-up New York deli vibe.

Smoothies range from strawberry and basil to pineapple and lime, or you can order beer, wine and cocktails. (www.joemolese. com; Steingasse 16a; dishes €5-12; ☺11am-11pm Sun-Thu, to midnight Fri & Sat)

'S' Kastanie German €€

A panoramic terrace provides sweeping views of the river at this gorgeous 1904-built former hunting lodge, with stained glass and timber panelling, set in the forest near the castle. Chef Sven Schönig's stunning creations include a sweet potato and goats cheese tower with papaya, and goose-stuffed ravioli. (📞06221-728 0343; www.restaurant-s-kastanie.de; Elisabethenweg 1; 2-course lunch menu €9, mains €12-28; 🕐11.30am-2.30pm & 6-10pm Wed-Fri, 5-10pm Sat, 11.30am-8pm Sun)

Café Weinstube Burkardt — Cafe €€

Charming Burkardt's latest incarnation sees it hitting its stride. A superb selection of wines from villages around Heidelberg are available by the glass, and the food is first-rate: paella, risotto with mushroom and asparagus, roast gnocchi with ham and rocket, and spinach frittata. The courtyard abuts the house where Friedrich Ebert, German president during the Weimar Republic, was born. (www.burkardt-heidelberg.de; Untere Strasse 27; mains €7.50-22; 🕐9am-11pm Tue-Sat, to 6pm Sun)

Zur Herrenmühle Heidelberg — German €€€

A flour mill from 1690 has been turned into an elegant and highly cultured place to enjoy refined 'country-style' cuisine –
including dishes such as saffron-crusted dorade royale with baby spinach and creamed potato – beneath weighty, 300-year-old wooden beams with candles flickering on the tables. Book ahead. (📞06221-602 909; www.herrenmuehle-heidelberg.de; Hauptstrasse 239; mains €23-31, 3-/4-/5-/6-course menus from €46/72/82/92; 🕐6-10pm Tue-Sat)

🍷 DRINKING & NIGHTLIFE

Zum Roten Ochsen — Pub

Fronted by a red-painted, blue-grey-shuttered facade, Heidelberg's most historic student pub has black-and-white frat photos on the dark wooden walls and names carved into the tables. Traditional dishes focus on regional fare, such as deer ragout with cranberries, croquettes and red cabbage. Along with German luminaries, visitors who've raised a glass here include Mark Twain, John Wayne and Marylin Monroe. (Red Ox Inn; www.roterochsen.de; Hauptstrasse 217; mains €11.90-24.50; 🕐5pm-12.30am Tue-Sat)

Zum Roten Ochsen

KulturBrauerei   Microbrewery

With its wood-plank floor, chairs from a Spanish monastery and black iron chandeliers, this brewpub is an atmospheric spot to quaff the house brews (including many seasonal specialities) in the enchanting beer garden. Soak them up with time-tested local dishes such as homemade sausages with cream cheese, radish and dark bread. It also has some lovely hotel rooms. (www.heidelberger-kulturbrauerei. de; Leyergasse 6; ⏰7am-midnight)

Chocolaterie Yilliy   Cafe

Especially when the weather's chilly, this is a wonderful spot to warm up with a wickedly thick house-speciality hot chocolate in flavours like hazelnut, cointreau, chilli or praline. The airy space has a laid-back lounge-room vibe, with a book swap, piano and regular acoustic gigs. (www.chocolaterie-heidelberg.de; Haspelgasse 7; ⏰10am-8pm Sat-Thu, to 10pm Fri)

❂ ENTERTAINMENT

The city's effervescent cultural scene includes concerts, films and dance and theatre performances. **Zigaretten Grimm** (☎06221-209 09; Sophienstrasse 11; ⏰9am-7pm Mon-Fri, 10am-5pm Sat), a tobacco shop at Bismarckplatz (east of the Alstadt), sells tickets for concerts and other cultural events.

ℹ INFORMATION

Tourist Office (☎06221-584 4444; www. heidelberg-marketing.de) There are branches at **Hauptbahnhof** (Willy-Brandt-Platz 1;

Where to Stay

Bargains are thin on the ground in Heidelberg and its popularity with tourists means finding a bed can be tricky, so booking ahead is advisable any time of year but especially in summer and during the Christmas season. Many places to stay don't include breakfast in the rate but can provide it for an extra charge.

⏰9am-7pm Mon-Sat, 10am-6pm Sun Apr-Oct, 9am-6pm Mon-Sat Nov-Mar), right outside the main train station, and on **Marktplatz** (Marktplatz 10; ⏰8am-5pm Mon-Fri, 10am-5pm Sat), in the old town.

ℹ GETTING THERE & AWAY

TRAIN

From the Hauptbahnhof (Willy-Brandt-Platz), 3km west of the Schloss, there are at least hourly train services to/from Frankfurt (€18 to €29, one hour to 1½ hours) and Stuttgart (€19 to €39, 40 minutes to 1½ hours).

BUS

The fastest way to reach Frankfurt airport is the eight-seat **Lufthansa Airport Shuttle** (www. lufthansa.com; Kurfürsten-Anlage 1-3, Crowne Plaza Hotel; one-way €25). It runs every 1½ hours; journey time is one hour.

THE BLACK
FOREST

The Black Forest

Home of the cuckoo clock, the Schwarzwald (Black Forest) gets its name from its dark, slightly sinister canopy of evergreens: this is where Hansel and Gretel encountered the wicked witch. The vast expanse of hills, valleys, rivers and forests stretch from the swish spa town of Baden-Baden to the Swiss border, and from the Rhine almost to Lake Constance.

Twenty minutes' walk, or a five-minute bike ride, from populated spots will almost always put you out in nature – in the middle of quiet countryside dotted with traditional farmhouses and amiable dairy cows, perhaps, or in a thick forest where Little Red Riding Hood's wolf may lurk.

☑ In This Section

➡ Arriving in the Black Forest

Karlsruhe-Baden-Baden Airport Handles mainly budget flights; 15km from Baden-Baden.

Stuttgart International Airport A major hub for Germanwings; 13km south of the city.

Freiburg Hauptbahnhof The main train station for accessing the Black Forest handles local and national services.

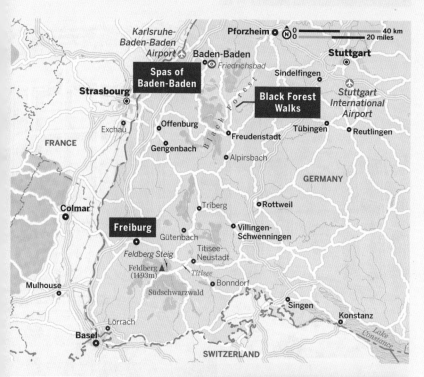

From left: Westweg (p165); the Black Forest in winter; Schiltach (p172)

JUERGEN WACKENHUT/SHUTTERSTOCK © ANDY BRANDL/GETTY IMAGES © DEATONPHOTOS/SHUTTERSTOCK/GETTY IMAGES ©

Historisches Kaufhaus

WERNER DIETERICH/GETTY IMAGES ©

Freiburg's Medieval Altstadt

Sitting plump at the foot of the Black Forest's wooded slopes and vineyards, Freiburg is a sunny, cheerful university town, its medieval Altstadt a story-book tableau of gabled town houses, cobblestone lanes and cafe-rimmed plazas.

Great For...

☑ Don't Miss

Look out for pavement mosaics in front of many shops denoting what is sold there.

Freiburger Münster

With its lacy spires, cheeky gargoyles and intricate entrance portal, Freiburg's 11th-century **minster** (Freiburg Minster; ☏0761-202 790; www.freiburgermuenster.info; Münsterplatz; tower adult/concession €2/1.50; ☺9.30am-5pm, tower 9.30am-4.45pm Mon-Sat, 1-5pm Sun) cuts an impressive figure above the central market square. It has dazzling kaleidoscopic stained-glass windows that were mostly financed by medieval guilds and a high altar with a masterful triptych by Dürer protege Hans Baldung Grien. Square at the base, the tower becomes an octagon higher up and is crowned by a filigreed 116m-high spire. On clear days you can spy the Vosges Mountains in France.

Freiburger Münster

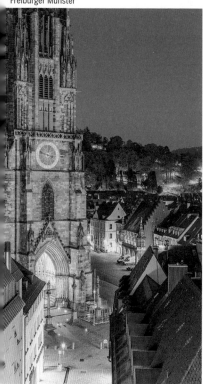

❶ Need to Know

Freiburger Münster is closed for visits during services (exact times are available at the info desk inside).

✕ Take a Break

There is a cafe overlooking the cloister at the Augustinermuseum where you can sip a drink and soak up the monastic vibe.

★ Top Tip

A €7 ticket is available which is valid for all museums in Freiburg.

Closer to the ground, near the main portal in fact, note the medieval wall measurements used to ensure that merchandise (eg loaves of bread) were of the requisite size.

Augustinermuseum

Dip into the past as represented by artists working from the Middle Ages to the 19th century at this superb **museum** (☑0761-201 2531; Auginerplatz 1; adult/concession/under 18yr €6/4/free; ☺10am-5pm Tue-Sun) in a sensitively modernised monastery. The Sculpture Hall on the ground floor is especially impressive for its fine medieval sculpture and masterpieces by Renaissance artists Hans Baldung Grien and Lucas Cranach the Elder. Head upstairs for eye-level views of mounted gargoyles.

Historisches Kaufhaus

Facing the Münster's south side and embellished with polychrome tiled turrets is the arcaded brick-red **Historisches Kaufhaus** (Münsterplatz), an early 16th-century merchants' hall. The coats of arms on the oriels and the four figures above the balcony symbolise Freiburg's allegiance to the House of Habsburg.

City Gates

Freiburg has two intact medieval gates. The **Martinstor** (Martin's gate) rises above Kaiser-Joseph-Strasse, while the 13th-century **Schwabentor** (Schwabenring), on the Schwabenring, is a massive city gate with a mural of St George slaying the dragon and tram tracks running under its arches.

Trinkhalle

Spas of Baden-Baden

Baden-Baden's air of old-world luxury and curative waters have attracted royals, the rich and celebrities over the years – Obama and Bismarck, Queen Victoria and Victoria Beckham included.

Great For...

☑ Don't Miss

Baden-Baden is criss-crossed with walking trails – one leads 3km to the 11th-century Altes Schloss.

This Black Forest town boasts grand colonnaded buildings and whimsically turreted art nouveau villas spread across the hillsides and framed by forested mountains. The bon vivant spirit of France, just across the border, is tangible in the town's open-air cafes, chic boutiques and pristine gardens fringing the Oos River. And with its temple-like thermal baths – which put the *Baden* (bathe) in Baden – and palatial casino, the allure of this *grande dame* of German spa towns is as timeless as it is enduring.

Friedrichsbad

If it's the body of Venus and the complexion of Cleopatra you desire, abandon modesty (and clothing) to wallow in thermal waters

ⓘ Need to Know

Bus 205 runs hourly between the Bahnhof and the airport, less frequently at weekends.

✖ Take a Break

Weinstube im Baldreit (p171) is one of the best places to eat in town.

★ Top Tip

Drink Baden-Baden's mineral-rich water for free at the Fettquelle near Römerplatz.

spring water. For those who dare to bare, saunas range from the rustic 'forest' to the roasting 95°C 'fire' variety.

Trinkhalle

Standing proud above a manicured park, the neoclassical Trinkhalle (Pump Room; Kaiserallee 3; ⏰10am-5pm Mon-Sat, 2-5pm Sun) was built in 1839 as an attractive addition to the Kurhaus. The 90m-long portico is embellished with 19th-century frescos of local legends. Baden-Baden's elixir of youth, some say, is the free curative mineral water that gushes from a faucet linked to the Friedrichsbad spring.

What's Nearby?

The sublime **casino** (www.casino-baden-baden.de; admission €5, guided tour €7; ⏰2pm-2am Sun-Thu, 2pm-3am Fri & Sat, guided tours 9.30-11.45am) seeks to emulate – indeed, outdo – the gilded splendour of Versailles. Marlene Dietrich called it 'the most beautiful casino in the world'. Gents must wear a jacket and tie. If you're not much of a gambler and want to simply marvel at the opulence, hook onto a 40-minute guided tour.

at **Friedrichsbad** (☎07221-275 920; www.carasana.de; Römerplatz 1; 3hr ticket €25, incl soap & brush massage €37; ⏰9am-10pm, last admission 7pm), a palatial 19th-century marble-and-mosaic-festooned spa. As Mark Twain put it, 'after 10 minutes you forget time; after 20 minutes, the world', as you slip into the regime of steaming, scrubbing, hot-cold bathing and dunking in the Roman-Irish bath.

Caracalla Spa

Modern, glass-fronted **Caracalla Spa** (☎07221-275 940; www.carasana.de; Römerplatz 11; 2/3/4hr €15/18/21; ⏰8am-10pm, last admission 8pm) has a cluster of indoor and outdoor pools, grottoes and surge channels, making the most of the mineral-rich

The Black Forest

Black Forest Walks

As locals will tell you, the essence of visiting the Black Forest is getting geared up and hitting the many trails that criss-cross the region. Well-marked routes take you to some of the most picturesque areas, some far from the main tourist hot spots.

Great For...

ⓘ Need to Know

Outdoor equipment shops are widespread in southern Germany and stock high-quality gear.

★ **Top Tip**

Make use of the Schwarzwaldverein's free tour planner at www.wander service-schwarzwald.de.

If you do decide to pull on walking boots and get out there, local tourist information offices in towns on or near the trails can help out with more info such as guides and maps.

It's also worth checking out the Schwarzwaldverein (www.schwarzwaldverein.de), whose well-marked paths reach even the darkest depths of the Black Forest. They produce maps and guides, have over 500 qualified hiking guides on their books, can arrange luggage transfer between overnight stays and oversee 24,000km of hiking trails across the region. They also look after the Black Forest's mountain-biking routes.

The Black Forests trails have a simple marking system. A red, blue-red or white-red diamond signifies you are on a long-distance path, a blue diamond means you're hiking on a regional trail and a yellow diamond marks a local route. Trails are pretty easy to follow with arrows and signposts at strategic points.

From gentle half-day strolls to multiday treks, we've cherry-picked the region for a few of our favourites.

Panoramaweg

If you want to appreciate Baden-Baden and the northern Black Forest from its most photogenic angles, this 40km-long high-level ridge trail weaves past waterfalls and viewpoints, through orchards and woodland. If you don't fancy doing the whole route in one go it can be easily split up into sections measuring 5km to 7km.

Waterfall in a branch of Wutachschlucht

Gütenbach-Simonswäldertal

Tucked-away Gütenbach, 22km south of Triberg, is the trailhead for one of the Black Forest's most beautiful half-day hikes (13km). From here a forest trail threads to Balzer Herrgott, where a sandstone figure of Christ has grown into a tree. Walking downhill from here to the Simonswälder Valley, fir-draped hills rise like a curtain before you. Return by veering north to Teichschlucht gorge, where a brook cascades through primeval forest lined with sheer cliffs and moss-strewn boulders. Head upstream to return to Gütenbach.

☑ **Don't Miss**

There are over 70 official campsites within the Black Forest, great for planning hikes around.

ALEXANDER SCHNURER/GETTY IMAGES ©

Westweg

Up for a bit of an adventure? This famous long-distance trail, marked with a red diamond, stretches for 280km from Pforzheim in the northern Black Forest to Basel in Switzerland. Highlights include the steep Murg Valley, Titisee and Feldburg. See www.westweg.de for maps and further details.

Wutachschlucht

This wild gorge, carved out by a fast-flowing river and flanked by near-vertical rock faces, lies near Bonndorf, close to the Swiss border and 15km east of Schluchsee. The best way to experience its unique microclimate, where you might just spot orchids, ferns, rare butterflies and lizards, is on this 14km-long trail leading from Schattenmühle to Wutachmühle. For more details, visit www.wutachschlucht.de.

Feldberg Steig

Orbiting Feldberg, the Black Forest's highest peak at 1493m, this 12km-long walk traverses a nature reserve that's home to chamois and wildflowers. On clear days the views of the Alps are glorious. It's possible to snowshoe part of the route in winter.

Martinskapelle

A scenic and easy-going walk, this 10km loop kicks off at a hilltop chapel called the Martinskapelle, which sits 11km southwest of Triberg. The well-marked path wriggles through forest to tower-topped Brendturm (1149m), which rewards walkers with views reaching from Feldberg to the Vosges and the Alps when the weather is playing ball. Continue via Brendhäusle and Rosseck for stunning vistas of the overlapping mountains and forest.

✗ **Take a Break**

The Schwarzwaldverein maintains a list of over 100 special picnic spots along the trails.

Freiburg

Historically engaging Freiburg is the gateway to the Black Forest and its de facto capital. Its cobbled lanes are definitely worth a couple of days' exploration (see p158 for information about Freiburg's Aldstadt) before striking out into the wilds of the surrounding countryside.

Blessed with 2000 hours of annual sunshine, this is Germany's warmest city. Indeed, while neighbouring hilltop villages are still shovelling snow, the trees in Freiburg are clouds of white blossom, and locals are already imbibing in canalside beer gardens. This eco-trailblazer has shrewdly tapped into that natural energy to generate nearly as much solar power as the whole of Britain, making it one of the country's greenest cities.

SIGHTS

Schlossberg   Viewpoint
The forested Schlossberg dominates Freiburg. Take the footpath opposite the Schwabentor, leading up through sun-dappled woods, or hitch a ride on the recently restored Schlossbergbahn cable car. For serious hikers, several trails begin here including those to St Peter (17km) and Kandel (25km).

The little peak is topped by the ice-cream-cone-shaped Aussichtsturm (look-out tower). From here, Freiburg spreads photogenically before you – the spire of the Münster soaring above a jumble of red gables, framed by the dark hills of the Black Forest. (Schlossbergring; cable car one way/return €3/5; ⊙9am-10pm, shorter hours in winter)

Rathausplatz   Square
Join locals relaxing in a cafe by the fountain in chestnut-shaded Rathausplatz, Freiburg's prettiest square. Pull out your camera to snap pictures of the ox-blood-red 16th-century Altes Rathaus (Old Town Hall) with the tourist office, the step-gabled 19th-century Neues Rathaus (New Town Hall) and the medieval Martinskirche with its modern interior. (Town Hall Square)

Freiburg

RICHARD FAIRLESS/GETTY IMAGES ©

Haus zum Walfisch   Landmark
The marvellously extravagant Haus zum Walfisch sports a late-Gothic oriel garnished with two impish gargoyles. (House of the Whale; Franziskanerstrasse)

Archäologisches Museum   Museum
In a sculpture-dotted park sits the neo-Gothic Colombischlössle. Built for the Countess of Colombi in 1859, the whimsical red-sandstone villa now harbours this archaeology-focused museum. From the skylit marble entrance, a cast-iron staircase ascends to a stash of finds from Celtic grave offerings to Roman artefacts. (www.museen.freiburg.de; Rotteckring 5; adult/concession €3/2; ⊙10am-5pm Tue-Sun)

Museum für Stadtgeschichte   Museum
The sculptor Christian Wentzinger's baroque town house, east of the Historisches Kaufhaus, now shelters this museum, spelling out in artefacts Freiburg's eventful past. Inside, a wrought-iron staircase guides the eye to an elaborate ceiling fresco. (Münsterplatz 30; adult/concession €3/2; ⊙10am-5pm Tue-Sun)

Museum für Neue Kunst   Gallery
Across the Gewerbekanal, this gallery highlights 20th-century expressionist and abstract art, including emotive works by Oskar Kokoschka and Otto Dix. (Marienstrasse 10; adult/concession €3/2; ⊙10am-5pm Tue-Sun)

✖ EATING

Edo's Hummus Küche   Vegetarian €
Edo's pulls in the midday crowds by doing what it says on the tin – superb homemade hummus served with warm pitta, as well as lentil salad and falafel. The basic hummus plate for €4.30 is a meal in itself. (www.thehummuscorner.com; Atrium Auginerplatz; light meals €2.50-8.50; ⊙11.30am-9pm Mon-Sat; 🍴)

⌐▷☞ Great Drives in the Black Forest

Spoiled with pastoral settings of fir-cloaked hills, peaceful river valleys, crystalline lakes, dense forests and other equally lyrical landscapes, there's no better way to appreciate the Black Forest's beauty than by careening along its many scenic routes:

Schwarzwald-Hochstrasse (Black Forest Hwy; www.schwarzwaldhochstrasse.de) Swoon over views of the mist-wreathed Vosges Mountains, heather-flecked forests and glacial lakes like Mummelsee on this high-altitude road, meandering 60km from Baden-Baden to Freudenstadt on the B500.

Badische Weinstrasse (Baden Wine Rd; www.deutsche-weinstrassen.de) From Baden-Baden south to Lörrach, this 160km-long route corkscrews through the red-wine vineyards of Ortenau, the Pinot noir of Kaiserstuhl and Tuniberg, and the white-wine vines of Markgräflerland.

Schwarzwald-Tälerstrasse (Black Forest Valley Rd) What scenery! Twisting 100km from Rastatt to Alpirsbach, this road dips into the forest-cloaked hills and half-timbered towns of the Murgtal and Kinzigtal valleys.

Deutsche Uhrenstrasse (German Clock Rd; www.deutscheuhrenstrasse.de) A 320km-long loop starting in Villingen-Schwenningen that revolves around the story of clockmaking in the Black Forest. Stops include Furtwangen and cuckoo-crazy Triberg.

Spring in the Black Forest
ANDREAS ZERNDL/GETTY IMAGES ©

Silent Heights

Escape the crowds and enjoy the view at these Baden-Baden lookouts:

Neues Schloss (Schlossstrasse) Vine-swathed steps lead from Marktplatz to the 15th-century Neues Schloss, the former residence of the Baden-Baden margraves, which is set to reopen as a luxury hotel in late 2017. The lookout affords far-reaching views over Baden-Baden's rooftops and spires to the Black Forest beyond.

Mt Merkur (funicular one-way/return €2/4; ⊙10am-10pm) Though modest in height, 668m Mt Merkur commands wide-screen views of Baden-Baden and the Murg Valley. It's a popular spot for paragliding, gentle hiking and family picnics. Buses 204 and 205 stop near the funicular, which has been trundling to the top since 1913.

Florentinerberg The Romans used to cool off here; check out the ruins of the original baths at the foot of the hill. Nowadays, the serene botanical gardens nurture wisteria, cypress trees, orange and lemon groves.

Paradies am Annaberg These Italian-ate gardens are the perfect spot to un-wind, with their soothing fountains and waterfalls. There are fine views of the Altstadt and wooded hills from these heights. Bus 205 to Friedrichshöhe runs nearby.

Markthalle   Market €

Eat your way around the world – from curry to sushi, oysters to antipasti – at the food counters in this historic market hall, nicknamed 'Fressgässle'. (www.markthalle-freiburg.de; Martinsgasse 235; light meals €4-8; ⊙8am-8pm Mon-Thu, to midnight Fri & Sat)

Gasthaus zum Kranz   German €€

There's always a good buzz at this quintes-sentially Badisch tavern. Pull up a chair at one of the wooden tables for well-prepared regional faves like roast suckling pig, *Maultaschen* (pork and spinach ravioli) and *Sauerbraten* (beef pot roast with vinegar, onions and peppercorns). (☎0761-217 1967; www.gasthauszumkranz.de; Herrenstrasse 40; mains €13-24; ⊙11.30am-3pm & 5.30pm-midnight Mon-Sat, noon-3pm & 5.30pm-midnight Sun)

Zirbelstube   French €€€

Freiburg's bastion of fine dining is this can-dlelit restaurant, decorated in warm Swiss pine. Chefs of exacting standards allow each ingredient to shine in specialities like Black Forest chateaubriand with red wine jus and chanterelles, and Breton turbot filet with artichoke-octopus salsa – all perfectly matched with quality wines. (☎0761-210 60; www.colombi.de; Rotteckring 16; mains €45-59; ⊙noon-2pm & 7pm-midnight Mon-Sat)

ⓘ INFORMATION

Tourist Office (☎0761-388 1880; www.freiburg.de; Rathausplatz 2-4; ⊙8am-8pm Mon-Fri, 9.30am-5pm Sat, 10.30am-3.30pm Sun)

ⓘ GETTING THERE & AROUND

AIR

Freiburg shares **EuroAirport** (BSL; ☎In France 03 89 90 31 11; www.euroairport.com) with Basel (Switzerland) and Mulhouse (France). Low-cost airline easyJet flies from here to destinations including London, Berlin, Rome and Alicante.

BUS

The **airport bus** (☎0761-500 500; www.freiburger-reisedienst.de; one-way/return €26/42) goes hourly from Freiburg's bus station to EuroAirport.

Südbaden Bus (www.suedbadenbus.de) and RVF (www.rvf.de) operate bus and train links to towns and villages throughout the southern Black Forest. Single tickets for one/two/three zones cost €2.20/3.80/5.40; a 24-hour Regio24 ticket costs €5.50 for one person and €11 for two to five people.

Bus and tram travel within Freiburg is operated by VAG (www.vag-freiburg.de) and charged at the one-zone rate. Buy tickets from the vending machines or from the driver and validate upon boarding.

TRAIN

Freiburg is on a major north–south rail corridor, with frequent departures for destinations such as Basel (€19 to €24.20, 45 minutes) and Baden-Baden (€18.10 to €25.80, 45 minutes to one hour). Freiburg is also the western terminus of the Höllentalbahn to Donaueschingen via Neustadt (€5.40, 38 minutes, twice an hour). There's a local connection to Breisach (€5.40, 26 minutes, at least hourly).

Baden-Baden

'So nice that you have to name it twice', enthused Bill Clinton about Baden-Baden. 'Nice', however, could never convey the amazing grace of this Black Forest town, with its grand colonnaded buildings and whimsically turreted art nouveau villas spread across the hillsides and framed by forested mountains.

And with its temple-like thermal baths (p160) – which put the *Baden* (bathe) in Baden – and palatial casino, the allure of this grand dame of German spa towns is as timeless as it is enduring.

◎ SIGHTS

Kurhaus   Landmark
Corinthian columns and a frieze of mythical griffins grace the belle époque facade of the Kurhaus, which towers above well-groomed gardens. An alley of chestnut trees, flanked by two rows of boutiques, links the Kurhaus with Kaiserallee. (www.kurhaus-baden-baden.de; Kaiserallee 1; tour €5)

Corinthian columns and mythical griffins grace the belle époque facade of the Kurhaus

Kurhaus

Triberger Wasserfälle (p172)

Kloster Lichtenthal — Abbey
Lichtentaler Allee concludes at the Kloster Lichtenthal, a Cistercian abbey founded in 1245, with an abbey church where generations of the margraves of Baden lie buried. (Lichtentaler Allee)

Museum Frieder Burda — Gallery
A Joan Miró sculpture guards the front of this architecturally innovative gallery, designed by Richard Meier. The star-studded collection of modern and contemporary art, featuring Picasso, Gerhard Richter and Jackson Pollock originals, is complemented by temporary exhibitions, such as recent ones spotlighting neo-expressionist Georg Baselitz and the striking light and shadow works of Heinz Mack. (www.museum-frieder-burda.de; Lichtentaler Allee 8b; adult/concession €12/10; ⊙10am-6pm Tue-Sun)

Staatliche Kunsthalle — Gallery
Sidling up to the Museum Frieder Burda is this sky-lit gallery, which showcases rotating exhibitions of contemporary art in neoclassical surrounds. Recently it zoomed in on the highly experimental works of Czech artist Eva Kot'átková and the expressionistic painting of Beijing-based artist Li Songsong. (www.kunsthalle-baden-baden.de; Lichtentaler Allee 8a; adult/concession €7/5, Fri free; ⊙10am-6pm Tue-Sun)

Stiftskirche — Church
The centrepiece of cobbled Marktplatz is this pink church, a hotchpotch of Romanesque, late Gothic and, to a lesser extent, baroque styles. Its foundations incorporate some ruins of the former Roman baths. Come in the early afternoon to see its stained-glass windows cast rainbow patterns across the nave. (Marktplatz; ⊙8am-6pm)

Römische Badruinen — Ruin
The beauty-conscious Romans were the first to discover the healing properties of Baden-Baden's springs in the city they called Aquae Aureliae. Slip back 2000 years on a tour of the well-preserved ruins of their baths. (Römerplatz; adult/concession €2.50/1; ⊙11am-noon & 3-4pm mid-Mar–mid-Nov)

EATING

Café König Cafe €
Liszt and Tolstoy once sipped coffee at this venerable cafe, which has been doing a brisk trade in Baden-Baden's finest cakes, tortes, pralines and truffles for 250 years. black forest gateau topped with clouds of cream, fresh berry tarts, moist nut cakes – oh, decisions! (Lichtentaler Strasse 12; cake €3.50-5; ☺8.30am-6.30pm)

Weinstube im Baldreit German €€
Tucked down cobbled lanes, this wine-cellar restaurant is tricky to find, but worth looking for. Baden-Alsatian fare such as *Flammkuchen* (Alsatian pizza) topped with Black Forest ham, Roquefort and pears is expertly matched with local wines. Eat in the ivy-swathed courtyard in summer, and the vaulted interior in winter. (☑07221-231 36; Küferstrasse 3; mains €12.50-19; ☺5-10pm Tue-Sat)

ⓘ INFORMATION

Branch Tourist Office (Kaiserallee 3; ☺10am-5pm Mon-Sat, 2-5pm Sun) In the Trinkhalle. Sells events tickets.

Main Tourist Office (☑07221-275 200; www.baden-baden.com; Schwarzwaldstrasse 52; ☺9am-6pm Mon-Sat, 9am-1pm Sun) Situated 2km northwest of the centre. If you're driving from the northwest (from the A5) this place is on the way into town. Sells events tickets.

ⓘ GETTING THERE & AWAY

Karlsruhe-Baden-Baden Airport (Baden Airpark; ☑07229-66 20 00; www.badenairpark.de), 15km west of Baden-Baden, serves destinations including London Stansted, Rome and Málaga by Ryanair.

Buses to Black Forest destinations depart from the bus station, next to the Bahnhof.

Baden-Baden is close to the A5 (Frankfurt–Basel autobahn) and is the northern starting point of the zigzagging Schwarzwald-Hochstrasse, which follows the B500.

🐦 Black Forest National Park

An outdoor wonderland of heather-speckled moors, glacial cirque lakes, deep valleys, mountains and near-untouched coniferous forest, the the **Nationalpark Schwarzwald** (www.schwarzwald-nationalpark.de; Schwarzwald-hochstrasse 2, Seebach; ☺10am-6pm Tue-Sun May-Sep, 10am-5pm Tue-Sun Oct-Apr), which finally got the seal of approval (national park status) on 1 January 2014, is the Schwarzwald at its wildest and untamed best. Nature is left to its own devices in this 100-sq-km pocket of forest in the northern Black Forest, tucked between Baden-Baden and Freudenstadt and centred on the Schwarzwaldhochstrasse (Black Forest High Road), the Murgtal valley and Mummelsee lake.

Hiking and cycling trails abound, as do discovery paths geared towards children. Details of guided tours and online maps are also available on the website.

Baden-Baden is on a major north–south rail corridor. Twice-hourly destinations include Freiburg (€21 to €41, 45 to 90 minutes) and Karlsruhe (€11 to €16, 15 to 30 minutes).

Gutach

The **Schwarzwälder Freilichtmuseum** (☑07831-935 60; www.vogtsbauernhof.org; adult/concession/child/family €9/8/5/25; ☺9am-6pm late Mar-early Nov, to 7pm Aug, last entry 1hr before closing) spirals around the Vogtsbauernhof, an early 17th-century farmstead. Farmhouses shifted from their original locations have been painstakingly reconstructed, using techniques such as thatching and panelling, to create this authentic farming hamlet and preserve age-old Black Forest traditions.

Explore barns filled with wagons and horn sleds, *Rauchküchen* (kitchens for smoking fish and meat) and the Hippenseppenhof (1599), with its chapel and massive hipped roof constructed from 400 trees. It's a great place for families, with inquisitive farmyard animals to pet, artisans on hand to explain their crafts, and frequent demonstrations, from sheep shearing to butter-making.

The self-controlled bobs of the **Schwarzwald Rodelbahn** (Black Forest Toboggan Run; Singersbach 4; adult/child €2.50/2; ⊘10am-6pm Apr-early Nov), 1.5km north of Gutach, are faster than they look. Lay off the brakes for extra speed.

Schiltach

Sitting smugly at the foot of wooded hills and on the banks of the Kinzig and Schiltach Rivers, medieval Schiltach looks too perfect to be true. The meticulously restored half-timbered houses, which once belonged to tanners, merchants and raft builders, are a riot of crimson geraniums in summer.

Centred on a trickling fountain, the sloping, triangular Marktplatz is Schiltach at its picture-book best. The frescos of its step-gabled, 16th-century Rathaus depict scenes from local history.

The **tourist office** (⊘07836-5850; www. schiltach.de; Marktplatz 6; ⊘9am-noon & 2-4pm Mon-Thu, 9am-noon Fri) in the Rathaus can help find accommodation and offers free internet access.

Triberg

Home to Germany's highest waterfall, heir to the original 1915 black forest gateau recipe and nesting ground of the world's biggest cuckoos, Triberg leaves visitors reeling with superlatives.

◉ SIGHTS

Triberger Wasserfälle   Waterfall
Niagara they ain't but Germany's highest waterfalls do exude their own wild romanticism. The Gutach River feeds the seven-tiered falls, which drop a total of

Schiltach

163m and are illuminated until 10pm. (adult/
concession/family €4/3.50/9.50; ☺9am-7pm
Mar-early Nov, 25-30 Dec)

1. Weltgrösste
Kuckucksuhr   Landmark

The 'world's oldest-largest cuckoo clock'
kicked into gear in 1980 and took local
clockmaker Joseph Dold three years to
build by hand. A Dold family member is
usually around to the explain the mech-
anism. (First World's Largest Cuckoo Clock;
☏07722-4689; www.1weltgroesstekuckucksuhr.
de; Untertalstrasse 28, Schonach; adult/conces-
sion €1.20/0.60; ☺9am-noon & 1-6pm)

EATING

Café Schäfer   Cafe €

Confectioner Claus Schäfer uses the
original 1915 recipe for black forest gateau
to prepare this sinful treat that layers
chocolate cake perfumed with cherry
brandy, whipped cream and sour cherries
and wraps it all in more cream and shaved
chocolate. Trust us, it's worth the calories.
(☏07722-4465; www.cafe-schaefer-triberg.de;
Hauptstrasse 33; cake €3-4; ☺9am-6pm Mon,
Tue, Thu & Fri, 8am-6pm Sat, 11am-6pm Sun)

Where to Stay

Baden-Baden is crammed with hotels,
but bargains are rare. The tourist office
has a room-reservation service, for a
10% fee.

Charismatic hotels abound in
Freiburg's Altstadt but it's wise to book
ahead in summer. The tourist office
offers a booking service (€3) and has a
list of good-value private guesthouses.

ⓘ INFORMATION

Tourist Office (☏07722-866 490; www.
triberg.de; Wallfahrtstrasse 4; ☺9am-5pm
Mon-Fri, 10am-5pm Sat & Sun) Inside the
Schwarzwald-Museum. Stocks walking (€3),
cross-country ski trail (€2) and mountain bike
(€6.90) maps.

ⓘ GETTING THERE & AWAY

The Schwarzwaldbahn train line loops southeast
to Konstanz (€23.50, 1½ hours, hourly), and
northwest to Offenburg (€12.10, 46 minutes,
hourly).

DRESDEN

Dresden

There are few city silhouettes more striking than Dresden's. The classic view from the Elbe's northern bank takes in spires, towers and domes belonging to palaces, churches and stately buildings.

Dresden's cultural heyday came under the 18th-century reign of Augustus the Strong (August der Starke) and his son Augustus III when the Saxon capital was known as the 'Florence of the north'. Their vision produced many of Dresden's iconic buildings, including the Zwinger and the Frauenkirche. The devastating bombing raids in 1945 levelled most of these treasures. But Dresden is a survivor and many of the most important landmarks have since been rebuilt, including the elegant Frauenkirche. Today, there's a constantly evolving arts and cultural scene and zinging pub and nightlife quarters, especially in the Outer Neustadt.

☑ In This Section

➡ Arriving in Dresden

Dresden International Airport Handles many domestic flights but only a handful of international connections.

Dresden Hauptbahnhof To the south of the Altstadt, is served by national and regional trains.

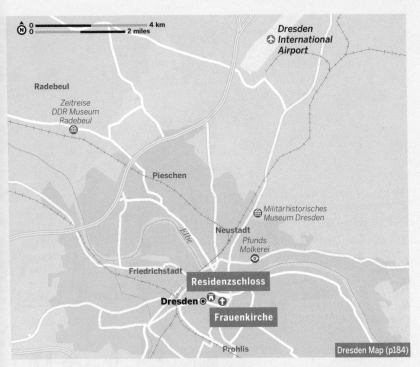

From left: Dresden Christmas market; Frauenkirche (p178); the Albertinum (p182)

Frauenkirche

JORG GREUEL/GETTY IMAGES ©

Frauenkirche

Dresden's top sight, the unmissable Frauenkirche has become a symbol of East Germany's post-communist renewal. Destroyed by Allied bombs in 1945, it was a heap of baroque rubble until rebuilding work began in 1994.

Standing in perfect baroque wedding-cake symmetry on Dresden's pretty Neumarkt, the domed Frauenkirche – Dresden's most beloved symbol – returned to Dresden's cityscape in 2005 after almost a decade of building work. The original had graced its skyline for two centuries before collapsing after the WWII bombing raid which turned Dresden into an inferno and destroyed most of the city centre. It had been left as a war memorial – the East German authorities weren't keen on rebuilding churches – but once the DDR's regime had been swept away in 1989, plans for the church's comeback, which had been drawn up in 1985, were quickly accelerated.

Great For...

☑ **Don't Miss**

The altar, reassembled from nearly 2000 fragments, is especially striking.

Original Building

The original Frauenkirche dated back to the first half of the 18th century but a

Dome of the Frauenkirche

ⓘ Need to Know

Church of Our Lady; www.muenchner-dom. de; Frauenplatz 1; ⊘ 7am-7pm Sat-Wed, to 8.30pm Thu, to 6pm Fri; Ⓢ Marienplatz

✕ Take a Break

The Frauenkirche is almost ringed with cafes that spill out onto the Neumarkt in summer.

★ Top Tip

At the visitors Centre you can watch an interesting documentary about the church's history.

den a smouldering shell. The Frauenkirche stood throughout the two days of the raid until finally collapsing on 15 February.

Resurrection

The reconstruction work cost €180 million and was financed largely by donations raised by the Society to Promote the Reconstruction of the Church of Our Lady and Dresdner Bank. In a symbolic act of reconciliation, the cross and orb that tops the Frauenkirche were created by a British goldsmith whose father was involved in the February 1945 air raid.

A spitting image of the original, it may not bear the gravitas of age but that only slightly detracts from its festive beauty inside and out. The cupola can be climbed. The galleried interior is a wonderful place for concerts, meditations and services. Check the website (www.frauen-kirche-dresden.de) for the current schedule or stop by the Frauenkirche Visitors Centre.

church had stood on this spot since the 11th century. The design you see today replaced a smaller building and was completed in 1743. Its most striking feature is the 96m-high dome, made of sandstone and weighing 12,000 tonnes. It was a remarkable feat of engineering for the time, comparable to the dome of St Paul's in London. The rounded structure is a prominent feature on the Dresden skyline.

Destruction

Dresden city centre was (in)famously destroyed in a massive air raid launched by British and American planes on 13 February 1945. Some 3900 tonnes of explosives were hurled down on the city from over 1200 bombers. The resulting firestorm killed around 25,000 people and left Dres-

Residenzschloss

Residenzschloss

One of the highlights of any visit to Dresden, the Residenzschloss occupies a hefty chunk of the Altstadt. The residence of Saxony's rulers for over 400 years, it's a safe box for the city's art.

Great For...

☑ **Don't Miss**

In the Historisches Grünes Gewölbe look out for the priceless Moor with Emerald Cluster.

History

A fortress of some sort had stood on the site since the 13th century, but following a major fire a new baroque residence was commissioned in the early 18th century by Augustus II the Strong. This was then given a neo-Renaissance makeover in 1914, just in time for Saxony's ruling dynasty to move out at the end of WWI. The palace suffered almost complete destruction in the American and British air raids of February 1945, after which the building was left as a pile of rubble. Some reconstruction began in the 1960s but it wasn't until the end of the Cold War that serious efforts were made to bring the Residenzschloss back to life. Work wasn't completed until 2013.

Dresden's extraordinary city palace now shelters multiple precious collections, including the unmissable Grünes Gewölbe

Lion-head door knocker, Residenzschloss

DIRK FREDER/GETTY IMAGES ©

Elbe River

Terrassenufer

Schlossplatz

Residenzschloss

ⓘ Need to Know

📞0351-4914 2000; www.skd.museum;
Schlossplatz; adult/concession €12/9;
🕙10am-6pm Wed-Mon

✕ Take a Break

There are many cafes and restaurants
in the streets and squares around the
Residenzschloss.

★ Top Tip

Buy timed tickets for the Historisches
Grünes Gewölbe at www.skd.museum.

(Green Vault), a real-life Aladdin's cave
spilling over with precious objects wrought
from gold, ivory, silver, diamonds and jewels. The entire renovated building, including
its unique murals and baroque towers, is
quite simply spectacular.

Collections

If you are intent on seeing everything
at the Residenzschloss, you'll need to
set aside a whole day to do so. There's
so much on display that two separate
treasure chambers are needed to show
off the extraordinary wealth of the Saxon
rulers' private collections. Established by
Augustus II the Strong in 1723, the Historisches **Grünes Gewölbe** (Historic Green
Vault; admission incl audioguide €14) and the
Neues Grünes Gewölbe (New Green Vault;
adult/under 17yr incl audioguide €14/free)

contain one of Europe's largest treasure
collections and the former was one of
Europe's first public museums. Sections
in the Historisches Grünes Gewölbe are
named after precious materials such as
gold, silver, amber and ivory. Also housed
here is the **Kupferstich-Kabinett**, which
counts around half a million prints and
drawings by 20,000 artists (including
Dürer, Rembrandt, Michelangelo, Tou-
louse-Lautrec and Picasso) in its possession. Numismatists might want to drop by
the **Münzkabinett** (Coin Cabinet) in the
palace tower for a small array of historic
coins and medals.

The **Türckische Cammer** (Turkish
Chamber), one of the richest collections
of Ottoman art outside Turkey, is also
here. A huge three-mast tent made of
gold and silk is one standout among
many. The **Riesensaal** (Giant's Hall)
houses a spectacular 10,000-piece
collection of armour, and the display includes re-creations of jousting
tournaments.

◎ SIGHTS

Zwinger   Palace

A collaboration between the architect
Matthäus Pöppelmann and the sculptor
Balthasar Permoser, the Zwinger was
built between 1710 and 1728 on the orders
of Augustus the Strong, who having
returned from seeing Louis XIV's palace at
Versailles, wanted something similar for
himself. Primarily a party palace for royals,
the Zwinger has ornate portals that lead
into the vast fountain-studded courtyard,
which is framed by buildings lavishly
festooned with evocative sculpture. Today
it houses three superb museums within its
baroque walls.

Atop the western pavilion stands a
tense-looking Atlas. Opposite him is a
cutesy carillon of 40 Meissen porcelain
bells, which emit a tinkle every 15 minutes.
Entry to the magnificent courtyard is
free, but all three museums are ticketed.
The Gemäldegalerie Alte Meister (Old
Masters Gallery) and Porzellansammlung
(Porcelain Collection) are unmissable,
while the historic scientific instruments

(globes, clocks, telescopes etc) at the
Mathematisch-Physikalischer Salon are
perhaps more for the scientifically minded.
(☑0351-4914 2000; www.der-dresdner-zwinger.
de; Theaterplatz 1; ☉10am-6pm Tue-Sun) FREE

Albertinum   Museum

After massive renovations following severe
2002 flood damage, the Renaissance-era
former arsenal became the stunning home
of the Galerie Neue Meister (New Masters
Gallery), which displays an arc of paintings
by some of the great names in art from the
18th century on. Caspar David Friedrich
and Claude Monet's landscapes compete
with the abstract visions of Marc Chagall
and Gerhard Richter, all in gorgeous rooms
orbiting a light-filled courtyard. There's also
a superb sculpture collection spread over
the lower floors. (☑0351-4914 2000; www.
skd.museum; enter from Brühlsche Terrasse or
Georg-Treu-Platz 2; adult/concession/under 17yr
€10/7.50/free; ☉10am-6pm Tue-Sun; P)

Semperoper   Historic Building

One of Germany's most famous opera
houses, the Semperoper opened in 1841

Zwinger

and has hosted premieres of famous works by Richard Strauss, Carl Maria von Weber and Richard Wagner. Guided 45-minute tours operate almost daily (the 3pm tour is in English); exact times depend on the rehearsal and performance schedule. Buy advance tickets online to skip the queue.

The original Semperoper burned down a mere three decades after its inauguration. After reopening in 1878, the neo-Renaissance jewel entered its most dazzling period. Alas, WWII put an end to the fun and it wasn't until 1985 that music again filled the grand hall. (📞0351-320 7360; www.semperoper-erleben.de; Theaterplatz 2; tour adult/concession €10/6; ⏰hours vary)

Militärhistorisches Museum Dresden   Museum

Even devout pacifists will be awed by this engaging museum that reopened in 2011 in a 19th-century arsenal bisected by a bold glass-and-steel wedge designed by Daniel Libeskind. Exhibits have been updated for the 21st century, so don't expect a roll call of military victories or parade of weapons. Instead, you'll find a progressive – and often artistic – look at the roots and ramifications of war and aggression.

Exhibits in the Libeskind wedge focus on such sociocultural aspects as women in war, animals in war, war-themed toys, the economy of war and the suffering brought on by war. The historical wing presents a chronology of German wars from the Middle Ages to the 20th century. Standouts among the countless intriguing objects are a 1975 Soyuz landing capsule, a V2 rocket, and personal items of concentration camp victims. Allow at least two hours to do this amazing museum justice. (📞0351-823 2803; www.mhmbw.de; Olbrichtplatz 2; adult/ concession €5/3; ⏰10am-6pm Thu-Tue, to 9pm Mon; 🚋7 or 8 to Stauffenbergallee)

Pfunds Molkerei   Architecture

The Guinness Book–certified 'world's most beautiful dairy shop' was founded in 1880 and is a riot of hand-painted tiles

 Dresden & WWII

Between 13 and 15 February 1945, British and American planes unleashed 3900 tonnes of explosives on Dresden in four huge air raids. Bombs and incendiary shells whipped up a mammoth firestorm, and ashes rained down on villages 35km away. When the blazes had died down and the dust settled, tens of thousands of Dresdners had lost their lives and 20 sq km of this once elegant baroque city lay in smouldering ruins.

Historians still argue over whether this constituted a war crime committed by the Allies on an innocent civilian population. Some claim that with the Red Army at the gates of Berlin, the war was effectively won, and the Allies gained little military advantage from the destruction of Dresden. Others have said that as the last urban centre in the east of the country left intact, Dresden could have provided shelter for German troops returning from the east and was a viable target.

WWII ruins in Dresden
RGLINSKY/GETTY IMAGES ©

and enamelled sculpture, all handmade by Villeroy & Boch. The shop sells replica tiles, wines, cheeses and other milk products. Not surprisingly, the upstairs cafe-restaurant has a strong lactose theme. Slip in between coach tours for a less shuffling look round. (📞0351 808 080; www. pfunds.de; Bautzner Strasse 79; ⏰10am-6pm Mon-Sat, 10am-3pm Sun) FREE

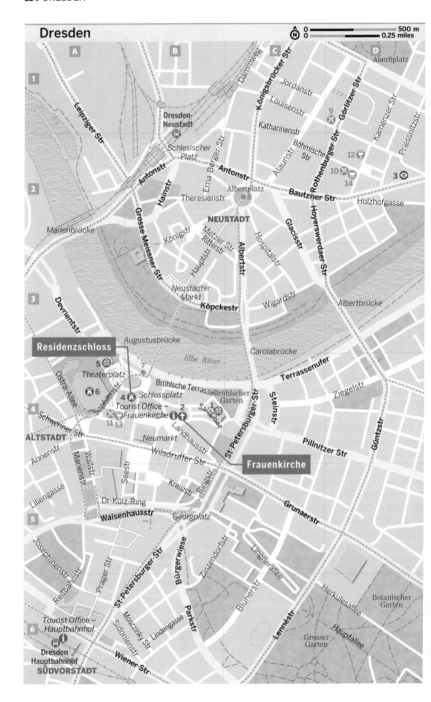

Dresden

0 — 500 m
0 — 0.25 miles

Alaunplatz

Leipziger Str

Dresden-Neustadt

Schlesischer Platz

Antonstr

Marienbrücke

Grosse Meissner Str

Hainstr

Dammweg

Königsbrücker Str

Jordanstr

Louisenstr

Katharinenstr

Antonstr

Erna-Berger-Str

Albertplatz ● 8

Theresienstr

NEUSTADT

Königstr

Metzer Str

Ritterstr

Hauptstr

Albertstr

Jordanstr

Alaunstr

Böhmische Str

Rothenburger Str

Görlitzer Str

Kamenzer Str

Priessnitzstr

12 🏨

10 ✕ 14

3 ◉

Bautzner Str

Holzhofgasse

Glacisstr

Hospitalstr

Hoyerswerdaer Str

Devrientstr

Neustädter Markt

Köpckestr

Wigardstr

Albertbrücke

Residenzschloss

Augustusbrücke

Elbe River

Carolabrücke

Terrassenufer

Ziegelstr

Günzstr

Ostra-Allee

5 🏛

Theaterplatz

7 ●

🏛 6

Schlossplatz

4 🏛

Brühlsche Terrasse

Brühlscher Garten

Steinstr

Sophienstr

✕ 🍴
11 13

Frauenkirche

2

Salzgasse

🛈 🛈

Landhausstr

St-Petersburger Str

Pillnitzer Str

Schweriner Str

ALTSTADT

Annenstr

Wallstr

Marienstr

Neumarkt

Wilsdruffer Str

Seestr

Kreuzstr

Ringstr

Dr-Külz-Ring

Liliengasse

Georgplatz

Grunaerstr

Waisenhausstr

Josephinenstr

Reitbahnstr

Prager Str

Bürgerwiese

St-Petersburger Str

Parkstr

Zinzendorfstr

Blüherstr

Lingnerallee

Lennéstr

Herkulesallee

Botanischer Garten

Tourist Office – Hauptbahnhof
🛈

Dresden Hauptbahnhof
SÜDVORSTADT

Moszinsky Str

Sidonienstr

Lindengasse

Wiener Str

Grosser Garten

Hauptallee

Dresden

TOURS

Grosse Stadtrundfahrt   Bus Tour
Narrated hop-on, hop-off tour with 22 stops and optional short guided tours ticks off all major sights. Buses leave every 15 to 30 minutes. (0351-899 5650; www. stadtrundfahrt.com; Theaterplatz; day pass adult/concession €20/18; 9.30am-10pm Apr-Oct, to 8pm Nov-Mar)

Trabi Safari   Car Tour
Get behind the wheel of the ultimate GDR-mobile for this 1½-hour guided drive around the city, taking in sights from all eras. The price depends on the number of people in the car: four people to a car is the best value. (0351-8990 0110; www.trabi-safari.de; Bremer Strasse 35; per person €34-60)

Nightwalk Dresden   Walking Tour
See street art, learn about what life was like in East Germany and visit fun pubs and bars in the Outer Neustadt on this super fun tour. Nightwalk also have the exclusive rights to take visitors to the slaughterhouse where Kurt Vonnegut survived the bombing of Dresden in 1945 and which he later immortalised in *Slaughterhouse-Five*. (www. nightwalk-dresden.de; Albertplatz; tours 9pm; tours €15)

❌ EATING

Cafe Continental   Cafe, International €
If the greenly lit openings behind the bar remind you of aquariums, you've hit the nail on the head, for buzzy 'Conti' was a pet

store back in GDR days. Today, it's a great place to hit no matter the hour for anything from cappuccino and cocktails to home-made cakes or a full meal. Breakfast is served until 4pm. (www.cafe-continental-dresden.de; Görlitzer Strasse 1; 24; dishes €4-15)

Restaurant Genuss-Atelier   German €€
Lighting up Dresden's culinary scene of late is this fantastic place that's well worth the trip on the No 11 tram. The creative menu is streets ahead of most offerings elsewhere, although the best way to experience the 'Pleasure-Atelier' is to book a surprise menu (three/four/five courses €35/45/55) and let the chefs show off their craft. Reservations essential. (0351-2502 8337; www.genuss-atelier.net; Bautzner Strasse 149; mains €16-20; noon-11pm Wed-Sun; 11 to Waldschlösschen)

Raskolnikoff   International €€
An artist squat before the Wall came down, Raskolnikoff now brims with grown-up artsy-bohemian flair, especially in the sweet little garden at the back, complete with bizarre water feature. The seasonally calibrated menu showcases the fruits of regional terroir in globally inspired dishes, and the beer is brewed locally. Breakfast is served until 2pm, with an excellent brunch (€14.90) on Sundays.

Upstairs are seven handsomely done-up rooms. (0351-804 5706; www.raskolnikoff.de; Böhmische Strasse 34; mains €10-15; 11am-2am Mon-Fri, 9am-2am Sat & Sun)

Peeking Behind the Iron Curtain

Not far from Dresden, in Radebeul and Pirna, two museums offer a fascinating glimpse into an extinct society. We're talking the GDR, the 'other' Germany that ceased to exist with reunification in 1990. Bafflingly eclectic collections of socialist-era flotsam and jetsam – including flags and posters, typewriters and radios, uniforms and furniture, dolls and detergents – have been assembled in these two privately managed 'time capsules'.

DDR Museum Pirna (03501-774 842; www.ddr-museum-pirna.de; Rottwerndorfer-strasse 45; adult/child €7/6; 10am-6pm Tue-Sun Apr-Oct, 10am-5pm Tue-Thu, Sat & Sun Nov-Mar) In a former army barracks, you can snoop around a furnished apartment, sit in a classroom with a portrait of GDR leader Walter Ulbricht glowering down at you, or find out how much a Junge Pioniere youth organisation uniform cost. Thousands of objects are creatively arranged and while most are self-explanatory, others would benefit from informational text.

Zeitreise DDR Museum Radebeul (0351-835 1780; www.ddr-museum-dres-den.de; Wasastrasse 50; adult/concession €8.50/7.50; 10am-6pm Tue-Sun) Large and well organised, each of the four floors here is dedicated to a particular theme, such as work, daily life and state institutions. This is rounded off by a fabulous collection of Trabi cars, Simson motorbikes and other vehicles. A timeline charts milestones in Cold War history and there's a restaurant serving GDR-era cuisine.

Sophienkeller Saxon €€
The 1730s theme with waitresses trussed up in period garb may be a bit overcooked but the local specialties certainly aren't. Most of it is rib-sticking fare, like the boneless half duck with red cabbage or the spit-roasted suckling pig. Wash it down with a mug of dark Bohemian Krušovice. Great ambience amid vaulted ceilings in the Taschenbergpalais building. (0351-497 260; www.sophienkeller-dresden.de; Taschenberg 3; mains €10-15; 11am-1am)

🍸 DRINKING & NIGHTLIFE

If you're up for a night on the razzle, head out to the Äussere Neustadt, which is chock-a-block with cafes and bars. Alaunstrasse, Louisenstrasse and Görlitzer Strasse are where it's happening.

Bottoms Up Bar
This is one of Neustadt's most popular and happening bars. There's an outside beer garden, cider on tap, choices of beers ranging from fancy Belgian to local German, and a cosy interior that gets packed at night. The weekend brunch is excellent. (Martin-Luther-Strasse 31; 5pm-5am Mon-Fri, 10am-5am Sat & Sun)

Lloyd's Cafe, Bar
In a quiet corner of the Neustadt, Lloyd's oozes grown-up flair thanks to stylish cream-coloured leather furniture, huge mirrors and fanciful chandeliers. It's a solid pit stop from breakfast to that last expertly poured cocktail; it even does a respectable afternoon tea and cake by the fireplace. (0351-501 8775; www.lloyds-cafe-bar.de; Martin-Luther-Strasse 17; 8am-1am)

Karl May Bar Bar
Cocktail connoisseurs gravitate to this sophisticated old-school bar inside the Taschenbergpalais hotel. Sink into a heavy burgundy-coloured leather chair to sip tried-and-true classics, or sample one of the 100 whiskies at the curved, dark wood bar. Live music Friday and Saturday; happy hour 6pm to 8pm. (0351-491 20; www. kempinski.com; Taschenberg 3; 6pm-2am)

Dresden park by the Elbe River

INFORMATION

Dresden's hotels can be horrendously expensive, with rates among the highest in Germany. Thankfully there are plenty of cheap beds available at the city's superb hostels.

Tourist Office – Hauptbahnhof (Map p184; 0351-501 501; www.dresden.de; Wiener Platz; 8am-8pm) Small office inside the main train station.

Tourist Office – Frauenkirche (Map p184; 0351-501 501; www.dresden.de; QF Passage, Neumarkt 2; 10am-7pm Mon-Fri, to 6pm Sat, to 3pm Sun) Go to the basement of the shopping mall to find the city's most central tourist office. Helpful English-speaking staff can give you advice, book rooms and tours, rent out audioguides and sell the excellent value Dresden Cards.

GETTING THERE & AWAY

AIR

Dresden International (DRS; www.dresden-airport.de) has flights to many German cities and such destinations as Moscow, Vienna and Zurich.

TRAIN

Fast trains make the trip to Dresden from Berlin-Hauptbahnhof in two hours (€40) and Leipzig in 1¼ hours (€24.50). The S1 local train runs half-hourly to Meissen (€6, 40 minutes).

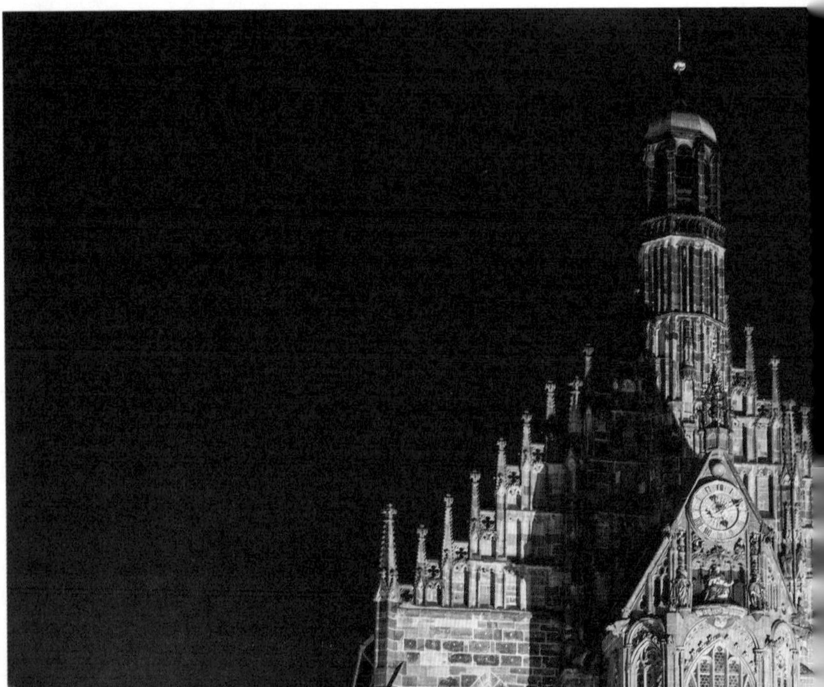

Christkindlesmarkt (p199)

NUREMBERG

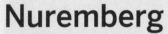

Nuremberg

Nuremberg (Nürnberg), Bavaria's second-largest city and the unofficial capital of Franconia, is an energetic place where the nightlife is intense and the beer is as dark as coffee. As one of Bavaria's biggest draws it is alive with visitors year-round, but especially during the spectacular Christmas market.

For centuries, Nuremberg was the undeclared capital of the Holy Roman Empire and the preferred residence of most German kings. Stuffed with architectural wonders, it was also a magnet for famous artists, though the most famous of all, Albrecht Dürer, was actually born here. By the 19th century, the city had become a powerhouse in Germany's industrial revolution.

The Nazis saw a perfect stage for their activities in working-class Nuremberg. It became the site of their famous rallies and, after the war, the place where their leaders were tried for war crimes.

☑ In This Section

➡ Arriving in Nuremberg

Albrecht Dürer Airport Handles domestic and some international flights.

Nuremberg Hauptbahnhof Major hub in the city centre served by local and national trains.

Main bus station Important stop for many national and international services. Located in the city centre.

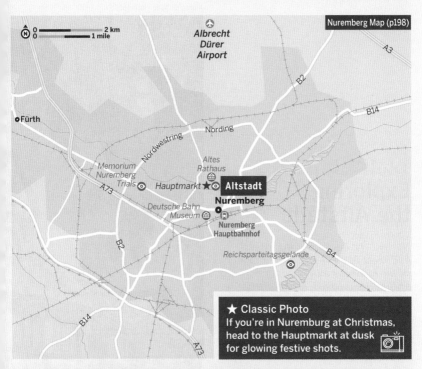

Nuremberg Map (p198)

N 0 ——— 2 km
0 ——— 1 mile

✈ Albrecht
Dürer
Airport

A3

B2

B14

○ Fürth

Nording

Nordwestring

Memorium
Nuremberg
Trials ◎

Altes
Rathaus

🏛

Hauptmarkt ★◎ **Altstadt**

Nuremberg

A73

Deutsche Bahn
Museum 🏛

🚉
Nuremberg
Hauptbahnhof

B2

Reichsparteitagsgelände
◎

B4

B14

A73

★ **Classic Photo**
If you're in Nuremburg at Christmas,
head to the Hauptmarkt at dusk
for glowing festive shots. 📷

From left: Zeppelinfeld (p197); St Sebalduskirche (p194); Nuremberg's Altstadt (p192)
DENNIS MACDONALD/GETTY IMAGES © STUDIO ONE-ONE/GETTY IMAGES © SEANPAVONEPHOTO/GETTY IMAGES ©

Albrecht-Dürer-Haus (p195)

Exploring the Altstadt

Nuremberg has one of the largest and most history-packed old towns in the business and a wander around its crooked, steep lanes, covered bridges and intact city defences is one of the highpoints of any visit to Bavaria.

Great For...

ⓘ Need to Know

The Altstadt is served by the Weisser Turm and Lorenzkirche U-Bahn stations.

★ **Top Tip**

The two-day Nürnberg+Fürth Card (€25) gives admission to all museums and attractions.

Kaiserburg

An enormous castle complex above the Altstadt, **Kaiserburg** (Imperial Castle; ☏0911-244 6590; www.kaiserburg-nuernberg.de; Auf der Burg; adult/concession incl Sinwell Tower €7/6, Palas & Museum €5.50/4.50; ⊙9am-6pm Apr-Sep, 10am-4pm Oct-Mar) poignantly reflects Nuremberg's medieval might. The main attraction is a tour of the newly renovated **Palas** (residential wing) to see the lavish Knights' and Imperial Hall, a Romanesque double chapel and an exhibit on the inner workings of the Holy Roman Empire. This segues to the **Kaiserburg Museum**, which focuses on the castle's military and building history. Elsewhere, enjoy panoramic views from the Sinwell Tower or peer 48m down into the Deep Well.

For centuries the castle, which has origins in the 12th century, also sheltered the crown jewels (crown, sceptre, orb etc) of the Holy Roman Empire, which are now kept at Hofburg palace in Vienna. It also played a key role in the drawing up of Emperor Charles IV's Golden Bull, a document that changed the way Holy Roman Emperors were elected. The exhibition contains an original statue taken from Prague's Charles Bridge of Charles IV who spent a lot of time in both Bohemia and Franconia during his reign.

St Sebalduskirche

Nuremberg's oldest church, **St Sebalduskirche** (www.sebalduskirche.de; Albrecht-Dürer-Platz 1; ⊙9.30am-4pm Jan-Mar, to 6pm Apr-Dec) was built in rusty pink-veined sandstone in the 13th century. Its exterior is replete with religious sculptures and sym-

Kaiserburg

ools; check out the ornate carvings over
he **Bridal Doorway** to the north, showing
the Wise and Foolish Virgins. Inside, the
bronze shrine of St Sebald (Nuremberg's
own saint) is a Gothic and Renaissance
masterpiece that took its maker, Peter
Vischer the Elder, and his two sons more
than 11 years to complete.

Stadtmuseum Fembohaus

Offering an entertaining overview of
the city's history, highlights of the
Stadtmuseum Fembohaus (☎0911-231
2595; Burgstrasse 15; adult/child €5/3; ⊙10am-

☑ Don't Miss

The Ehekarussell Brunnen (Weisser
Turm U-Bahn) is a grotesque sculptur-
al work depicting six interpretations
of marriage.

5pm Tue-Fri, 10am-6pm Sat & Sun) include the
restored historic rooms of this 16th-century
merchant's house. Also here, **Noricama**
takes you on a flashy Hollywoodesque
multimedia journey (in German and English) through Nuremberg's history.

Hauptmarkt

This bustling square in the heart of the
Altstadt is the site of daily markets as
well as the famous *Christkindlesmarkt*
(Christmas Markets; p199). At the eastern
end is the ornate Gothic **Frauenkirche**
(church). Daily at noon crowds crane their
necks to witness the clock's figures enact a
spectacle called the *Männleinlaufen* (Little
Men Dancing).

Albrecht-Dürer-Haus

Dürer, Germany's most famous Renaissance draughtsman, lived and worked at
the **Albrecht-Dürer-Haus** (☎0911-231 2568;
Albrecht-Dürer-Strasse 39; adult/concession
€5/3; ⊙10am-5pm Fri-Wed, to 8pm Thu) from
1509 until his death in 1528. After a multimedia show, there's an audioguide tour of
the four-storey house, which is narrated by
'Agnes', Dürer's wife.

Germanisches Nationalmuseum

Spanning prehistory to the early 20th
century, this museum is the German-
speaking world's biggest and most
important museum of Teutonic culture.
The **Germanisches Nationalmuseum**
(German National Museum; ☎0911-133 10; www.
gnm.de; Kartäusergasse 1; adult/concession
€8/5; ⊙10am-6pm Tue & Thu-Sun, to 9pm Wed)
features works by German painters and
sculptors, an archaeological collection,
arms and armour, musical and scientific
instruments, and toys.

HEINZ WOHNER / LOOK-FOTO/GETTY IMAGES ©

✖ Take a Break

Altstadt-based Bratwursthäusle (p200)
is the best place to sample Nuremberg's
famous sausages.

⊙ SIGHTS

Deutsche Bahn Museum   Museum

Forget Dürer and Nazi rallies, Nuremberg is a railway town at heart. Germany's first passenger trains ran between here and Fürth, a fact reflected in the unmissable German Railways Museum which explores the history of Germany's legendary rail system. The huge exhibition which continues across the road is one of Nuremberg's top sights.

If you have tots aboard, head straight for KIBALA (Kinder-Bahnland – Children's Railway World), a recently refashioned part of the museum where lots of hands-on, interactive choo-choo-themed attractions await. There's also a huge model railway, one of Germany's largest, set in motion every hour by a uniformed controller. (☏0800-3268 7386; www.db-museum.de; Lessingstrasse 6; adult/child €5/2.50; ⊙9am-5pm Tue-Fri, 10am-6pm Sat & Sun)

Altes Rathaus   Historic Building

Beneath the Altes Rathaus (1616–22), a hulk of a building with lovely

Renaissance-style interiors, you'll find the macabre **Mittelalterliche Lochgefängnisse** (Medieval Dungeons; ☏0911-231 2690; adult/concession €3.50/1.50; ⊙tours 10am-4.30pm Tue-Sun). This 12-cell death row and torture chamber must be seen on a 30-minute guided tour (held every half-hour) and might easily put you off lunch. (Rathausplatz 2)

Memorium Nuremberg Trials   Memorial

Göring, Hess, Speer and 21 other Nazi leaders were tried for crimes against peace and humanity by the Allies in **Schwurgerichtssaal 600** (Court Room 600) of this still-working courthouse. Today the room forms part of an engaging exhibit detailing the background, progression and impact of the trials using film, photographs, audiotape and even the original defendants' dock.

The initial and most famous trial, held from 20 November 1945 until 1 October 1946, resulted in three acquittals, 12 sentences to death by hanging, three life sentences and four long prison sentences.

Pegnitz River

Hermann Göring, the Reich's field marshall, famously cheated the hangman by taking a cyanide capsule in his cell hours before his scheduled execution. Although it's easy to assume that Nuremberg was chosen as a trial venue because of its sinister key role during the Nazi years, it was actually picked for practical reasons since the largely intact Palace of Justice was able to accommodate lawyers and staff from all four Allied nations. Note that Court Room 600 is still used for trials and may be closed to visitors.

To get here, take the U1 towards Bärenschanze and get off at Sielstrasse. (📞0911-3217 9372; www.memorium-nuremberg. de; Bärenschanzstrasse 72; adult/concession incl audioguide €5/3; ⏰10am-6pm Wed-Mon)

Reichsparteitagsgelände Historic Site
If you've ever wondered where the infamous black-and-white images of ecstatic Nazi supporters hailing their Führer were taken, it was here in Nuremberg. Much of the grounds were destroyed during Allied bombing raids, but enough remain to get a sense of the megalomania behind it, especially after visiting the excellent **Dokumentationszentrum** (Documentation Centre) served by tram 9 from the Hauptbahnhof.

In the north wing of the partly finished Kongresshalle (Congress Hall), the Documentation Centre examines various historical aspects, including the rise of the NSDAP (Nazi Party), the Hitler cult, the party rallies and the Nuremberg Trials.East of here is the **Zeppelinfeld**, where most of the big Nazi parades, rallies and events took place. It is fronted by a 350m-long grandstand, the Zeppelintribüne, where you can still stand on the very balcony from where Hitler incited the masses. It now hosts sporting events and rock concerts, though this rehabilitation has caused controversy.

The grounds are bisected by the 2km-long and 40m-wide **Grosse Strasse** (Great Road), which was planned as a military

Nuremburg & the Third Reich

The Nazis saw a perfect stage for their activities in working class Nuremberg. It was here that the fanatical party rallies were held, the boycott of Jewish businesses began and the infamous Nuremberg Laws outlawing Jewish citizenship for people were enacted. History buffs will want to visit the Reichsparteitagsgelände, site of fanatical Nazi-party rallies.

After WWII the city was chosen as the site of the war crimes tribunal, now known as the Nuremberg Trials. You can see where the Nazi leaders were trialled at the Memorium Nuremberg Trials.

parade road. Zeppelinfeld, Kongresshalle and Grosse Strasse are all protected landmarks for being significant examples of Nazi architecture. The Reichsparteitagsgelände is about 4km southeast of the city centre. (Luitpoldhain; 📞0911-231 5666; www.museen-nuernberg.de; Bayernstrasse 110; grounds free, documentation centre adult/concession incl audioguide €5/3; ⏰grounds 24hr, documentation centre 9am-6pm Mon-Fri, 10am-6pm Sat & Sun)

🕐 TOURS

Old Town
Walking Tours Walking Tour
English-language old town walking tours are run by the tourist office – tours leave from the Hauptmarkt branch and take two hours. (www.nuernberg-tours.de; adult/child €9/free; ⏰1.30pm May-Oct)

Geschichte für Alle Cultural Tour
Intriguing range of themed English-language tours by a nonprofit association. The 'Albrecht Dürer' and 'Life in Medieval Nuremberg' tours come highly

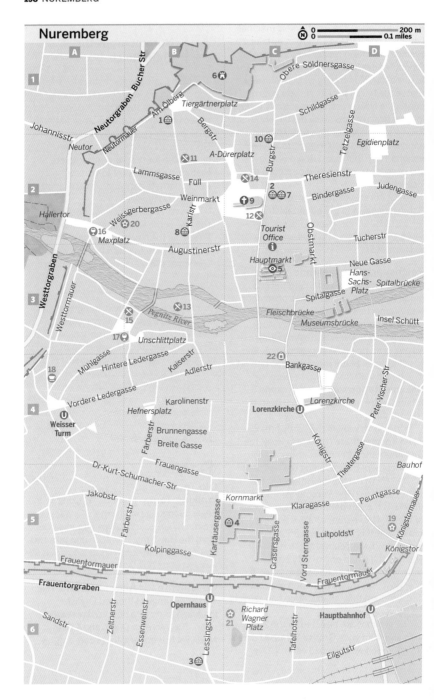

Nuremberg

N 0 ———— 200 m
0 ———— 0.1 miles

Obere Söldnersgasse

Schildgasse

Tetzelgasse

Egidienplatz

Neutorgraben Bucher Str

Johannisstr

Neutor

Neutormauer

Am Olberg

6

Tiergärtnerplatz

Bergstr

1

A-Dürerplatz

Burgstr

10

Theresienstr

Bindergasse

Judengasse

Lammsgasse

Füll

11

14

Weinmarkt

2

9

7

Karlstr

12

Weissgerbergasse

Hallertor

20

16

Maxplatz

8

Augustinerstr

Tourist
Office

Obstmarkt

Tucherstr

Hauptmarkt
5

Neue Gasse

Hans-
Sachs-
Platz

Spitalbrücke

Westtorgraben

Westtormauer

Pegnitz River

13

15

Spitalgasse

Fleischbrücke

Museumsbrücke

Insel Schütt

17

Unschlittplatz

Mühlgasse

Hintere Ledergasse

Kaiserstr

Adlerstr

22

Bankgasse

18

Vordere Ledergasse

Karolinenstr

Lorenzkirche

Lorenzkirche

Peter-Vischer-Str

Weisser
Turm

Hefnersplatz

Färberstr

Brunnengasse

Breite Gasse

Königstr

Theatergasse

Bauhof

Dr-Kurt-Schumacher-Str

Frauengasse

Jakobstr

Färberstr

Kornmarkt

Kartäusergasse

4

Klaragasse

Grasersgasse

Vord Sterngasse

Luitpoldstr

Peuntgasse

19

Königstormauer

Königstor

Kolpinggasse

Frauentormauer

Frauentorgraben

Frauentormauer

Sandstr

Zeltnerstr

Essenweinstr

Lessingstr

Opernhaus

Richard
Wagner
Platz

21

Tafelhofstr

Hauptbahnhof

Eilgutstr

3

A B C D

1 2 3 4 5 6

Nuremberg

recommended. (☑0911-307 360; www.
geschichte-fuer-alle.de; adult/concession €8/7)

Nuremberg Tours   Walking Tour
Four-hour walking and public transport
tours taking in the city centre and the
Reichsparteitagsgelände. Groups meet at
the entrance to the Hauptbahnhof. (www.
nurembergtours.com; adult/concession €19/17;
⊗11.15am Mon, Wed & Sat Apr-Oct)

🔒 SHOPPING

From late November to Christmas Eve,
the Hauptmarkt is taken over by the most
famous **Christkindlesmarkt** (www.christ-
kindlesmarkt.de) in Germany. Yuletide
shoppers descend on the 'Christmas City'
from all over Europe to seek out unique
gifts at the scores of colourful timber
trinket stalls that fill the square.

   The aroma of mulled wine and roast sausages permeates the chilly air, while special
festive events take place across the city.

🍴 EATING

Café am Trödelmarkt   Cafe €
A gorgeous place on a sunny day, this
multilevel waterfront cafe overlooks the
covered Henkersteg bridge. It's especially
popular for its continental breakfasts, and
has fantastic cakes, as well as good blackboard lunchtime specials between 11am

and 2pm. (Trödelmarkt 42; dishes €4-8.50;
⊗9am-6pm Mon-Sat, 11am-6pm Sun)

**Naturkostladen
Lotos**   Organic, Buffet €
Unclog arteries and blast free radicals with
a blitz of grain burgers, spinach soup or
vegie pizza at this health-food shop. The
fresh bread and cheese counter is a treasure
chest of nutritious supplies. (www.naturkost-
laden-lotos.de; Am Unschlittplatz 1; dishes €3-6;
⊗9.30am-6pm Mon-Fri, to 4pm Sat; 🖉)

**Albrecht Dürer
Stube**   Franconian €€
This unpretentious and intimate restaurant
has a Dürer-inspired dining room, prettily
laid tables, a ceramic stove keeping things
toasty when they're not outside and a menu
of Nuremburg sausages, steaks, sea fish,
seasonal specials, Franconian wine and
Landbier (regional beer). There aren't many
tables so booking ahead at weekends is
recommended. (☑0911-227 209; www.albre-
cht-duerer-stube.de; cnr Albrecht-Dürer-Strasse
& Agnesgasse; mains €7-15; ⊗6pm-midnight Mon-
Sat, 11.30am-2.30pm Fri & Sun)

**Goldenes
Posthorn**   Franconian €€
Push open the heavy copper door to find a
real culinary treat that has hosted royals,
artists and professors (including Albrecht
Dürer) since 1498. You can't go wrong

sticking with the miniature local sausages, but the pork shoulder and also the house speciality – vinegar-marinated ox cheeks – are highly recommended as well. (0911-225 153; Glöckleinsgasse 2, cnr Sebalder Platz; mains €9-19; 11am-11pm;)

Bratwursthäusle German €€
Seared over a flaming beech-wood grill, the little links sold at this rustic inn arguably set the standard across the land. You can dine in the timbered restaurant or on the terrace with views of the Hauptmarkt. Service can be flustered at busy times. (www.die-nu-ernberger-bratwurst.de; Rathausplatz 1; meals €7.20-12.90; 10am-10pm Mon-Sat)

American Diner American €€
For the juiciest burgers in town, head for this retro diner in the Cinecitta Cinema, Germany's biggest multiplex. (Gewerbemuse-umsplatz 3; burgers €8-11; 11am-1am)

> *Yuletide shoppers descend on the 'Christmas City' from all over Europe*

DRINKING & NIGHTLIFE

Kettensteg Beer Garden
At the end of the chain bridge and in the shadow of the Halletor you'll find this classic Bavarian beer garden complete with gravel floor, folding slatted chairs, fairy-lights, tree shade and river views. Zirndorf-er, Lederer and Tucher beers are on tap and some of the food comes on heart-shaped plates. (www.restaurant-biergarten-kettensteg.de; Maxplatz 35; 11am-11pm)

Kloster Pub
One of Nuremberg's best drinking dens is all dressed up as a monastery replete with ecclesiastic knick-knacks including coffins emerging from the walls. The monks here pray to the god of *Landbier* (regional beer) and won't be up at 5am for matins, that's for sure. (Obere Wörthstrasse 19; 5pm-1am)

Treibhaus Cafe
Off the path of most visitors, this bustling cafe is a Nuremberg institution and one of the most happening places in town. Set yourself down in the sun on a yellow

Christmas gingerbread at the Christkindlesmarkt (p199)

JUERGEN SACK/GETTY IMAGES ©

director's chair out front or warm yourself with something strong around the huge zinc bar inside. (📞0911-223 041; Karl-Grillenberger-Strasse 28; light meals €5-10; ⊙9am to last customer; 📶)

⊛ ENTERTAINMENT

The excellent *Plärrer* (www.plaerrer.de), available at newsstands throughout the city and from the tourist office, is the best source of information on events around town.

Mata Hari Bar   Live Music
This bar with live music and DJ nights is a Nuremberg institution. After 9pm it's usually standing-room only and the party goes on well into the early hours. (www.mataharibar.de; Weissgerbergasse 31; ⊙from 8pm Wed-Sun)

Staatstheater   Theatre
Nuremberg's magnificent state theatre serves up an impressive mix of dramatic arts. The renovated art nouveau opera house presents opera and ballet, while the Kammerspiele offers a varied program of classical and contemporary plays. The Nürnberger Philharmoniker also performs here. (www.staatstheater-nuernberg.de; Richard-Wagner-Platz 2)

Filmhaus   Cinema
This small indie picture house shows foreign-language movies, plus reruns of cult German flicks and films for kids. (📞0911-231 5823; www.kunstkulturquartier.de; Königstrasse 93)

Where to Stay

Accommodation gets tight and rates rocket during the Christmas market and the toy fair (trade only) in late January to early February. At other times, cheap rooms can be found, especially if you book ahead.

ⓘ INFORMATION
Tourist Office (📞0911-233 60; www.tourismus.nuernberg.de; Hauptmarkt 18; ⊙9am-6pm Mon-Sat year-round, also 10am-4pm Sun Apr-Oct)

ⓘ GETTING THERE & AWAY
AIR
Nuremberg airport (www.airport-nuernberg.de), 5km north of the centre, is served by regional and international carriers, including Ryanair, Lufthansa, Air Berlin and Air France. U-Bahn 2 runs every few minutes from the Hauptbahnhof to the airport (€2.40, 13 minutes). A taxi to/from the airport will cost you about €16.

TRAIN
Rail connections from Nuremberg include the following:

Berlin €100, five hours, at least hourly

Frankfurt €55, 2½ hours, at least hourly

Munich €36 to €55, one hour, twice hourly

ROTHENBURG OB DER TAUBER

Rothenburg ob der Tauber

A medieval gem, Rothenburg ob der Tauber (meaning 'above the Tauber River') is a top tourist stop along the Romantic Road. With its web of cobbled lanes, higgledy-piggledy houses and towered walls, this town is the fairy-tale Germany the hordes of Japanese and Korean tourists came to see. Urban conservation orders here are the strictest in Germany – and at times it feels like a medieval theme park – but all's forgiven in the evenings, when the yellow lamplight casts its spell long after the last tour buses have left.

☑ **In This Section**

➡ **Arriving in Rothenburg ob der Tauber**

Rothenburg train station Only handles local services to Steinach where you can change.

Romantic Road Coach Stops in the main bus park at the train station and on the more central Schrannenplatz.

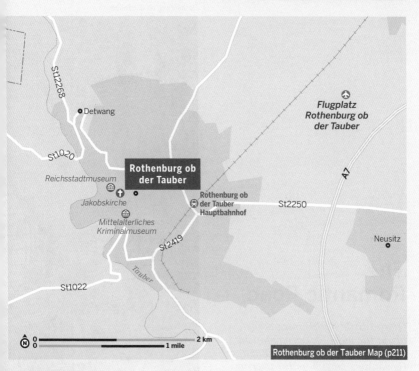

St12268

● Detwang

St1020

Reichsstadtmuseum

Rothenburg ob der Tauber

🏛

✝

Jakobskirche

🏛

Mittelalterliches Kriminalmuseum

St2419

Tauber

St1022

🚉 **Rothenburg ob der Tauber Hauptbahnhof**

St2250

✈ *Flugplatz Rothenburg ob der Tauber*

A7

Neusitz ◉

Ⓝ 0 ———————— 2 km
0 ———————— 1 mile

Rothenburg ob der Tauber Map (p211)

From left: Stadtmauer (p210); Nutcrackers for sale; Rödergasse
ANDREW BAIN/GETTY IMAGES © DANITA DELIMONT/GETTY IMAGES © CALLE MONTES/GETTY IMAGES ©

Rothenburg ob der Tauber

The Romantic Road

Quaint little Rothenburg is just about the most engaging stop on the 350km-long Romantic Road, Germany's most popular touring route. Here we list other highlights of the trip extending from Würzburg to Füssen.

Great For...

ⓘ Need to Know

Deutsche Touring's Romantic Road Coach (p307) runs daily from April to October between Frankfurt and Füssen.

★ **Top Tip**

If you've got the time, consider doing the route by bike for a slower, more bucolic experience.

Würzburg

This scenic town straddles the Main River and is renowned for its art, architecture and delicate wines.

Würzburg was a Franconian duchy when, in 686, three Irish missionaries tried to persuade Duke Gosbert to convert to Christianity, and ditch his wife. Gosbert was mulling it over when his wife had the three bumped off. When the murders were discovered decades later, the martyrs became saints and Würzburg was made a pilgrimage city, and, in 742, a bishopric.

For centuries the resident prince-bishops wielded enormous power and wealth, and the city grew in opulence. Their crowning glory is the **Residenz**, one of the finest baroque structures in Germany and a Unesco World Heritage Site.

Rothenburg ob der Tauber

This is the Romantic Road's quaintest stop with its ring of medieval town walls, cobbled lanes and old taverns (p210). Visit in the quieter times for a taste of romance minus the tourists.

Dinkelsbühl

Some 40km south of Rothenburg, immaculately preserved Dinkelsbühl proudly traces its roots to a royal residence founded by Carolingian kings in the 8th century. Saved from destruction in the Thirty Years War and ignored by WWII bombers, this is arguably the Romantic Road's most authentically medieval halt. For a good overall impression of the town, walk along the fortified walls with their 18 towers and four gates.

The Residenz, Würzburg

Nördlingen

Charmingly medieval, Nördlingen sees fewer tourists than its better-known neighbours. The town lies within the **Ries Basin**, a massive impact crater gouged out by a meteorite more than 15 million years ago. The crater is one of the best preserved on earth, and has been declared a special 'geopark'. Nördlingen's 14th-century **walls**, all original, mimic the crater's rim and are almost perfectly circular.

Donauwörth & Harburg

Donauwörth is a medieval rebuild, largely destroyed during WWII. Nearby **Schloss**

> ☑ **Don't Miss**
>
> Schloss Weikersheim (www. schloss-weikersheim.de) is one of the finest palaces on the Romantic Road.

FRANS SELLIES/GETTY IMAGES ©

Harburg looms over the Wörnitz River, its medieval covered parapets, towers, turrets, keep and red-tiled roofs so perfectly preserved they almost seem like a film set. Tours tell the building's long tale and evoke the ghosts that are said to haunt the castle.

Augsburg

The largest city on the Romantic Road is is also one of Germany's oldest, founded by the stepchildren of Roman emperor Augustus over 2000 years ago. It is an engaging stop, though one with a grittier, less quaint atmosphere than others along the route. Top billing here goes to the **Fuggerei**, Augsburg's Catholic welfare settlement, the oldest in existence.

Wieskirche

The ecclesiastical climax of the Romantic Road is the Baroque **Wieskirche** located in the village of Wies, just off the B17 between Füssen and Schongau. It's one of Bavaria's best-known baroque churches and a Unesco-listed heritage site. About one million visitors a year flock here to see this monumental opus by the legendary artist-brothers Dominikus and Johann Baptist Zimmermann.

Neuschwanstein & Hohenschwangau Castles

The Romantic Road comes to a fittingly idyllic crescendo at Germany's most popular tourist attraction, Neuschwanstein (p134) and Hohenschwangau castles.

Füssen

The town of Füssen (p140) is worth half a day's exploration. You can easily escape from the crowds into a landscape of gentle hiking trails and Alpine vistas.

> ✕ **Take a Break**
>
> The Romantic Road has every kind of dining experience, from gourmet to kebabs.

◉ SIGHTS

Jakobskirche   Church

One of the few places of worship in Bavaria to charge admission, Rothenburg's Lutheran parish church was begun in the 14th century and finished in the 15th. The building sports some wonderfully aged stained glass windows but the top attraction is Tilman Riemenschneider's **Heilig Blut Altar** (Altar of the Holy Blood). The gilded cross above the main scene depicting the Last Supper incorporates Rothenburg's most treasured reliquary – a rock crystal capsule said to contain three drops of Christ's blood. (Church of St Jacob; Klingengasse 1; adult/concession €2.50/1.50; ⊙9am-5.15pm Mon-Sat, 10.45am-5.15pm Sun)

Mittelalterliches Kriminalmuseum   Museum

Medieval implements of torture and punishment are on show at this gruesomely fascinating museum. Exhibits include chastity belts, masks of disgrace for gossips, a cage for cheating bakers, a neck brace for quarrelsome women and a beer-barrel pen for drunks. You can even snap a selfie in the stocks! (Medieval Crime & Punishment Museum; www.kriminalmuseum.eu; Burggasse 3; adult/concession €5/3.50; ⊙10am-6pm May-Oct, shorter hours Nov-Apr)

Deutsches Weihnachtsmuseum   Museum

If you're glad Christmas comes but once every 365 days, then stay well clear of the Käthe Wohlfahrt Weihnachtsdorf, a Yuletide superstore that also houses this Christmas Museum. This repository of all things 'Ho! Ho! Ho!' traces the development of various Christmas customs and decorations, and includes a display of 150 Santa figures, plus lots of retro baubles and tinsel – particularly surreal in mid-July when the mercury outside is pushing 30°C. (Christmas Museum; ☏09861-409 365; www.weihnachtsmuseum. de; Herrngasse 1; adult/child/family €4/2.50/7; ⊙10am-5pm daily Easter-Christmas, shorter hours Jan-Easter)

Stadtmauer   Historic Site

With time and fresh legs, a 2.5km circular walk around the Stadtmauer, the town's unbroken ring of walls, gives a sense of the importance medieval man placed on defending his settlement. A great lookout point is the eastern tower, the **Röderturm** (Rödergasse; adult/child €1.50/1; ⊙9am-5pm Mar-Nov), but for the most impressive views head to the west side of town, where a sweeping view of the Tauber Valley includes the Doppelbrücke, a double-decker bridge.

Alt-Rothenburger Handwerkerhaus   Historic Building

Hidden down a little alley is the Alt-Rothenburger Handwerkerhaus, where numerous artisans – including coopers, weavers, cobblers and potters – have their workshops today, and mostly have had for the house's more than 700-year existence. It's half museum, half active workplace and you can easily spend an hour or so watching the craftsmen at work. (Alter Stadtgraben 26; adult/concession €3/2.50; ⊙11am-5pm Mon-Fri, from 10am Sat & Sun Easter-Oct, 2-4pm daily Dec)

Reichsstadtmuseum   Museum

Highlights of the Reichsstadtmuseum, housed in a former Dominican convent, include the *Rothenburger Passion* (1494), a cycle of 12 panels by Martinus Schwarz, and the oldest convent kitchen in Germany, as well as weapons and armour. Outside the main entrance (on your right as you're facing the museum), you'll see a spinning barrel, where the nuns distributed bread to the poor – and where women would leave babies they couldn't afford to keep. (www. reichsstadtmuseum.rothenburg.de; Klosterhof 5; adult/concession €4.50/3.50; ⊙9.30am-5.30pm Apr-Oct, 1-4pm Nov-Mar)

Rathausturm   Historic Building

The Rathaus on Marktplatz was begun in Gothic style in the 14th century and was completed during the Renaissance. Climb the 220 steps of the medieval town hall to the viewing platform of the Rathausturm to be rewarded with widescreen views of the Tauber. (Town Hall Tower; Marktplatz; adult/

Rothenburg ob der Tauber

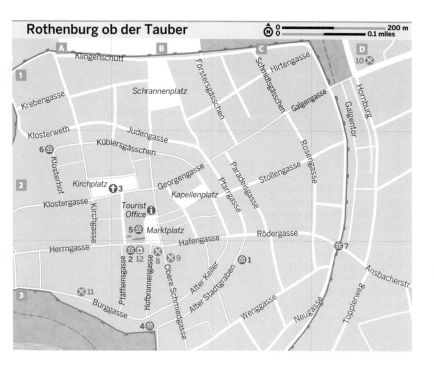

Rothenburg ob der Tauber

⊙ Sights	
1 Alt-Rothenburger Handwerkerhaus.........	C3
2 Deutsches Weihnachtsmuseum	B3
3 Jakobskirche.......................................	B2
4 Mittelalterliches Kriminalmuseum............	B3
5 Rathausturm......................................	B2
6 Reichsstadtmuseum..............................	A2
7 Röderturm..	D3

⊗ Eating	
8 Diller's Schneeballen	B3
9 Gasthof Goldener Greifen..........................	B3
10 Mittermeier	D1
11 Zur Höll	A3

⊕ Shopping	
12 Käthe Wohlfahrt Weihnachtsdorf.............	B3

concession €2/0.50; ⊙9.30am-12.30pm &
1-5pm daily Apr-Oct, 10.30am-2pm & 2.30-6pm
daily Dec, noon-3pm Sat & Sun rest of year)

🕜 TOURS

The tourist office runs 1½-hour walking
tours (€7; in English) at 2pm from April
to October. Every evening a lantern-toting
Nachtwächter (Night Watchman) dressed
in traditional costume leads an entertaining tour of the Altstadt; English tours (€7)
meet at the Rathaus just before 8pm.

🛍 SHOPPING

**Käthe Wohlfahrt
Weihnachtsdorf**　　Decorations

With its mind-boggling assortment of
Yuletide decorations and ornaments, this
huge shop lets you celebrate Christmas
every day of the year. Many of the items
are handcrafted with amazing skill and
imagination; prices are correspondingly
high. (www.wohlfahrt.com; Herrngasse 1;
⊙9am-6pm)

Bottoms up for Freedom

In 1631 the Thirty Years War – pitching Catholics against Protestants – reached the gates of Rothenburg ob der Tauber. Catholic General Tilly and 60,000 of his troops besieged the Protestant market town and demanded its surrender. The town resisted but couldn't stave off the onslaught of marauding soldiers, and the mayor and other town dignitaries were captured and sentenced to death.

And that's about where the story ends and the legend begins. As the tale goes, Rothenburg's town council tried to sate Tilly's bloodthirstiness by presenting him with a 3L pitcher of wine. Tilly, after taking a sip or two, presented the men with an unusual challenge, saying 'If one of you has the courage to step forward and down this mug of wine in one gulp, then I shall spare the town and the lives of the councilmen!' Mayor Georg Nusch accepted – and succeeded! And that's why you can still wander though Rothenburg's wonderful medieval lanes today.

It's pretty much accepted that Tilly was really placated with hard cash. Nevertheless, local poet Adam Hörber couldn't resist turning the tale of the Meistertrunk into a play, which, since 1881, has been performed every Whitsuntide (Pentecost), the seventh Sunday after Easter. It's also re-enacted several times daily by the clock figures on the tourist office building.

Rothenburg ob der Tauber
ANDREW BAIN/GETTY IMAGES ©

✖ EATING

Rothenburg's most obvious speciality is *Schneeballen*, ribbons of dough loosely shaped into balls, deep-fried then coated in icing sugar, chocolate and other dentist's foes. Some 27 different types are produced at **Diller's Schneeballen** (Hofbronnengasse 16; ⊙10am-6pm); a more limited range is available all over town.

Mittermeier Bavarian €€
Supporters of the slow food movement and deserved holders of a Michelin Bib Gourmand, this hotel restaurant pairs punctilious craftsmanship with top-notch ingredients, sourced regionally whenever possible. There are five different dining areas including a black-and-white tiled 'temple', an alfresco terrace and a barrel-shaped wine cellar. The wine list is one of the best in Franconia. (☎09861-945 430; www.villamittermeier.de; Vorm Würzburger Tor 7; mains €12-19; ⊙6-10.30pm Tue-Sat; P🛜)

Zur Höll Franconian €€
This medieval wine tavern is in the town's oldest original building, with sections dating back to the year 900. The menu of regional specialities is limited but refined, though it's the superb selection of Franconian wines that people really come for. (☎09861-4229; www.hoell.rothenburg.de; Burggasse 8; mains €6.80-20; ⊙5-11pm)

Gasthof Goldener Greifen Franconian €€
Erstwhile home of Heinrich Toppler, one of Rothenburg's most famous medieval mayors (the dining room was his office), the 700-year-old Golden Griffin is the locals' choice in the touristy centre serving a hearty menu of Franconian favourites in an austere semi-medieval setting and out back in the sunny and secluded garden. (☎09861-2281; www.gasthof-greifen-rothen-burg.de; Obere Schmiedgasse 5; mains €8-17; ⊙11am-9.30pm)

Dinkelsbühl (p208)

ℹ INFORMATION

Tourist Office (☎09861-404 800; www.touris-mus.rothenburg.de; Marktplatz 2; ☉9am-6pm Mon-Fri, 10am-5pm Sat & Sun May-Oct, 9am-5pm Mon-Fri, 10am-1pm Sat Nov-Mar) Helpful office offering free internet access.

ℹ GETTING THERE & AWAY

BUS

The Romantic Road Coach (p307) stops in the main bus park at the Hauptbahnhof and on the more central Schrannenplatz.

CAR & MOTORCYCLE

The A7 autobahn runs right past town.

TRAIN

You can go anywhere by train from Rothenburg, as long as it's Steinach. Change there for services to Würzburg (€13.30, one hour and 10 minutes). Travel to and from Munich (from €31, three hours) can involve up to three different trains.

ℹ GETTING AROUND

The city has five car parks right outside the walls. The town centre is closed to non-resident vehicles, although hotel guests are exempt.

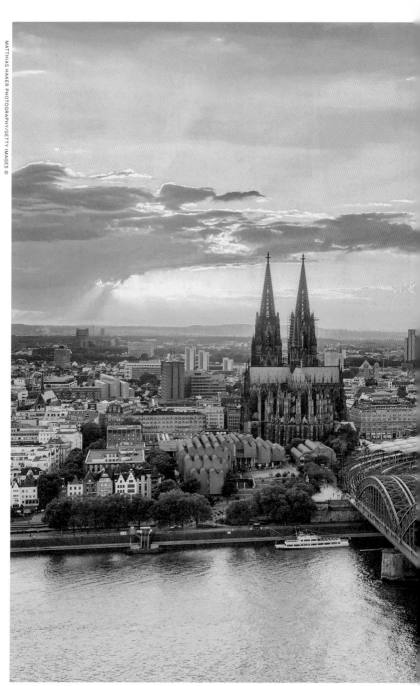

COLOGNE

Cologne

Cologne (Köln) offers seemingly endless attractions, led by its famous cathedral whose filigree twin spires dominate the skyline. It's regularly voted the country's single most popular tourist attraction. The city's museum landscape is especially strong when it comes to art but also has something in store for fans of chocolate, sports and even Roman history.

Cologne is like a 3D textbook on history and architecture. Drifting about town you'll stumble upon an ancient Roman wall, medieval churches, nondescript postwar buildings, avant-garde structures and even a new postmodern quarter. Germany's fourth-largest city was founded by the Romans in 38 BC and given the lofty name Colonia Claudia Ara Aggripinensium. It grew into a major trading centre, a tradition it solidified in the Middle Ages and continues to uphold.

☑ In This Section

➡ Arriving in Cologne

Cologne-Bonn Airport Receives domestic as well as many European flights.

Cologne Hauptbahnhof A major stop on the German rail network handling countless local, regional and national services.

Central bus station Handles national and international coach services. Near the Hauptbahnhof.

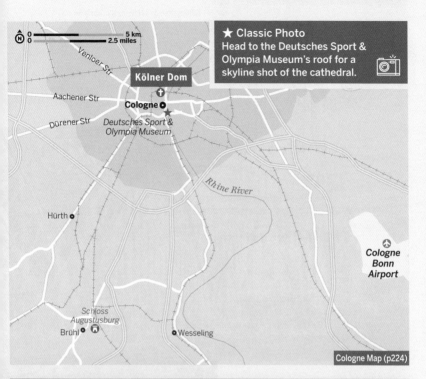

★ **Classic Photo**
Head to the Deutsches Sport &
Olympia Museum's roof for a
skyline shot of the cathedral.

N
0 —————— 5 km
0 —————— 2.5 miles

Venloer Str

Kölner Dom

Aachener Str

Cologne

Dürener Str

*Deutsches Sport &
Olympia Museum*

Rhine River

Hürth

Cologne
Bonn
Airport

*Schloss
Augustusburg*

Brühl

Wesseling

Cologne Map (p224)

From left: Restaurants in Cologne; inside the Kölner Dom (p218); Kranhauser (crane houses) on the Rhine, Cologne
JULIAN ELLIOTT PHOTOGRAPHY/GETTY IMAGES © MERTEN SNIJDERS/GETTY IMAGES © STUART LECHE/GETTY IMAGES ©

Kölner Dom and Hohenzollernbrücke

THOMAS WINZ/GETTY IMAGES ©

Kölner Dom

Cologne's geographical and spiritual heart – and its single-biggest tourist draw – is the magnificent Kölner Dom. With its soaring twin spires, this is the Mt Everest of cathedrals, jam-packed with art and treasures.

The Dom is Germany's largest cathedral and must be circled to truly appreciate its dimensions. Note how its lacy spires and flying buttresses create a sensation of lightness and fragility despite its mass and height.

This sensation continues inside, where a phalanx of pillars and arches supports the lofty nave. Soft light filters through the medieval stained-glass windows as well a much-lauded recent one by contemporary artist Gerhard Richter in the transept. A kaleidoscope of 11,500 squares in 72 colours, Richter's abstract design has been called a 'symphony of light'. In the afternoon especially, when the sun hits it just so, it's easy to understand why.

Great For...

☑ **Don't Miss**

The underground Domforum visitor centre is a good source of info and tickets.

History

Construction began in 1248 in the French Gothic style but proceeded slowly and was

Kölner Dom

MERTEN SNIJDERS/GETTY IMAGES ©

ⓘ Need to Know

Cologne Cathedral; www.koelner-dom.de; tower adult/concession €4/2; ⊘6am-9pm May-Oct, to 7.30pm Nov-Apr, tower 9am-6pm May-Sep, to 5pm Mar-Apr & Oct, to 4pm Nov-Feb

✗ Take a Break

There are several cafes and restaurants in and around the square which the Dom dominates.

★ Top Tip

To get more out of your visit, invest €1 in the information pamphlet or join a guided tour.

eventually halted in 1560 when funds ran out. The half-built church lingered for nearly 300 years and even suffered a stint as a horse stable and prison when Napoleon occupied the town. A few decades later, a generous cash infusion from Prussian King Friedrich Wilhelm IV finally led to its completion in 1880, 632 years after it started. Luckily, it escaped WWII bombing raids with nary a shrapnel wound and has been a Unesco World Heritage Site since 1996.

Shrine of the Three Kings

The pièce de résistance among the cathedral's bevy of treasures is the Shrine of the Three Kings behind the main altar, a richly bejewelled and gilded sarcophagus said to hold the remains of the kings who followed the star to the stable in Bethlehem where Jesus was born. The bones were

spirited out of Milan in 1164 as spoils of war by Emperor Barbarossa's chancellor and instantly turned Cologne into a major pilgrimage site.

South Tower

For an exercise fix, climb the 533 steps up the Dom's south tower to the base of the steeple that dwarfed all buildings in Europe until Gustave Eiffel built a certain tower in Paris. During your climb up to the 95m-high viewing platform, take a breather and admire the 24-tonne Peter Bell (1923), the world's largest free-swinging working bell.

Other Highlights

Other highlights include the Gero Crucifix (970), notable for its monumental size and an emotional intensity rarely achieved in those early medieval days; the choir stalls from 1310, richly carved from oak; and the altar painting (c 1450) by Cologne artist Stephan Lochner.

Kolumba (p223)

Walking Tour: Exploring Cologne

Cologne's history is everywhere, as you'll see on this walk, which circles through the heart of the bustling city. You can view Roman or medieval ruins.

Distance: 2km
Duration: 3 hours

✗ **Take a Break**
You'll always be near somewhere to pause for refreshments.

Start Kölner Dom

❶ Kölner Dom

Cologne's biggest drawcard is the historically and architecturally impressive **Kölner Dom** (p218). Visitors can climb the 533 steps up its south tower to the base of the steeple which once towered over all of the buildings in Europe, until it was overtaken with the construction of Paris' Eiffel Tower. The underground Domforum visitor centre is a good source of info and tickets.

❷ Altes Rathaus

Dating to the 15th century and much restored, the **old city hall** (Rathausplatz; ⊙8am-4pm Mon, Wed & Thu, to 6pm Tue) has fine bells that ring daily at noon and 5pm. The Gothic tower is festooned with statues of old city notables.

❸ Archäologische Zone & Future Jüdisches Museum

Cologne used the construction of the U-Bahn line to expand the **Archäologische Zone** and to build the grand new **Future Jüdisches Museum** (Archaeological Zone/Jewish Museum; ☎0221-2213 3422; Kleine Budengasse 2; adult/concession €3.50/3; ⊙10am-5pm Tue-Sun), which is located under the Rathausplatz and fully ecompasses two major parts of the city history.

At the deepest level is the Praetorium, which has relics of a Roman governor's palace. One level up you'll find relics from the Jewish community that was here in the Middle Ages, including a *mikveh* (community bath). Although work is ongoing, there is usually some access to the site.

❹ Wallraf-Richartz-Museum

The **Wallraf-Richartz-Museum** (p222) houses a significant collection of European

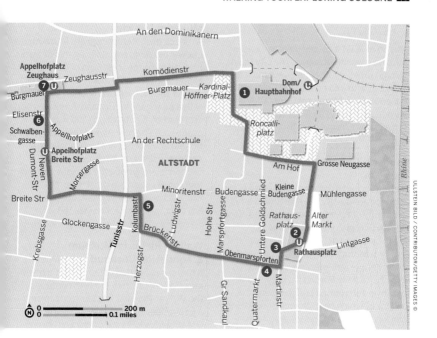

art. The top floor shines the spotlight on the 19th century with Germany's largest collection of impressionist paintings, including masterpieces by Monet, Van Gogh, Cezanne, Gauguin and all the other heavy hitters of the genre.

5 Kolumba

Home to a wide array of religious treasures, **Kolumba** (p223) also contains the ruins of the late-Gothic church of St Kolumba and has foundations that date back to the days of the Romans.

6 NS Dokumentationszentrum

Cologne's Third Reich history is poignantly documented in the **NS Documentation Centre** (☎0221-2212 6332; www.museenkoeln. de; Appellhofplatz 23-25; adult/concession €4.50/2; ☺10am-6pm Tue-Fri, 11am-6pm Sat & Sun). In the basement of this otherwise

mundane-looking building was the local Gestapo prison where scores of people were interrogated, tortured and killed. Inscriptions on the basement cell walls offer a gut-wrenching record of the emotional and physical pain endured by inmates. Executions often occurred in the courtyard.

7 Kölnisches Stadtmuseum

The **Kölnisches Stadtmuseum** (Cologne City Museum; ☎0221-2212 2398; www.museen-koeln.de; Zeughausstrasse 1-3; adult/concession €5/3; ☺10am-8pm Tue, to 5pm Wed-Sun), in the former medieval armoury, explores all facets of Cologne history. There are exhibits on Carnival, Kölsch (the local beer), eau de cologne and other things that make the city unique. A model re-creates the city of 1571; it's huge yet minutely detailed.

Finish Kölnisches Stadtmuseum

◉ SIGHTS

Plan on at least a couple days to explore Cologne's wealth of sights. The city maintains an excellent website (www.museenkoeln.de) with info on most of Cologne's museums. The **MuseumsCard** (€18/30 per person/family) includes most of the museums and is good for two consecutive days.

Römisch-Germanisches Museum   Museum

Sculptures and ruins displayed outside the entrance are merely the overture to a full symphony of Roman artefacts found along the Rhine. Highlights include the giant Poblicius tomb (AD 30–40), the magnificent 3rd-century Dionysus mosaic, and astonishingly well-preserved glass items. Insight into daily Roman life is gained from toys, tweezers, lamps and jewellery, the designs of which have changed surprisingly little since Roman times. (Roman Germanic Museum; ☎0221-2212 4438; www.museenkoeln. de; Roncalliplatz 4; adult/concession €9/5; ◷10am-5pm Tue-Sun)

Museum Ludwig   Museum

A mecca of contemporary art, Museum Ludwig presents a tantalising mix of works from all major phases. Fans of German expressionism (Beckmann, Dix, Kirchner) will get their fill here as much as those with a penchant for Picasso, American pop art (Warhol, Lichtenstein) and Russian avant-garde painter Alexander Rodchenko. Rothko and Pollock are highlights of the abstract collection, while Gursky and Tillmanns are among the reasons the photography section is a must-stop. (☎0221-2212 6165; www.museum-ludwig.de; Heinrich-Böll-Platz; adult/concession €11/7.50, more during special exhibits; ◷10am-6pm Tue-Sun)

Wallraf-Richartz-Museum & Fondation Corboud   Museum

A famous collection of European paintings from the 13th to the 19th centuries, the Wallraf-Richartz-Museum occupies a postmodern cube designed by the late OM Ungers. Works are presented chronologically, with the oldest on the 1st floor where standouts include brilliant examples from the Cologne School, known for its

Crossing Hohenzollernbrücke

distinctive use of colour. The most famous painting is Stefan Lochner's *Madonna of the Rose Bower*. (📞0221-2212 1119; www.wallraf.museum; Obenmarspforten; adult/concession €8/4.50; ⏱10am-6pm Tue, Wed & Fri-Sun, to 9pm Thu)

Museum Schnütgen   Museum

East of the Neumarkt, the Cultural Quarter encompasses the Museum Schnütgen, a repository of medieval religious art and sculpture. Part of the exhibit shows the beautiful setting of the Romanesque Cäcilienkirche (Cecily Church). Also part of the atrium complex is the Rautenstrauch-Joest-Museum. (📞0221-2212 2310; www.museen koeln.de; Cäcilienstrasse 29; adult/concession €6/3.50; ⏱10am-6pm Tue-Sun, to 8pm Thu)

Kolumba   Museum

Art, history, architecture and spirituality form a harmonious tapestry in this spectacular collection of religious treasures of the Archdiocese of Cologne. Called Kolumba, the building encases the ruins of the late-Gothic church of St Kolumba, layers of foundations going back to Roman times and the Madonna in the Ruins chapel, built on the site in 1950. Exhibits span the arc of religious artistry from the early days of Christianity to the present. Don't miss the 12th-century carved ivory crucifix.

Other exhibits include Coptic textiles, Gothic reliquaries and medieval painting juxtaposed with works by Bauhaus legend Andor Weiniger in edgy room installations.

The museum is yet another magnificent design by Swiss architect Peter Zumthor, 2009 winner of the Pritzker Prize, the 'architectural Oscar'. (📞0221-933 1930; www.kolumba.de; Kolumbastrasse 4; adult/child €5/free; ⏱noon-5pm Wed-Mon)

Schokoladenmuseum   Museum

At this high-tech temple to the art of chocolate-making, exhibits on the origin of the 'elixir of the gods', as the Aztecs called it, and the cocoa-growing process are followed by a live-production factory tour and a stop at a chocolate fountain for a sample. (Chocolate Museum; 📞0221-931 8880; www.

⚥ LGBT Cologne

Next to Berlin, Cologne is Germany's most gay-and-lesbian-friendly city. The rainbow flag flies especially proudly in the so-called 'Bermuda Triangle' around Rudolfplatz, which explodes into a nonstop party zone at weekends. Another major romping ground is the Heumarkt area (especially Pipinstrasse), which draws more sedate folks and leather and fetish lovers. **Cologne Pride** (www.colognepride.de; ⏱Jun) basically serves as a warm-up for the **Christopher Street Day** (⏱early Jul), which brings more than a million people to Cologne.

Christopher Street Day parade
YULIA REZNIKOV/SHUTTERSTOCK ©

schokoladenmuseum.de; Am Schokoladenmuseum 1a; adult/concession €9/6.50; ⏱10am-6pm Tue-Fri, 11am-7pm Sat & Sun, last entry 1hr before closing; 👪)

🏃 ACTIVITIES

Cologne's dense network of bike routes along the Rhine and throughout the city make it a fine place to cycle. Pick up a bike map at the tourist office.

Radstation   Bicycle Rental

Bike rental place under the train station. It offers excellent three-hour tours (Marksmann-gasse; tours €17.50; ⏱1.30pm Apr-Oct) in English that start from a small stand in the Altstadt on the Rhine near the Deutzer Brücke. (📞0221-139 7190; www.radstation-koeln.de; Breslauerplatz, Hauptbahnhof; rental per 3hr/day €5/10; ⏱5.30am-10.30pm Mon-Fri, 6.30am-8pm Sat, 8am-8pm Sun)

Cologne

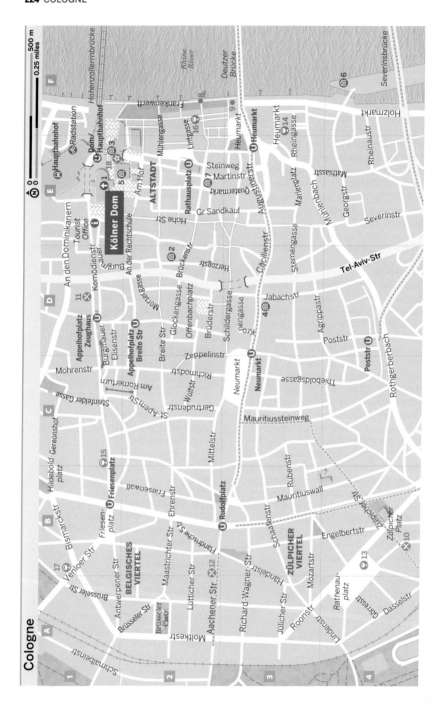

Cologne

ⓕ TOURS

KD River Cruises   Boat Tour

One of several companies offering one-hour spins taking in the splendid Altstadt panorama; other options include brunch and sunset cruises. (☏0221-258 3011; www.k-d.com; Frankenwerft 35; adult/concession €10/6; ◷10.30am-5pm Apr-Oct)

ⓐ SHOPPING

Hohe Strasse is one of Germany's oldest pedestrianised shopping strips, and along with its side street In der Höhle, it's where you'll find all the mainstream chains and department stores. Smaller fashion and shoe shops culminate in Schildergasse in the Neumarkt, where the Neumarkt-Galerie mall is easily recognised by the upturned ice-cream cone on the roof, designed by Claes Oldenburg and Coosje van Brugge.

Mittelstrasse and Pfeilstrasse are lined with exclusive fashion, jewellery and home-accessory shops, while Ehrenstrasse is easily Cologne's most creative strip, with designer boutiques mixing with more offbeat fare. Funky music shops, vintage clothing dealers and the-next-hot-desginer-shops are scattered about the streets near Belgisches Viertel and Brüsseler Platz.

⊗ EATING

Cologne's multiculturalism lets you take a culinary journey around the world. The Belgisches Viertal and streets in and around Zülpicher Platz and Ehrenstrasse are ideal areas for making a tasty discovery.

Cologne's unmissable beer halls (p226) offer not only the local brew but also excellent meals at good prices. And be sure to sample some of Cologne's *Schwarzbrot* (black bread), which many claim is Germany's best.

Salon Schmitz   Modern European €€
Spread over three historic row houses, the Schmitz empire is your one-stop shop for excellent food and drink. From the casual bistro to excellent seasonal meals in the restaurant to the take-out deli, you'll find something you like at Schmitz almost any time of day. Wash it all down with the house-brand *Kölsch*. (☏0221-9229 9594; www.salonschmitz.com; Aachener Strasse 28; mains from €10; ◷9am-late, hours vary by venue)

Bei Oma Kleinmann   German €€
Named for its long-time owner, who was still cooking almost to her last day at age 95 in 2009, this perennially booked, grafitti-covered restaurant serves oodles of schnitzel, made either with pork or veal and paired with homemade sauces and sides. Pull up a seat at the small wooden tables for a classic Cologne night out.

 Kölsch Beer

Cologne has its own style of beer, *Kölsch*, which is unlike any other in Germany. It's light and hoppy and slightly sweet, always crisp, and served cool. Unlike the vast steins used elsewhere for suds serving, in Cologne your *Kölsch* comes in *stangen* (skinny, straight glasses that only hold 0.2L).

In traditional Cologne beer halls and pubs you don't order beer so much as subscribe. The constantly prowling waiters will keep dropping off the little glasses of beer until you indicate you've had enough by placing a beer mat on top of your glass.

A ceaseless flow of *stangen* filled with *Kölsch*, coupled with earthy humour and platters of meaty local foods are the hallmarks of Cologne's iconic beer halls. Look for the days when each place serves glorious potato pancakes (*Kartoffelpuffer* or *Reibekuchen* in local dialect).

Cologne brewery
PATRIK STOLLARZ / STAFF/GETTY IMAGES ©

(📞0221-232 346; www.beiomakleinmann.de; Zülpicher Strasse 9; mains €13-21; ⏰5pm-midnight Tue-Thu & Sun, to 1am Fri & Sat)

Bistrot B   European €€€

Classic French cooking by chef Jean-Claude Bado stars at this prim little bistro that's one of Cologne's most popular restaurants. The dishes are inventive, seasonal and remarkably good value given the talents at work in the kitchen. Bentwood chairs add curvaceous charm to the simple dining room. (📞0221-1398 6777; www.lapoe-ledor.de; Komödienstrasse 50; menus from €31; ⏰noon-2pm & 5-10pm Tue-Sat)

🍷 DRINKING & NIGHTLIFE

Päffgen   Beer Hall

Busy, loud and boisterous, Päffgen has been pouring *Kölsch* since 1883 and hasn't lost a step since. In summer you can enjoy the refreshing brew and local specialities beneath starry skies in the beer garden. (📞0221-135 461; www.paeffgen-koelsch.de; Friesenstrasse 64-66; ⏰10am-midnight Sun-Thu, to 12.30am Fri & Sat)

Biergarten Rathenauplatz   Beer Garden

A large, leafy park has one of Cologne's best places for a drink: a community-run beer garden. Tables sprawl under huge, old trees, while simple snacks such as salads and very good *frikadelle* (spiced hamburger) issue forth from a cute little hut. Prices are cheap; beers come from nearby Hellers Brewery – try the organic lager. Proceeds help maintain the park. (📞0221-801 7349; www.rathenauplatz.de; Rathenauplatz; ⏰noon-11pm Apr-Oct)

Stadtgarten   Club

Surrounded by a small park, this Belgisches Viertel favourite hosts vibrant dance parties and live jazz, soul and world music concerts in its cellar hall, but is also a great spot for a drink (summer beer garden). (📞0221-952 9940; www.stadtgarten.de; Venloer Strasse 40; ⏰hours vary)

Brauerei Zur Malzmühle   Beer Hall

Expect plenty of local colour at this convivial beer hall off the beaten tourist track. It brews *Kölsch* with organic ingredients and is also known for its lighter *Malzbier* (malt beer, 2% alcohol). (📞0221-210 117; www.muehlenkoelsch.de; Heumarkt 6; ⏰10am-midnight)

🎭 ENTERTAINMENT

Major listings are in the mainstream *Kölner Illustrierte* (www.koelner.de) and the alternative *StadtRevue* (www.stadtrevue.de). Buy tickets at www.koelnticket.de.

Papa Joe's Jazzlokal Lounge

Jazz riffs nightly in this museum-like place where the smoky brown walls are strewn with yesteryear's photographs. There really is a Joe and he is a true jazz lover. There's a second, less intimate location, Papa Joe's Klimperkasten, on Alter Markt. (☎0221-257 7931; www.papajoes.de; Buttermarkt 37; ☺8pm-3am)

Kölner Philharmonie Classical Music

The famous Kölner Philharmoniker is the 'house band' in this grand, modern concert hall below the Museum Ludwig. (☎0221-280 280; www.koelner-philharmonie.de; Bischofsgartenstrasse 1)

ℹ INFORMATION

Cologne often hosts trade shows, which can cause hotel rates to double and triple. Otherwise, you'll find good-value options across the walkable central area.

The excellent **Tourist Office** (☎0221-346 430; www.cologne-tourism.com; Kardinal-Höffner-Platz 1; ☺9am-8pm Mon-Sat, 10am-5pm Sun) is located near the cathedral. The app is well-done.

ℹ GETTING THERE & AWAY

AIR

About 18km southeast of the city centre, **Cologne-Bonn Airport** (Köln Bonn Airport; www.koeln-bonn-airport.de) has direct flights to 130 cities and is served by numerous airlines, with destinations across Europe. The S13 train connects the airport and the Hauptbahnhof every 20 minutes (€2.80, 15 minutes). Taxis charge about €30.

TRAIN

Services are fast and frequent in all directions. A sampling: Berlin (€117, 4¼ hours), Frankfurt (€71, 1¼ hours) and Munich (€142, 4½ hours).

Cologne is like a 3D textbook on history and architecture.

Cologne's Altstadt (old town)

THE ROMANTIC RHINE VALLEY

The Romantic Rhine Valley

Between Rüdesheim and Koblenz, the Rhine cuts deeply through the Rhenish slate mountains, meandering between hillside castles and steep fields of wine to create a magical mixture of beauty and legend. Idyllic villages appear around each bend, their neat half-timbered houses and Gothic church steeples seemingly plucked from the world of fairy tales.

High above the river, busy with barge traffic, and the rail lines that run along each bank, are the famous medieval castles, some ruined, some restored, all mysterious vestiges of a time that was anything but tranquil. In 2002 Unesco designated these 67km of riverscape, more prosaically known as the Oberes Mittelrheintal (Upper Middle Rhine Valley; www.welterbe-mittelrheintal.de), as a World Heritage Site.

☑ In This Section

➡ Arriving in the Rhine Valley

Koblenz Hauptbahnhof Handles services from destinations north and from along the Rhine Valley.

Bingen Hauptbahnhof Services from the Rhine Valley and destinations south call in here.

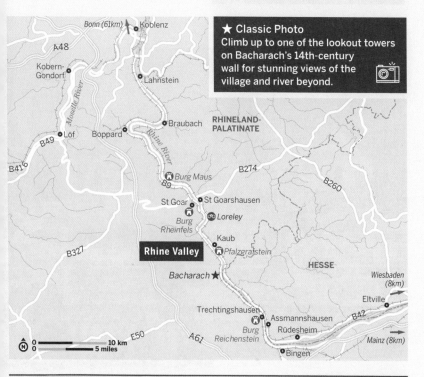

Bonn (61km)
Koblenz
A48
Kobern-Gondorf
Lahnstein
Moselle River
B49 Löf
Boppard
Braubach
RHINELAND-PALATINE
Rhine River
B41
B274
B260
Burg Maus
B9
St Goar
St Goarshausen
Loreley
Burg Rheinfels
B327
Kaub
Rhine Valley
Pfalzgrafstein
HESSE
Bacharach ★
Wiesbaden (8km)
Eltville
Trechtingshausen
Assmannshausen
B42
Burg Reichenstein
Rüdesheim
Mainz (8km)
E50
A61
Bingen

N 0 — 10 km
0 — 5 miles

★ Classic Photo
Climb up to one of the lookout towers on Bacharach's 14th-century wall for stunning views of the village and river beyond.

From left: Peterskirche (p236), Bacharach; Altes Haus (p236), Bacharach; Loreley (p237)
ULLSTEIN BILD/GETTY IMAGES © H & D ZIELSKE/LOOK-FOTO GETTY IMAGES © BRIGITTE MERZ/LOOK-FOTO/GETTY IMAGES ©

Hiking & Cycling in the Rhine Valley

The Rhine Valley is superb territory for hikers and cyclists. There are many options for two-wheelers and boots, and slow travel will enable you to enjoy this beautiful region.

Great For...

☑ Don't Miss

A tough hilly stretch of the Rheinsteig between Rüdesheim and Loreley is considered the most invigorating.

Hiking

Two challenging but achingly beautiful long-distance hiking trails run along the Romantic Rhine, with variants continuing downriver to Bonn and upriver to Mainz and beyond. The first is the 199km **Rhein-BurgenWeg** (www.rheinburgenweg.com), linking Rolandsbogen, near Bonn, with Bingen, passing some 40 castles.

The other is the 320km **Rheinsteig** (www.rheinsteig.de), which links Wiesbaden with Bonn, hugging the river valley for most of the way and considered by many to be one of the best hiking trails in all Germany, and certainly one of its prettiest. And this being the Rhine, no day on the trail would be complete without a wine-tasting session in a wine-producing village or wine cellar. On any stretch of

Rheingau Riesling Path

INA PETERS/GETTY IMAGES ©

the river a one-way hike can be turned into a circuit by combining walking with ferries, trains and buses. Other trails which intersect the above two are the **Rheinhöhenweg**, the **Limes-Wanderweg**, the **Gebückwanderweg**, the **Rhine Panorama Way**, the **Rheingau Riesling Path** and several local nature trails.

Cycling

The **Rhein-Radweg** (www.rheinradweg.eu; Euro Velo route 15) stretches for 1230km (900km of which are in Germany) from Andermatt in Switzerland to the Hoek van Holland, near Rotterdam – from the source of the Rhine to where it meets the North Sea. Between Bingen and Koblenz it runs along the left (more or less west)

bank, as well as on a growing number of sections of the right bank. It links up with two other long-distance bike paths: the 207km **Nahe-Hunsrück-Mosel-Radweg** (www.naheland-radtouren.de), which follows the Nahe River from Bingen southwest to Trier, and the 311km **Mosel-Radweg** (www.mosel-radweg.de), which runs along the banks of the Moselle River from Koblenz to Traben-Trarbach, Bernkastel-Kues, Trier and on to Thonville in France. Note that you cannot cycle on several sections of the hiking trails detailed above for safety reasons (usually where they are deemed too narrow to accommodate both riders and walkers).

Bicycles can be taken on Regional trains, car ferries and river ferries, making it possible to ride one way (such as down the valley) and take public transport the other. Bike repair shops are common in large towns, less so in smaller communities. The website www.bettundbike.de helps you find bike-friendly accommodation (hotels and guesthouses with bike storage facilities, bike tools, drying facilities etc). You can search according to town or long-distance cycling trail.

Rüdesheim

Rüdesheim, part of the Rheingau wine region (famous for its superior rieslings), is deluged by some three million day-tripping coach tourists a year. The tunnel-like Drosselgasse alley is the Rhine at its most colourfully touristic – music blares from the pubs, which heave with rollicking crowds. At the top of Drosselgasse, Oberstrasse is similarly overloaded. To get away from the throngs all you have to do is wander a few blocks in any direction.

Situated 50m to the left from the top of Drosselgasse **Siegfried's Mechanisches Musikkabinett** (www.smmk.de; Oberstrasse 29; tour adult/child €6.50/3; ⊙10am-6pm Mar-Dec) has a fun and often surprising collection of 18th- and 19th-century mechanical musical instruments that play themselves as you're shown around.

For a stunning Rhine panorama, head up the wine slopes west of Rüdesheim to the **Niederwald Monument**. Erected between 1877 and 1883, this bombastic monument celebrates the Prussian victory in the Franco-Prussian War and the creation of the German Reich, both in 1871. You can walk up via the Rüdesheimer Berg vineyards – sign-posted trails include one that begins at the P2 car park (one block above Oberstrasse) – but to save climbing 203 vertical metres, it's faster to glide above the vineyards aboard the 1400m-long **Seilbahn cable car** (Kabinenbahn; www.seilbahn-ruedesheim.de; Oberstrasse 37; adult/child one-way €5/2.50, return €7/3.50, with Sesselbahn €8/4; ⊙10am-5.30pm Mon-Fri, to 6pm Sat & Sun May-Sep, 10am-5pm Mon-Fri, to 5.30pm Sat & Sun Apr & Oct).

The **tourist office** (🖉06722-906 150; www.ruedesheim.de; Rheinstrasse 29a; ⊙8.30am-6.30pm Mon-Fri, 10am-4pm Sat & Sun Apr-Oct, 10am-4.30pm Mon-Fri Nov-Mar) is at the eastern edge of the town centre.

Rüdesheim is connected to Bingen by passenger and car ferries.

Bingen

Thanks to its strategic location at the confluence of the Nahe and Rhine Rivers, Bingen has been coveted by warriors

Autumn vineyards opposite Bingen

and merchants since its founding by the Romans in 11 BC. These days it's an attractive, flowery town that's less touristy – and less cute – than its smaller neighbours.

◉ SIGHTS

Museum am Strom   Museum
On Bingen's riverside promenade, this one-time power station now displays exhibits on Rhine romanticism, both engraved and painted. Other highlights include a set of surgical instruments – from scalpels and cupping glasses to saws – left behind by a Roman doctor in the 2nd century AD. (Museumsstrasse 3; adult/child €3/2; ⊙10am-5pm Tue-Sun)

Mäuseturm   Castle
The Mouse Tower, on an island near the confluence of the Nahe and Rhine, is where – according to legend – Hatto II, the 10th-century archbishop of Mainz, was devoured alive by mice as punishment for his oppressive rule. In fact, the name is probably a mutation of *Mautturm* (toll tower), which reflects the building's medieval function. (⊙closed to the public)

❶ INFORMATION

Tourist Office (☎06721-184 205; www.bingen. de; Rheinkai 21; ⊙9am-6pm Mon-Fri, 9am-5pm Sat, 10am-1pm Sun May-Oct, 9am-6pm Mon, 9am-4pm Tue-Thu, 9am-1pm Fri Nov-Mar, 9am-6pm Mon-Fri, 9am-1pm Sat Apr)

Burg Reichenstein

Looming above the village of Trechtingshausen, mighty **Burg Reichenstein** (☎06721-6117; www.burg-reichenstein.de; adult/child €5/3.50; ⊙10am-6pm Tue-Sun Mar–mid-Nov, 10am-5pm Tue-Sun mid-Nov–Feb) harbours a lavish collection of furnishings, armour, hunting trophies and even cast-iron oven slabs. Situated 8km downriver from Bingen.

🗺 Getting Around the Rhine Valley

Boat

River travel is a relaxing and very romantic way to see the castles, vineyards and villages of the Romantic Rhine. From about Easter to October (winter services are very limited), passenger ships run by Köln-Düsseldorfer (www.k-d.com) link Rhine villages on a set timetable.

You can travel to the next village or all the way from Mainz to Koblenz (one-way/return €50/55, downstream/upstream 5½/8 hours). Within the segment you've paid for (eg Boppard–Rüdesheim, which costs €25.40/26.80 one-way/return), you can get on and off as many times as you like, but be sure to ask for a free stopover ticket each time you disembark.

Train

Villages on the Rhine's left bank (eg Bingen, Bacharach, Oberwesel and Boppard) are served hourly by local trains on the Koblenz–Mainz run.

Right-bank villages such as Rüdesheim, Assmannshausen, Kaub, St Goarshausen and Braubach are linked hourly to Koblenz' Hauptbahnhof and Wiesbaden by the RheingauLinie.

Car Ferry

No bridges span the Rhine between Koblenz and Mainz; the only way to cross the river along this stretch is by *Autofähre* (car ferry). Ferry services generally operate every 15 or 20 minutes during the day and every 30 minutes early in the morning and late at night:
Bingen–Rüdesheim (www.bingen-ruedesheimer.com)
Niederheimbach–Lorch (www.mittel-rhein-faehre.de)
Boppard–Filsen (www.faehre-boppard.de)
Oberwesel–Kaub (www.faehre-kaub.de)
St Goar–St Goarshausen (www.faehre-loreley.de)

Pfalzgrafenstein Toll Station

Across the river from Bacharach and about 8km upriver from Loreley, near the village of Kaub, stands the fairly-tale **Pfalzgrafenstein** (www.burg-pfalzgrafen-stein.de; adult/child €3/2; ⏱10am-6pm Tue-Sun Apr-Oct, 10am-5pm Mar, 10am-5pm Sat & Sun Nov, Jan & Feb, closed Dec), a boat-shaped toll castle perched on a narrow island – perfect for picnics – in the middle of the Rhine. To get out to there, hop on a **Fährboot** (adult/child €2.50/1; ⏱every 30min 10am-6pm Tue-Sun Apr-Oct, 10am-5pm Mar, 10am-5pm Sat & Sun Nov, Jan & Feb, closed Dec) next to the Kaub car ferry dock.

Pfalzgrafenstein
HANS GEORG EIBEN/GETTY IMAGES ©

Bacharach

One of the prettiest of the Rhine villages, tiny Bacharach – 24km downriver from Bingen – conceals its considerable charms behind a 14th-century wall. From the B9, go through one of the thick arched gateways under the train tracks and you'll find yourself in a medieval old town graced with half-timbered mansions such as the **Altes Haus**, the **Posthof** and the off-kilter **Alte Münze** – all are along Oberstrasse, the main street, which runs parallel to the Rhine, and all now house places to eat, drink and be merry.

◉ SIGHTS & ACTIVITIES

The best way to get a sense of the village and its hillside surrounds is to take a stroll on top of the walls – it's possible to walk almost all the way around the centre. The lookout tower on the upper section of the wall affords panoramic views.

The now-ruined Gothic Wernerkapelle was built between 1289 and 1430; the 12th-century **Burg Stahleck** (☎06743-1266; www.jugendherberge.de) is now a hostel.

Peterskirche   Church
This late Romanesque-style Protestant church has some columns with vivid capitals – look for the naked woman with snakes sucking her breasts (a warning about the consequences of adultery), at the altar end of the left aisle. (Blücher-strasse 1; ⏱10am-6pm Mar-Sep, to 4pm Nov-Feb)

🍷 DRINKING & NIGHTLIFE

Zum Grünen Baum   Wine Bar
Dating from 1421, this olde-worlde tavern serves some of Bacharach's best whites; the *Weinkarussel* (€22.50) lets you sample 15 of them. Its nearby **Vinothèque** (Koblenzer Strasse 1; ⏱3-5pm Mon-Fri, 11am-6pm Sat & Sun Apr-Oct, 3-5pm Mon-Fri Nov-Mar), by contrast, is state of the art. Owner Friedrich Bastian is a renowned opera singer, so music (and culinary) events take place year-round, including on Bastian's private river island with its own vineyard. (www.weingut-bastian-bacharach.de; Oberstrasse 63; ⏱noon-midnight Apr-Oct, reduced hours Nov-Mar)

❶ INFORMATION

Tourist Office (☎06743-919 303; www.rhein-nahe-touristik.de; Oberstrasse 10; ⏱9am-5pm Mon-Fri, 10am-3pm Sat & Sun Apr-Oct, 9am-1pm Mon-Fri Nov-Mar) Information about the entire area includes details of day hikes through the vineyards.

Loreley & St Goarshausen

Loreley, the most fabled spot on the Romantic Rhine, is an enormous, almost vertical slab of slate that owes its fame to a mythical maiden whose siren songs are said to have lured sailors to their death in the river's treacherous currents. A sculpture of the blonde, buxom beauty in question perches lasciviously below the outcrop, at the very tip of a narrow breakwater jutting into the Rhine.

◎ SIGHTS & ACTIVITIES

Loreley
Besucherzentrum Museum

On the edge of the plateau above the Loreley outcrop, 4km southeast of St Goarshausen, this visitors centre covers the Loreley myth and local flora, fauna, shipping and winemaking traditions through an English-signed multimedia exhibit and German-language 3D film. A 300m gravel path leads to a viewpoint at the tip of the Loreley outcrop, 190m above the river. From April to October, bus 595 runs from St Goarshausen's Marktplatz. Alternatively, the 400-step Treppenweg begins at the base of the breakwater. (☑06771-599 093; www.loreley-besucherzentrum.de; Loreleyring 7; adult/child €2.50/1.50, parking €2; ☉10am-6pm Apr-Oct, 10am-5pm Mar, 11am-4pm Sat & Sun Nov-Feb)

Burg Maus Castle

Two rival castles stand either side of the village of St Goarshausen. Burg Peterseck was built by the archbishop of Trier to counter the toll practices of the powerful Katzenelnbogen family. The latter responded by building a much bigger castle high on the other side of town, Burg Neukatzenelnbogen (dubbed Burg Katz, meaning 'Cat Castle'). Highlighting the obvious imbalance of power between the Katzenelnbogens and the archbishop, Burg Peterseck was soon nicknamed Burg Maus ('Mouse Castle'). (Burg Peterseck; ☉closed to the public)

> *Loreley, the most fabled spot on the Romantic Rhine... owes its fame to a mythical maiden*

Loreley and St Goarshausen

WESTEND61/GETTY IMAGES ©

EUGEN_Z/GETTY IMAGES ©

From left: The Rhine, near Boppard; Street art in Koblenz; Burg Rheinfels, St Goar

St Goar

A car ferry connects St Goarshausen with its twin across the river, St Goar. It's lorded over by the sprawling ruins of **Burg Rheinfels** (www.st-goar.de; adult/child €5/2.50; ☉9am-6pm mid-Mar–late Oct, 11am-5pm late Oct–mid-Nov), once the mightiest fortress on the Rhine. Built in 1245 by Count Dieter V of Katzenelnbogen as a base for his toll-collecting operations, its size and labyrinthine layout are astonishing. Kids (and adults) will love exploring the subterranean tunnels and galleries (bring a torch). It's a 20-minute uphill walk, or you can take the Burg Express Shuttle from St Goar's Marktplatz, or drive (parking €2).

Boppard

Thanks to its scenic location on a horse-shoe bend in the river – and the fact that the riverfront and historical centre are both on the same side of the train tracks – Boppard (pronounced bo-part) is one of the Romantic Rhine's prettiest and most enjoyable getaways.

◉ SIGHTS & ACTIVITIES

Just off Boppard's main commercial street, the pedestrianised, east–west oriented Oberstrasse, is the ancient Marktplatz, whose modern fountain is a favourite local hang-out.

The peculiar geography of the Vierseen-blick (Four-Lakes-View) panoramic outlook creates the illusion that you're looking at four separate lakes rather than a single river. The nearby Gedeonseck affords views of the Rhine's hairpin curve. To get up here you can either hike or – to save 240 vertical metres – take the 20-minute **Sesselbahn** (chairlift; www.sesselbahn-boppard.de; adult/child return €7.50/4.50, one-way €4.80/3; ☉10am-5pm Apr-Oct) over the vines from the upriver edge of town.

Römer-Kastell   Archaeological Site
A block south of the Marktplatz, the Roman Fort (also known as the Römer-park) has 55m of the original 4th-century Roman wall and graves from the Frankish era (7th century). A wall panel shows what the Roman town of Bodobrica looked like

1700 years ago. (Roman Fort; cnr Angert-strasse & Kirchgasse; ⊘24hr) FREE

EATING

Severus Stube   German €€
Smoked trout roasted in herb butter, pheasant with roast potatoes and bacon, braised beef in horseradish sauce, and warm apple strudel with vanilla custard are among the reasonably priced dishes served up at high-backed wooden booths in Severus Stube's cosy, timber-panelled dining room, and on the cobbled alleyway in summer. Reservations are recommended. (☏06742-3218; www.severus-stube.de; Untere Marktstrasse 7; mains €8.50-18.50; ⊘11.30am-2pm & 5-10pm Fri-Tue, 5-10pm Wed)

ⓘ INFORMATION

Tourist Office (☏06742-3888; www.boppard-tourismus.de; Marktplatz; ⊘9am-6.30pm Mon-Fri, 10am-2pm Sat May-Sep, 9am-5pm Mon-Fri Oct-Apr)

Koblenz

The modern, flowery, park-filled city of Koblenz sits at the confluence of the Rhine and Moselle Rivers. Its roots go all the way back to the Romans, who founded a military stronghold here (calling it Confluentes) because of the site's supreme strategic value.

◉ SIGHTS

Deutsches Eck   Square
At the point of confluence of the Moselle and the Rhine, the 'German Corner' is dominated by a soaring statue of Kaiser Wilhelm I on horseback, in the bombastic style of the late 19th century. After the original was destroyed in WWII, the stone pedestal remained empty – as a testament to lost German unity – until, post-reunification, a copy was re-erected in 1993. Flowery parks stretch southwest, linking up with a grassy riverfront promenade running southward along the Rhine.

Mittelrhein-Museum   Museum

Spread over 1700 sq metres of the striking new glass Forum Confluentes building, Koblenz' Mittelrhein-Museum's displays span 2000 years of the region's history, including artworks, coins, ceramics, porcelain, furniture, miniature art, textiles, militaria and more. Don't miss the collection of 19th-century landscape paintings of the Romantic Rhine by German and British artists. (www.mittelrhein-museum.de; Zentralplatz 1; adult/child €10/7; ⏰10am-6pm Tue-Sun)

Festung Ehrenbreitstein   Fortress

On the right bank of the Rhine, 118m above the river, this mighty fortress proved indestructible to all but Napoleonic troops, who levelled it in 1801. A few years later the Prussians, to prove a point, rebuilt it as one of Europe's mightiest fortifications. Today there are fabulous views from its ramparts and a regional museum and restaurants inside; an audioguide costs €2. It's accessible by car, on foot or by cable car. (www.diefestungehrenbreitstein.de; adult/ child €6/3, incl cable car €11.80/5.60; ⏰10am-6pm Apr-Oct, to 5pm Nov-Mar)

Schloss Stolzenfels   Castle

A vision of crenellated towers, ornate gables and medieval-style fortifications, Schloss Stolzenfels rises above the Rhine's left bank 5km south of the city centre. In 1823, the future Prussian king Friedrich Wilhelm IV had the castle – ruined by the French – rebuilt as his summer residence; guests included Queen Victoria. Today, the rooms remain largely as the king left them, with paintings, weapons, armour and furnishings from the mid-19th century. Take bus 650 from the Hauptbahnhof. (www.schloss-stolzenfels. de; adult/child €4/2.50; ⏰9am-6pm Apr-Sep, to 5pm Oct, Nov & Mar, 10am-5pm Sat & Sun Jan-Feb, closed Dec)

✖ EATING

Cafe Miljöö   Cafe €

Cosy cafe-restaurant 'Milieu' (pronounced like the French) has fresh flowers, changing art exhibits, and a fantastic selection of

Mittelrhein-Museum, Koblenz, designed by Benthem Crouwel Architects

coffees (40 kinds!), teas and homemade cakes. Ten different breakfasts (including Mediterranean, with feta, olives, salami, espresso and a glass of wine; Dutch, with chocolate sprinkles; Swiss, with hot chocolate and sliced apple and honey; 'hangover', with multivitamin juice) are available until 5pm. (www.cafe-miljoeoe.de; Gemüsegasse 8; mains €8-15; ☺kitchen 9am-10pm Apr-Oct, shorter hours Nov-Mar; 🗑🖊🖐)

ℹ INFORMATION

Tourist Office (🖊0261-194 33; www.koblenz-touristik.de; Zentralplatz 1; ☺10am-6pm) In the Forum Confluentes.

ℹ GETTING THERE & AWAY

Koblenz has two train stations, the main Hauptbahnhof on the Rhine's left bank about 1km south of the city centre, and Koblenz-Ehrenbreitstein on the right bank (right below Festung Ehrenbreitstein).

Day Trip to Braubach

Framed by forested hillsides, vineyards and Rhine-side rose gardens, the 1300-year-old town of Braubach, about 8km south of Koblenz on the right bank, is centred on the small, half-timbered Marktplatz. High above are the dramatic towers, turrets and crenellations of the 700-year-old **Marksburg** (www.marksburg.de; adult/child €6/4; ☺10am-5pm mid-Mar–Oct, 11am-4pm Nov–mid-Mar), one of the area's most interesting castles because, unique among the Rhine fortresses, it was never destroyed. Tours (in English at 1pm and 4pm from late March to October) take in the citadel, the Gothic hall and the large kitchen, plus a grisly torture chamber, with its hair-raising assortment of pain-inflicting nasties.

Cochem (p252)

THE MOSELLE VALLEY

The Moselle Valley

Wending between vertiginous vine-covered slopes, the Moselle (in German, Mosel) is narrower than its neighbour, the Rhine, and has a more intimate charm. The German section of the river, which rises in France then traverses Luxembourg, flows for 195km from Trier to Koblenz on a slow, winding course, with entrancing scenery around every hairpin bend: brightly coloured, half-timbered medieval villages, crumbling hilltop castles, elegant Jugendstil (art nouveau) villas, and ancient wine warehouses.

Wonderful walking trails allow you to explore the Moselle's banks and hillsides, where you'll find Europe's (and reputedly the world's) steepest vineyard, the Bremmer Calmont just north of Bremm, with a 65-degree gradient.

☑ In This Section

➡ Arriving in the Moselle Valley

Trier One of the gateways to the Moselle Valley at its southern end. Trier Hauptbahnhof handles many regional and national train services.

Koblenz At the northern end of the Moselle Valley with train connections to major cities in western Germany.

Cologne-Bonn Airport The most convenient airport for the Moselle Valley, though Luxembourg Airport is nearer to Trier and has many more international connections.

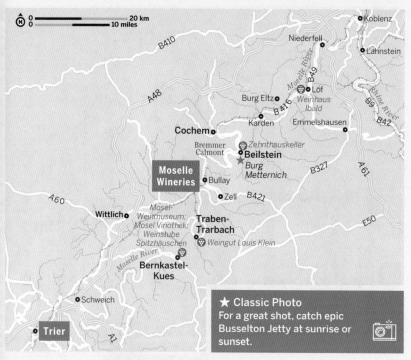

N
0 ———— 20 km
0 ———— 10 miles

B410

Koblenz

Niederfell

Lahnstein

Mosel River

B49

Burg Eltz

Löf

Weinhaus
Ibald

Cochem

Karden

Emmelshausen

B416

B89

Rhine River

B42

Bremmer
Calmont

Zehnthauskeller

Beilstein

*Burg
Metternich*

B327

A61

**Moselle
Wineries**

Bullay

Zell

B421

E50

Wittlich

Mosel-
Weinmuseum;
Mosel Vinothek;
Weinstube
Spitzhäuschen

A60

**Traben-
Trarbach**

Weingut Louis Klein

Moselle River

**Bernkastel-
Kues**

Schweich

Trier

A1

A48

A1

★ **Classic Photo**
For a great shot, catch epic
Busselton Jetty at sunrise or
sunset.

From left: Half-timbered houses, Bernkastel-Kues (p254); Cycling in Cochem (p252); Grevenburg (p253), Traben-Trarbach

WESTEND61/GETTY IMAGES ©; GABY WOJCIECH/GETTY IMAGES ©; GUY HEITMANN/DESIGN PICS/GETTY IMAGES ©

Porta Nigra

RAINPREL/GETTY IMAGES ©

Trier's Roman Monuments

A Unesco-protected site, Germany's oldest city (p256) is home to its finest ensemble of Roman monuments, among them a mighty gate, amphitheatre, thermal baths, Imperial throne room, and the country's oldest bishop's church, which retains Roman sections.

Great For...

☑ **Don't Miss**

The Konstantin Basilika's new organ, has 6500 pipes and generates a seven-fold echo.

Amphitheatre

Trier's Roman **amphitheatre** (Olewiger Strasse; adult/child €3/2; ☉9am-6pm Apr-Sep, to 5pm Mar & Oct, to 4pm Nov-Feb) could accommodate 20,000 spectators for gladiator tournaments and animal fights. Beneath the arena are dungeons where prisoners sentenced to death waited next to starving beasts for the final showdown.

Porta Nigra

This brooding 2nd-century Roman **city gate** (adult/child €3/2; ☉9am-6pm Apr-Sep, to 5pm Mar & Oct, to 4pm Nov-Feb) – blackened by time (hence the name, Latin for 'black gate') – is a marvel of engineering since it's held together by nothing but gravity and iron clamps. In the 11th century, the structure was turned into a church to

Kaiserthermen

ⓘ Need to Know

The three-day TrierCard (€9.90) gives 10% to 25% off museum and monument admissions and unlimited use of public transport.

✕ Take a Break

The Weinwirtschaft Friedrich-Wilhelm (p259) is the best place to refuel.

★ Top Tip

The Antiquities Card (two/four Roman sites and Rheinisches Landesmuseum €10/15) is a great deal.

honour Simeon, a Greek hermit who spent six years walled up in its east tower. After his death in 1134, he was buried inside the gate and later became a saint.

Kaiserthermen

Get a sense of the layout of this vast Roman **thermal bathing complex** (Imperial Baths; Weberbachstrasse 41; adult/child €3/2; ⏰9am-6pm Apr-Sep, to 5pm Mar & Oct, to 4pm Nov-Feb) with its striped brick-and-stone arches from the corner lookout tower, then descend into an underground labyrinth consisting of cavernous hot and cold water baths, boiler rooms and heating channels.

Konstantin Basilika

Constructed around AD 310 as Constantine's throne room, the brick-built **basilica**

(www.konstantin-basilika.de; Konstantinplatz 10; ⏰10am-6pm Mon-Sat, 1-4pm Sun Apr-Oct, 10am-noon & 2-4pm Mon-Sat, 1-4pm Sun Nov-Mar) is now an austere Protestant church. With built-to-impress dimensions, it's the largest remaining single-room Roman structure.

Römerbrücke

Spanning the Moselle, Germany's oldest **bridge** (Roman Bridge; western end of Karl Marx Strasse) uses 2nd-century stone pilings (AD 144–152), built from black basalt from the Eifel mountains, which have been holding it up since legionnaires crossed on chariots.

Thermen am Viehmarkt

Found by accident in 1987 during the construction of a parking garage and buried beneath WWII air-raid shelters, the remains of a 17th-century Capucinian monastery, one-time vineyards and cemeteries, these **thermal baths** (Viehmarktplatz; adult/child €3/2; ⏰9am-5pm Tue-Sun) are sheltered by a dramatic glass cube. The site is closed on Tuesday when Monday is a public holiday.

Vineyard overlooking Bernkastel-Kues (p254)

IAIN MASTERTON/GETTY IMAGES ©

Moselle Wine Experience

Disciples of the grape could do no worse in Germany than make a pilgrimage along the Moselle, sampling arguably the country's best whites as they go. Here we list some of the wine experiences on offer.

Great For...

☑ **Don't Miss**

Try some of the less well-known grape types such as Elbling, Dornfelder and Kerner.

Visiting the Wineries

Exploring the wineries of the Moselle Valley is an ideal way to get to know German culture, interact with locals and, of course, sample some truly exceptional wines.

Keep an eye out for signs reading Weingut, Weinprobe, Wein Probieren, Weinverkauf and Wein zu Verkaufen. In spring pale-purple wisteria flowers, trailing from stone houses, anticipate the bunches of grapes that will ripen in autumn.

From around April to mid-November, numerous wine festivals take place in the towns and villages; for a complete list visit www.mosel-weinfeste.de.

Vineyards beside the Moselle River

INA PETERS/GETTY IMAGES ©

Mosel Vinothek

In the cellar of the **Mosel Vinothek** (www.moselvinothek.de; ☉10am-6pm Apr-Oct, 11am-5pm Nov, Dec, Feb & Mar) in Bernkastel-Kues, you can indulge in an 'all you can drink' wine tasting (€18) with about 150 vintages to choose from. In winter the selection is more limited but costs just €12.

Weingut Louis Klein

Along with whites such as riesling, rivaner and Pinot blanc, **Weingut Louis Klein** (☎06541-6246; www.klein-wein.de; Enkircher Strasse 20, Trarbach; tastings per 6 wines €10; ☉10am-6pm Mon-Sat, 10am-noon Sun) is one of the few Moselle wine producers to specialise in reds, including Pinot Meunier, Pinot noir, Cabernet Dorio, cabernet sauvignon, merlot and Dornfelder. It occupies a monumental stone warehouse on the river; you can also arrange tastings in the vineyard amongst the vines. The winery is located in Traben-Trarbach (p253).

Weinhaus Ibald

Occupying a 1547 half-timbered building, wonderfully local **Weinhaus Ibald** (☎02605-2043; www.weinhaus-ibald.de; Moselstrasse 34, Hatzenport; ☉10am-11pm Easter-Oct, shorter hours Nov-Mar) in Hatzenport specialises in rieslings, sparkling

Must-Sees for Wine Lovers

Mosel-Weinmuseum

Part of the St-Nikolaus-Hospital (p255) complex in Bernkastel-Kues, the small **Moselle Wine Museum** (☎06531-4141; www.moselweinmuseum.de; Cusanusstrasse 2, Kues; adult/child €5/3; ☉10am-6pm Apr-Oct, 11am-5pm Nov, Dec, Feb & Mar) has interactive screens (best appreciated by German speakers) and features such as an Aromabar (you have to guess what you're smelling). The main event, though, is the cellar of the adjacent Vinothek.

Spätlese, Dornfelder reds, and Fruchsaft (fruit wine); the ultimate spot for a glass is on the vine-shaded terrace. Food ranges from homemade onion soup to sausage platters and gorgeous cakes including rhubarb topped with meringue.

You can also stay in its simple but comfortable rooms (doubles from €60).

Weinstube Spitzhäuschen

Wine bars don't come cuter than **Weinstube Spitzhäuschen** (☎ 06531-7476; www.spitzhaeuschen.de; Karlstrasse 13, Bernkastel; ☺ from 4pm Mon-Fri, from 3pm Sat & Sun Easter-Oct, from 3pm Sat Nov-Dec, other times by appointment) in its crooked half-timbered building (the Moselle's oldest, dating from 1416), which resembles a giant bird's house: its narrow base is topped by a much larger, precariously leaning upper floor which allowed carriages to pass through the narrow alley to the marketplace. Taste over 50 of the Schmitz family's local wines; small snacks are also available. It is located in Bernkastel-Kues (p254).

Zehnthauskeller

Starting in 1574, the **Zehnthauskeller** (www.zehnthauskeller.de; Marktplatz; ☺11am-10pm Tue-Sat, noon-10pm Sun) in Beilstein was used to store wine delivered as a tithe; it now houses a romantically dark, vaulted wine cellar where you can try six wines for €8.90, served by dirndl-wearing staff. Live music plays on summer evenings.

Moselle vineyards in autumn

Beilstein, a pint-sized village straight out of a storybook, is located on the right bank of the Moselle about 50km upriver from Koblenz. Centred on the Marktplatz, its cluster of half-timbered houses are surrounded by steep vineyards.

Moselle Transport

Driving is the easiest way to see the Moselle, which, unlike the Romantic Rhine, is spanned by plenty of bridges.

★ Top Tip

The hugely popular 275km-long cycling trail, Mosel Radweg (www.mosel-radweg), heads from Trier down the Moselle all the way to Koblenz and upriver along the Luxembourg border and into the French region of Lorraine.

Currently under construction, the Hochmoselbrücke (High Moselle Bridge) will link Ürzig and Zeltingen-Rachtig, with a carriageway stretching 158m above the river. It's part of a new highway connection, the Hochmoselübergang (B50), providing a fast link to the Frankfurt area and beyond. Environmental concerns have seen it beset by delays, but it's expected to open in 2018. Check its progress via webcam at www.b50hochmoselbruecke.de.

The valley is also well served by public transport:

◉ The rail line linking Koblenz with Trier (€22.70, 1½ to two hours, at least hourly) follows the Moselle (and stops at its villages) only as far upriver as Bullay. (Koblenz to Bullay €15.60, 45 minutes, hourly; Trier to Bullay €12.10, 45 minutes, two per hour.)

◉ From Bullay, small shuttle trains run along a spur line that terminates in Traben-Trarbach (€3.90, 20 minutes, up to four per hour).

◉ The villages between Traben-Trarbach and Trier, including Bernkastel-Kues, are served year-round by bus 333 (www.moselbahn.de, day ticket €5.80, six daily Monday to Friday, three daily Saturday and Sunday).

◉ Kolb (www.moselrundfahrten.de) is the Moselle's main boat operator, offering sightseeing cruises as well as one-way transport. Most services run from April to October.

ROMRODINKA/GETTY IMAGES ©

☑ Don't Miss

If you are tackling the Moselle Valley on foot, be sure to stop off at Ediger-Eller, Bremm, Zell, Kröv, Ürzig and Zeltingen-Rachtig, all of which are worth an hour's break from the trail. Some of these have tiny wine cellars where some of the best-kept wine secrets of the Moselle are hidden by small-scale vintners.

Cochem

Inundated with visitors most of the year, Cochem is the Moselle at its most touristy, with a bank of pastel-coloured, terrace-fronted restaurants lining the waterfront. Its tangle of narrow alleyways and dramatic castle precipitously perched on a rock, however, are well worth a stop.

◉ SIGHTS

Reichsburg   Castle

Like many others in the area, Cochem's original 11th-century castle fell victim to French troops in 1689, then stood ruined for centuries until wealthy Berliner Louis Ravene snapped it up for a pittance in 1868 and had it restored to its current – if not always architecturally faithful – glory. The 40-minute tours (in German but English leaflet/audioguide available) take in the decorative rooms that reflect 1000 years' worth of tastes and styles.

Its restaurant hosts four-hour banquets (€49) on Friday and Saturday evenings in summer, attended by costumed staff, with wine served in a clay tumbler that you get to keep and culminating in a knighting ceremony. (📞02671-255; www.burg-cochem. de; Schlossstrasse 36; tours adult/child €6/3; ⏲tours 9am-5pm mid-Mar–Oct, 10am-3pm Nov & Dec, 11am, noon & 1pm Wed, Sat & Sun Jan–mid-Mar)

✴ EATING

Alt Thorschenke   German €€

Wedged into the old medieval walls, away from the busy riverfront restaurants, Alt Thorschenke is a diamond find for regional specialities, such as herring with apple and onions, pork neck with mustard-cream sauce, and several different types of schnitzel, washed down with wines from local producers. Upstairs are 27 small but charming rooms (doubles from €99), some with four-poster beds. (📞02671-7059; www. thorschenke.de; Brückenstrasse 3; mains €10.50-19; ⏲kitchen 11am-10pm Apr-Oct, reduced hours Nov-Mar)

Reichsburg, Cochem

ℹ️ INFORMATION

Tourist Office (📞02671-600 40; www.cochem.
de; Endertplatz 1; 🕘9am-5pm Mon-Sat, 10am-
3pm Sun May-Oct, 9am-5pm Mon-Fri Apr, 9am-
1pm & 2-5pm Mon-Fri Nov-Mar)

Traben-Trarbach

Elegant Traben-Trarbach makes an excellent base for exploring the valley by bike
or car. A major centre of the wine trade a
century ago, the town's winemakers still
welcome visitors for tastings and sales.

Traben, on the Moselle's left bank, lost its
medieval appearance to three major fires
but was well compensated with beautiful
Jugendstil villas, many of them designed
by Berlin architect Bruno Möhring, whose
works also include the ornate 1898 bridge
gate, the medieval-style Brückentor, across
the river in Trarbach. The two towns united
in 1904.

◎ SIGHTS

Buddha Museum   Museum
A magnificent 1906 *Jugendstil* former
winery designed by architect Bruno
Möhring is the unlikely home of the
Buddha Museum, which has a beautifully
presented collection of over 2000 wood,
bronze and paper statues of the Buddha
from all over Asia. Upstairs the peaceful
rooftop garden has Moselle views. (www.
buddha-museum.de; Bruno-Möhring-Platz 1,
Trarbach; adult/child €15/7.50; 🕘10am-6pm
Tue-Sun)

Grevenburg   Ruin
The Grevenburg castle, built in the mid-
14th century, sits high in the craggy hills
above Trarbach, with incredible valley
views. Because of its strategic importance,
it changed hands 13 times, was besieged
six times and was destroyed seven times –
no wonder that two walls are all that remain. It's reached via a steep 500m-long
footpath, the Sponheimer Weg, that

🚲 Boat & Bike Combo

From May to October, boats run by **Kolb**
(📞02673-1515; www.moselrundfahrten.de)
link Bernkastel with Traben-Trarbach
(one-way/return €13/19, two hours, five
daily). You can take along a bicycle for
€2, making it easy to sail one way and
ride the 24km back.

In Traben-Trarbach, **Zweirad Wagner**
(📞06541-1649; www.zweirad-wagner.de;
Brückenstrasse 42, Trarbach; per day €8.50;
🕘9am-12.30pm & 2-6pm Mon-Fri, 9am-1pm
Sat) rents bikes; in Bernkastel-Kues
try **Fun Bike Team** (📞06531-940 24;
www.funbiketeam.de; Schanzstrasse 22,
Bernkastel; 7-speed/tandem per day €11/19;
🕘9am-6.30pm Mon-Fri & 9am-2pm Sat Mar-
Oct, 9am-1pm & 2-6.30pm Mon, Tue, Wed &
Fri, 1-6.30pm Thu, 9am-2pm Sat Nov-Mar).
Bernkastel-Kues (p254)

HANS GEORG EIBEN/GETTY IMAGES ©

begins a block north of the bridge (there's
no access by car). Its cafe serves wine,
beer and *Flammkuchen* (regional pizza).
(Trarbach)

Mont Royal   Ruin
Above Traben are the remains of the vast
Mont Royal fortress, constructed between
1687 and 1698 and designed by Vauban for
Louis XIV as a base from which to project
French power. Ruinously expensive, it
was dismantled before completion by the
French themselves under the Treaty of
Ryswick. The 1.5km-long footpath up to the
site begins at the upper end of Römer-
strasse. (Traben)

 ### Divine Brews

The Moselle might be better known for its wine but a former Cistercian monastery, founded in the 13th century, now houses an extraordinary brewery. **Kloster Machern** (www.klostermachern. de; An der Zeltinger Brücke, Zeltingen-Rachtig; ⊗bar 11am-2am Easter-Oct, reduced hours Nov-Easter) also has a bar made from a copper vat and strung with dry hops, a wicker-chair-filled terrace, and excellent local cuisine. Brews, including a Dunkel (dark), Hell (light) and Hefe-Weizen (wheat beer), are also sold at its **shop** (⊗noon to 5pm). Also here is a **museum** (⊗10am-6pm Easter-Oct, reduced hours Nov-Easter; adult/child €3/1.50) exhibiting religious iconography, plus puppets, toys and model railways. It's 7km north-west of Bernkastel-Kues.

Kloster Machern
ZOONAR GMBH/ALAMY STOCK PHOTO ©

✪ ACTIVITIES

From Traben-Trarbach, Bernkastel-Kues is 24km upriver by car but, because of the Moselle's hairpin curve, just 6.5km over the hill on foot. The walk up through the forest from Traben-Trarbach and down through the vineyards to Bernkastel-Kues is wonderfully scenic but poorly signposted, so be sure to pick up a map from the tourist office.

Wine tastings and cellar tours are available in Traben-Trarbach; contact the tourist office to find out what's on while you're in town. Weingut Louis Klein (p249) is worth a try.

✪ EATING

Alte Zunftscheune   German €€
Dine on delicious Moselle-style dishes like homemade black pudding and liver sausage, pork medallions with riesling cream sauce, or grilled rump steak with asparagus and fried potatoes in a series of wonderfully atmospheric rooms choc-full of rustic bric-a-brac, with beautiful timber staircases. Its cellar still has its original 1890s lighting. Reservations are recommended. Cash only. (☎06541-9737; www.zunftscheune.de; Neue Rathausstrasse 15, Traben; mains €11.50-20; ⊗kitchen 5-11pm Tue-Fri, 11.30am-3pm & 5-11pm Sat & Sun Easter-Oct, reduced hours Nov-Easter; ⏍)

ℹ INFORMATION

Tourist Office (☎06541-839 80; www.traben-trarbach.de; Am Bahnhof 5, Traben; ⊗10am-5pm Mon-Fri, 11am-3pm Sat May-Aug, 10am-6pm Mon-Fri, 11am-3pm Sat Sep & Oct, 10am-4pm Mon-Fri Nov-Apr; 🛜)

Bernkastel-Kues

These charming twin towns are the hub of the *Mittelmosel* ('Middle Moselle', ie Central Moselle) region. Bernkastel, on the right (eastern) bank, is a symphony in half-timber, stone and slate and teems with wine taverns. Kues, the birthplace of theologian Nicolaus Cusanus (1401–64), is less quaint but is home to some key historical sights.

◎ SIGHTS

The Kues shore has a lovely riverfront promenade.

Marktplatz   Square
Bernkastel's pretty Marktplatz, a block inland from the bridge, is enclosed by a romantic ensemble of half-timbered houses with beautifully decorated gables. Look for the medieval iron handcuffs, to which criminals were attached, on the facade of the old Rathaus. (Bernkastel)

Pfarrkirche St Michael Church

Facing the bridge, this partly 14th-century-Gothic church has an ornate interior and some colourful stained glass. The tower was originally part of the town's fortifications. (Bernkastel; ⏰9am-6pm)

Burg Landshut Ruin

A rewarding way to get your heart pumping is hoofing it from the Marktplatz up to Burg Landshut, a ruined 13th-century castle – framed by vineyards and forests – on a bluff above town. It's a very steep 750m from town; allow 30 minutes. You'll be rewarded with glorious river valley views and a refreshing drink in the beer garden. An hourly shuttle bus from the riverfront costs €5 uphill, €3.50 downhill or €7 return. (Bernkastel; ⏰beer garden 10am-6pm Fri-Wed Easter-Nov)

St-Nikolaus-Hospital Historic Building

Most of Kues' sights, including the Mosel Vinothek (p249), are conveniently grouped near the bridge in the late-Gothic St-Nikolaus-Hospital, an old-age home founded by Cusanus in 1458 for 33 men (one for every year of Jesus' life). You're free to explore the cloister and Gothic *Kapelle* (chapel) at leisure, but the treasure-filled library can only be seen on a guided tour. (www.cusanus.de; Cusanusstrasse 2, Kues; guided tours €5; ⏰9am-6pm Sun-Fri, 9am-3pm Sat, guided tours 10.30am Tue & 3pm Fri Apr-Oct) FREE

🔄 TOURS

The tourist office rents out audioguides (per three hours/day €6/8).

For a gentle bike ride, the Mosel-Maare-Radweg (www.maare-moselradweg.de), linking Bernkastel-Kues with Daun (in the Eifel Mountains), follows an old train line so the gradients are reasonable. From April to October, you can take RegioRadler bus 300 up (adult/bicycle transport €12.35/3, 1½ hours, every two hours) and ride the 57km back down to Bernkastel-Kues. Fun Bike Team (p253) rents bikes.

Bernkastel-Kues

Trierer Dom, Trier

> *Germany's oldest bishop's church still retains Roman sections*

🍴 EATING

Rotisserie Royale   Modern European €€
Seriously good cooking in this half-timbered house spans starters such as salmon carpaccio with lime and olive marinade, followed by mains such as pike perch with potato soufflé and riesling foam, or braised rabbit with snow peas, and decadent desserts like chocolate mousse on eggnog foam with walnut sorbet. (📞06531-6572; www.rotisserie-royale.de; Burgstrasse 19, Bernkastel; mains €13.50-19.50; ⏰noon-2pm & 5-9pm Thu-Tue)

🍷 DRINKING & NIGHTLIFE

Weinstube Spitzhäuschen (p250) is a cute wine bar. For a change from wine, don't miss the monastery-housed Kloster Machern (p254).

ℹ️ INFORMATION

Tourist Office (📞06531-500 190; www.bernkastel.de; Gestade 6, Bernkastel; ⏰9am-5pm Mon-Fri, 10am-5pm Sat, 10am-1pm Sun May-Oct, 9.30am-4pm Mon-Fri Nov-Apr) Reserves hotel rooms, sells hiking and cycling maps and has an ATM.

Trier

A Unesco World Heritage Site since 1986, Germany's oldest city is home to its finest ensemble of Roman monuments, among them a mighty gate, amphitheatre, elaborate thermal baths, Imperial throne room, and the country's oldest bishop's church, which retains Roman sections. Architectural treasures from later ages include Germany's oldest Gothic church, and Karl Marx' baroque birthplace.

Trier's mostly pedestrianised city centre is filled with cafes and restaurants, many inside gorgeous Gothic or baroque buildings. Wineries scatter throughout the surrounding vineyards.

The city's proximity to both Luxembourg and France is apparent in its cuisine and the local *esprit,* enlivened by some 15,000 students from its renowned university.

 SIGHTS

For Trier's Roman monuments, see p246.

Hauptmarkt Square
Anchored by a 1595 fountain dedicated to St Peter and the Four Virtues, Trier's central market square is surrounded by medieval and Renaissance architectural treasures such as the **Rotes Haus** (Red House), and the Steipe, which now houses a cafe and the **Spielzeugmuseum** (Toy Museum; www.spielzeugmuseum-trier.de; Dietrichstrasse 50/51; adult/child €4.50/2.50; ⊙11am-5pm Tue-Sun), as well as the Gothic **St-Gangolf-Kirche** (⊙7am-6.30pm). Small market stalls (flowers, sausages etc) set up most days, except Sunday.

Trierer Dom Cathedral
Looming above the Roman palace of Helena (Emperor Constantine's mother), Germany's oldest bishop's church still retains Roman sections. Today's edifice is a study in nearly 1700 years of church architecture with Romanesque, Gothic and baroque elements. Intriguingly, its floorplan is of a 12-petalled flower, symbolising the Virgin Mary.

To see some dazzling ecclesiastical equipment and peer into early Christian history, head upstairs to the **Domschatz** (Cathedral Treasury; adult/child €1.50/0.50; ⊙10am-5pm Mon-Sat, 12.30-5pm Sun Mar-Oct & Dec, 11am-4pm Tue-Sat, 12.30-4pm Sun & Mon Nov & Jan-Mar). The **Bischöfliches Dom-und Diözesanmuseum** (☎0651-710 5255; www.bistum-trier.de/museum; Windstrasse 6-8; adult/child €3.50/2; ⊙9am-5pm Tue-Sat, 1-5pm Sun) is also just around the corner. (☎0651-979 0790; www.dominformation.de; Liebfrauenstrasse 12, cnr of Domfreihof; ⊙6.30am-6pm Apr-Oct, to 5.30pm Nov-Mar) FREE

 Detour to Beilstein

Picture-perfect Beilstein (www.beilstein-mosel.de) is located about 50km upriver from Koblenz.

Above the village looms **Burg Metternich** (admission €2.50; ⊙9am-6pm Apr-Nov), a ruined hilltop castle reached via a staircase. Built in 1129, it was destroyed by French troops in the Nine Years' War (1688–97) in 1689. Today you can visit the ruins and have a glass of local wine at the courtyard cafe.

Beilstein is also home to the Zehnthauskeller (p250), an interesting place for wine tasting. The area has plenty of hiking trails.

Liebfrauenbasilika Church
Germany's oldest Gothic church was built in the 13th century. It has a cruciform structure supported by a dozen pillars symbolising the 12 apostles (look for the black stone from where all 12 articles of the Apostle's Creed painted on the columns are visible) and some colourful postwar stained glass. (Church of Our Lady; www.trierer-dom.de; Liebfrauenstrasse; ⊙10am-7pm Mon-Fri, 11am-4.30pm Sat, 12.30-6pm Sun Apr-Oct, 10am-5pm Mon-Fri, 11am-4.30pm Sat, 12.30-5pm Sun Nov-Mar)

Rheinisches Landesmuseum Museum
A scale model of 4th-century Trier and rooms filled with tombstones, mosaics, rare gold coins (including the 1993-discovered Trier Gold Hoard, the largest preserved Roman gold hoard in the world, with over 2600 gold coins) and some fantastic glass are highlights of this museum, which affords an extraordinary look at local Roman life. Admission includes an audioguide. (Roman Archaeological Museum; www.landesmuseum-trier.de; Weimarer Allee 1; adult/child €6/3; ⊙10am-5pm Tue-Sun)

€4/2.50; ◷10am-6pm daily Apr-Oct, 2-5pm Mon, 11am-5pm Tue-Sun Nov-Mar)

🗘 ACTIVITIES

Weinkulturpfad   Hiking
Panoramic views unfold from Petrisberg, the vine-covered hill just east of the amphitheatre. Halfway up, the Weinkulturpfad (Wine Culture Path) leads through the grapes to Olewig (1.6km). Next to the Petrisberg/Aussicht stop for buses 4 and 85 on Sickingenstrasse, a multilingual panel traces local history from the first known human habitation (30,000 years ago) through the last ice age to the Romans.

🗘 TOURS

City Walking Tour   Walking Tour
Guided 75-minute walking tours in English begin at the tourist office. (adult/child €6.50/3; ◷1pm May-Oct)

Kolb   Boat Tour
Cruise along the Moselle for 45 minutes across the border into Luxembourg (one-way/return €9/13), or choose from a range of river tours within Germany such as a 4¼-hour trip to Bernkastel (one-way/return €24/30). (📞0651-263 37; www.moselrund-fahrten.de; Georg-Schmitt-Platz 2; ◷Apr-Oct)

🗘 EATING

In the warmer months, cafes fill the Altstad's public squares, including the Hauptmarkt and Kornmarkt.

Traditional *Weinstuben* (wine taverns) scatter throughout the Olewig district, 3km southeast of the centre.

Kartoffel Kiste   German €
Fronted by a bronze fountain, local favourite Kartoffel Kiste specialises, as its name suggests, in baked, breaded, gratinéed, soupified and sauce-doused potatoes. If you're after something heartier (albeit pricier), it also does great schnitzel and steaks. (www.kiste-trier.de; Fahrstrasse 13-14; mains €6-17; ◷kitchen 11.30am-10pm; 🖋️🏠)

---

r⇗ꟼ **Fairy-Tale Burg Eltz**

Victor Hugo thought this fairy-tale castle, hidden away in the forest above the left bank of the Moselle, was 'tall, terrific, strange and dark'. Indeed, 850-year-old fairy-tale **Burg Eltz** (www.burg-eltz.de; Burg-Eltz-Strasse 1, Wierschem; tours adult/child €9/6.50; ◷9.30am-5.30pm Apr-Oct), owned by the same family for more than 30 generations, has a forbidding exterior somewhat softened by the turrets that crown it like candles on a birthday cake. The treasury features a rich collection of jewellery, porcelain and weapons.

By car, you can reach Burg Eltz – which has never been destroyed – via the village of Münstermaifeld. From the Eltz car park it's a shuttle-bus ride (€2) or 1.3km walk to the castle. From Koblenz, boats and trains also go to Moselkernvillage, from where it's a lovely 5km walk to the castle.

Burg Eltz
EDUCATION IMAGES/UIG/GETTY IMAGES ©

Karl Marx Haus   Historic Site
The early 18th-century baroque town house in which the author of *The Communist Manifesto* and *Das Kapital* was born in 1818 now houses exhibits that cover Marx' life, work, allies and enemies; social democracy; his decades of exile in London, where he died in 1883; and his intellectual and political legacy. Admission includes an audioguide that opens with the stirring cadences of *L'Internationale*. (www.fes.de/Karl-Marx-Haus; Brückenstrasse 10; adult/child

Traben-Trarbach (p253)

Food Market   Market €

The city centre's largest outdoor market is a perfect place to pick up fresh local produce for a riverside picnic. (Viehmarktplatz; ☺7am-2pm Tue & Fri Apr-Sep, from 8am Tue & Fri Oct-Mar)

Weinwirtschaft
Friedrich-Wilhelm Modern German €€

A historical former wine warehouse with exposed brick and hoists now houses this superb restaurant. Creative dishes incorporate local wines, such as trout poached in sparkling white wine with mustard sauce and white asparagus; local sausage with riesling sauerkraut and fried potatoes. Vines trail over the trellis-covered garden; the attached wine shop is a great place to stock up. (☎0651-9947 4800; www.weinwirtschaft-fw.de; Weberbach 75; mains €11-26; ☺kitchen noon-2pm & 6-10pm Mon-Sat, wine shop 9am-6pm Mon-Sat)

⭐ ENTERTAINMENT

The tourist office has details on concerts and other cultural activities and sells tickets.

TuFa   Performing Arts

This vibrant cultural events venue, housed in a former *Tuchfabrik* (towel factory), hosts cabaret, live music of all sorts, theatre and dance performances. (☎0651-718 2410; www.tufa-trier.de; Wechselstrasse 4-6)

ℹ️ INFORMATION

Tourist Office (☎0651-978 080; www.trier-info.de; ☺9am-6pm Mon-Sat, 10am-5pm Sun May-Oct, shorter hours Nov-Apr)

ℹ️ GETTING AROUND

The city centre is easily explored on foot. A bus ride (see www.swt.de) costs €2; a public transport day pass costs €5.80. The Olewig wine district is served by buses 7 and 84.

Bikes in tip-top condition can be rented at the Hauptbahnhof's **Radstation** (Fahrradservicestation; ☎148 856; adult/child/electric bike per day from €12/6/30; ☺9am-6pm mid-Apr–Oct, 10am-6pm Mon-Fri Nov–mid-Apr), next to track 11, and from the tourist office. Staff are enthusiastic about cycling and can provide tips on routes.

Olympiapark (p116), Munich

In Focus

Street art, Berlin (p35)

RADIOKAFKA/SHUTTERSTOCK ©

Germany Today

Europe's most populous nation, Germany is also its biggest economic power and has consequently taken on a more active role in global politics. A founding member of the European Union (EU), it is solidly committed to preserving the alliance and making sure it is poised to deal with the political and social challenges of this increasingly complex world.

Europe's Economic Engine

Germany weathered the recent global fiscal crisis better than most industrial nations, in large part because it now bears the fruits of decade-old key reforms, especially the liberalisation of its labour laws. It is the fourth-largest economy in the world (after the US, Japan and China) and the largest in the EU. With its solid manufacturing base and an economic backbone of small and medium-sized businesses, it has drawn worldwide admiration, as well as criticism, for its relentless reliance on exports (one in four euros is earned from exports) and for using the euro to serve its own interests.

The European Commission reported 0.7% growth in the German economy for the fourth quarter of 2014, while the Eurozone as a whole grew a mere 0.3%. GDP is expected to grow by 1.75% in 2015. Manufacturing orders and exports, especially to hungry markets in

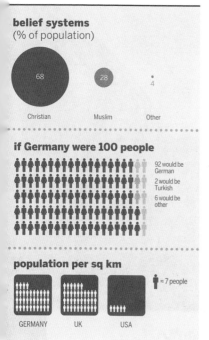

belief systems
(% of population)

68

28

4

Christian   Muslim   Other

if Germany were 100 people

92 would be German

2 would be Turkish

6 would be other

population per sq km

≈ 7 people

GERMANY   UK   USA

South America, Asia and Eastern Europe, are up, helped along by a weak euro. At the same time, the unemployment rate has dropped to around 6% (among the lowest in the EU), the property market is sizzling and consumer confidence is high.

Political Leadership

Aware of the burden of their country's 20th-century history, modern German leaders have traditionally avoided taking on a major political or military role in Europe. However, changing circumstances that pose a threat to European stability have led to a more assertive German foreign policy in recent years. Long accused of being reluctant to make tough decisions, Chancellor Angela Merkel has emerged as Europe's chief diplomat, demonstrating a commitment to a coherent European foreign policy and a willingness to take on a leadership role.

Together with French president François Hollande she has worked hard towards a peaceful resolution to the Russia–Ukraine conflict, which began in February 2014 with Russia's annexation of the Crimean Peninsula. Germany again took a leadership role in the Greek financial crisis, which began around 2010, when it became clear that Greece had taken on a much higher debt than previously disclosed and thus, at least in part, kicked off the euro crisis.

Land of Immigration

Some 15 million people living in Germany have an immigrant background (foreign-born or at least one immigrant parent), accounting for about 18% of the total population. The largest group are people of Turkish descent, a legacy of the post-WWII economic boom, when 'guest workers' were recruited to shore up the war-depleted workforce. Many stayed. Immediately after reunification, Germany welcomed large numbers of repatriates from the former USSR and refugees from war-ravaged Yugoslavia. In recent years, factors such as the economic stability and a high standard of living in Germany have attracted migrants from new EU member nations Romania and Bulgaria, as well as people from economically weaker countries like Spain, Greece and Italy.

Along with other European nations, Germany is also accommodating an enormous influx of refugees, especially from war-torn Syria, Libya and Afghanistan, as well as from non-EU countries such as Kosovo and Albania. Among certain population groups, the arrival of these new migrants and the perceived drain they put on Germany's economy and society has given rise to new nationalist and anti-immigrant movements despite the fact that an aging population and the world's lowest birthrate currently account for the fastest population decline among developed nations.

Kölner Dom (p218) and Hohenzollernbrücke, Cologne

History

Events in Germany have often dominated the European stage, but the country itself is a relatively recent invention: for most of its history Germany has been a patchwork of semi-independent principalities and city-states, ruled first by the Roman Empire, then the Holy Roman Empire and finally the Austrian Habsburgs. Perhaps because of this, many Germans retain a strong regional identity despite the momentous national events that have occurred since.

800–300 BC

Germanic tribes and Celts inhabit large parts of northern and central Germany.

AD 9

The Battle of the Teutoburg Forest halts Roman expansion eastwards.

482

Clovis becomes king of the Franks and lays the foundations for a Frankish Reich.

Tribes & the Romans

Early inhabitants on German soil were Celts and, later, the Germanic tribes. The tribes east of the Rhine and the Romans struggled for control of territory across the river until AD 9, when Roman general Varus lost three legions – about 20,000 men – in the bloody Battle of the Teutoburg Forest, putting paid to Roman plans to extend their rule eastwards. By AD 300, four main groups of tribes had formed: Alemanni, Franks, Saxons and Goths.

Frankish Reich

On the Rhine's western bank, the Frankish Reich became a key political power in early medieval Europe. Merovingian king Clovis laid the groundwork in the 5th century but it would be another three centuries before Charlemagne, the Reich's most important ruler, rose to power in 768. From his residence in Aachen, Charlemagne conquered Lombardy,

768–814	962	1241
The Carolingian Charlemagne is crowned Kaiser and under him the Frankish Reich grows in power and extent.	Otto I is crowned Holy Roman Emperor by the pope, reaffirming the precedent established by Charlemagne.	Hamburg and Lübeck create the basis for the powerful Hanseatic League.

Hanseatic League

The origins of the Hanseatic League go back to various guilds and associations established from about the mid-12th century by out-of-town merchants to protect their interests. After Hamburg and Lübeck signed an agreement in 1241 to protect their ships and trading routes, they were joined in their league by Lüneburg, Kiel and a string of Baltic Sea cities east to Greifswald.

By 1356 this had grown into the Hanseatic League, encompassing half a dozen other large alliances of cities, with Lübeck playing the lead role. At its zenith, the league had about 200 member cities. By the 15th century however, competition from Dutch and English shipping companies, internal disputes and a shift in the centre of world trade from the North and Baltic Seas to the Atlantic had caused decline.

won territory in Bavaria, waged a 30-year war against the Saxons in the north and was eventually crowned Kaiser (emperor) by the pope in 800.

The cards were reshuffled in the 9th century when attacks by Danes, Saracens and Magyars threw the eastern portion of Charlemagne's empire into turmoil and four dominant duchies emerged – Bavaria, Franconia, Swabia and Saxony. The Treaty of Verdun (843) saw a gradual carve-up of the Frankish Reich and when Louis the Child (r 900–11) – a grandson of Charlemagne's brother – died heirless, the East Frankish (ie German) dukes elected a king from their own ranks, thereby creating the first German monarch.

Early Middle Ages

Strong regionalism in Germany today has its roots in the early Middle Ages, when dynasties squabbled and intrigued over territorial spoils. The symbolic heart of power was the cathedral in Aachen, which hosted the coronations and burials of 31 German kings from 936 until 1531. The first to be crowned was Otto I who, in 962, renewed Charlemagne's pledge to protect the papacy and was rewarded by the pope with the imperial crown the same year.

This created the Holy Roman Empire and made the Kaiser and pope acrimonious bedfellows for the next 800 years until Kaiser Franz II abdicated the throne in 1806. Through the centuries, the empire variously encompassed present-day Netherlands, Belgium, Switzerland, Lorraine and Burgundy (in France), Sicily, Austria and an eastern swath of land that lies in the Czech Republic, Poland and Hungary.

In the 14th century, the basic structure of the Holy Roman Empire became more solidified. A key document was the Golden Bull of 1356 (so named for its golden seal), a decree issued by Emperor Charles IV that was essentially an early form of an imperial constitution. Most importantly, it set out precise rules for elections by specifying the seven Kurfürsten (prince-electors) entitled to choose the next king to be crowned Holy Roman Emperor by the pope. The privilege fell to the rulers of Bohemia, Brandenburg, Saxony and the Palatinate as well as to the archbishops of Trier, Mainz and Cologne.

1273	**1455**	**1517**
The House of Habsburg begins its rise to become Europe's most powerful dynasty.	Johannes Gutenberg of Mainz prints the Gutenberg Bible using a moveable type system, revolutionising book printing.	Martin Luther makes public his *Ninety-Five Theses* in the town of Wittenberg.

As the importance of the minor nobility declined, the economic power of the towns increased, especially after many joined forces in a strategic trading alliance called the Hanseatic League. The most powerful towns, such as Cologne, Hamburg, Nuremberg and Frankfurt, were granted Free Imperial City status, which made them beholden directly to the emperor.

Ordinary Germans, however, battled with panic lynching, pogroms against Jews and labour shortages – all sparked off by the plague (1348–50) that wiped out 25% of Europe's population. While death gripped the (Ger)man on the street, universities were being established all over the country around this time.

Reformation & the 30 Years' War

In 1517, German monk and theology professor Martin Luther (1483–1546) made public his *Ninety-Five Theses* critiquing not only the practice of selling indulgences to exonerate sins but also questioning papal infallibility, clerical celibacy and other elements of Catholic doctrine. This was the spark plug of the Reformation. Threatened with excommunication, Luther refused to recant, broke from the Catholic Church and was banned from the Reich.

It was not until 1555 that the Catholic and Lutheran churches were ranked as equals, thanks to Emperor Karl V (r 1520–58), who signed the Peace of Augsburg, allowing princes to decide the religion of their principality. The more secular northern principalities adopted Lutheran teachings, while the clerical lords in the south, southwest and Austria stuck with Catholicism.

But the religious issue refused to die. It degenerated into the bloody Thirty Years' War (1618–48) that left Europe drenched with the blood of millions. Calm was restored with the Peace of Westphalia (1648), signed in Münster and Osnabrück, but it left the Reich a nominal, impotent state. Switzerland and the Netherlands gained formal independence, France won chunks of Alsace and Lorraine, and Sweden helped itself to the mouths of the Elbe, Oder and Weser Rivers.

Age of Enlightenment

In the 18th century an intellectual movement called the Enlightenment swept through much of Europe. Leading thinkers like the philosophers Johann Gottfried von Herder, Immanuel Kant and Voltaire embraced humanist ideals and sought to understand and explain reality through reason and science rather than religion and faith. This went hand in hand with a flourishing of the arts and culture: rulers built stunning palaces and gardens; Goethe and Schiller penned their famous works; and Bach, Haydn, Händel and Mozart composed their immortal music.

One king who embraced the Enlightenment was Friedrich II (r 1740–86) – aka Frederick the Great – of Brandenburg-Prussia. When not waxing philosophical with his friend Voltaire, Frederick was busy on the battlefield, fighting tooth and nail for two decades to

1555	1618–48	1806
The Peace of Augsburg allows German rulers to decide their fiefdom's religion.	The Thirty Years' War sweeps through Germany and leaves it with a depleted population.	The Holy Roman Empire collapses and Napoleon creates the Confederation of the Rhine.

Topographie des Terrors, Berlin

★ **Third Reich Sites**

Dachau concentration camp (p118), near Munich

Nuremberg Trials courtroom (p196), Nuremberg

Topographie des Terrors (p69), Berlin

wrest Silesia (in today's Poland) from Austria and Saxony and thus for the first time positioning the Brandenburg-Prussian kingdom as a force to be reckoned with.

Napoleon & Revolutions

In the aftermath of the 1789 French Revolution, a diminutive Frenchman named Napoleon Bonaparte (Napoleon I) took control of Europe and significantly altered its fate through a series of wars. The defeat of Austrian and Russian troops in the Battle of Austerlitz in 1806 led to the collapse of the Holy Roman Empire. That same year, most German kingdoms, duchies and principalities aligned themselves with Napoleon in the Confederation of the Rhine. It was to be a short-lived alliance though, for many of its members switched allegiance again after Napoleon got trounced by Prussian, Russian, Austrian and Swedish troops in the bloody 1813 Battle of Leipzig.

In 1815, at the Congress of Vienna, Germany was reorganised into the *Deutscher Bund* (German Alliance), a confederation of 39 states with a central legislative assembly, the Reichstag, established in Frankfurt. Austria and Prussia dominated this alliance until a series of bourgeois democratic revolutions swept through German cities in 1848, resulting in Germany's first ever freely elected parliamentary delegation convening in Frankfurt's Paulskirche. Austria, meanwhile, broke away from Germany, came up with its own constitution and promptly relapsed into monarchism. As the revolutions fizzled out in 1850, the confederation resumed again with Prussia and Austria as dominant members.

Bismarck & the Birth of an Empire

The creation of a unified Germany with Prussia at the helm was the glorious ambition of Otto von Bismarck (1815–98), who had been appointed as Prussian prime minister by King Wilhelm I in 1862. An old-guard militarist, he used intricate diplomacy and a series of wars with neighbouring Denmark and France to achieve his aims. By 1871 Berlin stood as the proud capital of the Deutsches Reich (German Empire), a bicameral, constitutional

1834	1848	1871
The German Customs Union is formed under the leadership of Prussia.	Following the March Revolution, Germany's first parliamentary delegation meets in Frankfurt.	Through diplomacy and war, Bismarck creates a Prussia-led unified Germany.

monarchy. On 18 January 1871, Prussian king Wilhelm I was crowned Kaiser at Versailles, with Bismarck as his 'Iron Chancellor'.

When pressed, Bismarck made concessions to the growing and increasingly antagonistic socialist movement, enacting Germany's first modern social reforms, though this was not his true nature. When Wilhelm II (r 1888–1918) came to power, he wanted to extend social reform while Bismarck envisioned stricter antisocialist laws. By March 1890, the Kaiser had had enough and excised his renegade chancellor from the political scene. Bismarck's legacy as a brilliant diplomat unravelled as a wealthy, unified and industrially powerful Germany paddled into the new century.

World War I

The assassination of Archduke Franz Ferdinand, the heir to the Austrian throne, on 28 June 1914 triggered a series of diplomatic decisions that led to WWI, the bloodiest European conflict since the Thirty Years' War. Initial euphoria and faith in a quick victory soon gave way to despair as casualties piled up in the battlefield trenches and stomachs grumbled on the home front. When peace came with defeat in 1918, it also ended domestic stability, ushering in a period of turmoil and violence. On November 1918, Kaiser Wilhelm II abdicated, bringing an inglorious end to Germany's monarchy.

The seeds of acrimony and humiliation that later led to WWII were sown in the peace conditions of WWI. Germany, militarily broken, teetering on the verge of revolution and caught in a no man's land between monarchy and modern democracy, signed the Treaty of Versailles (1919), which made it responsible for all losses inflicted upon its enemies. Its borders were trimmed back and it was forced to pay high reparations.

Weimar Republic

In July 1919 the federalist constitution of the fledgling republic – Germany's first serious experiment with democracy – was adopted in the town of Weimar, where the constituent assembly had sought refuge from the chaos of Berlin. It gave women the vote and established basic human rights, but it also gave the chancellor the right to rule by decree – a concession that would later prove critical in Hitler's rise to power.

The Weimar Republic (1920–33) was governed by a coalition of left and centre parties but pleased neither communists nor monarchists. In fact the 1920s began as anything but 'golden', marked, as they were, by the humiliation of a lost war, social and political instability, hyperinflation, mass unemployment, hunger and disease.

Economic stability gradually returned after a new currency, the *Rentenmark*, was introduced in 1923 and with the Dawes Plan in 1924, which limited the crippling reparation payments. But the tide turned again when the US stock market crashed in 1929, plunging the world into economic depression. Within weeks, millions were jobless and riots and demonstrations again ruled Germany's streets.

1914–18	**1918–19**	**1933**
WWI: Germany, Austria-Hungary and Turkey go to war against Britain, France, Italy and Russia.	The 'war guilt' clause in the Treaty of Versailles holds Germany and its allies financially responsible for loss suffered by its enemies.	Hitler becomes chancellor of Germany and creates a dictatorship through the Enabling Law.

Hitler's Rise to Power

The volatile, increasingly polarised political climate provided fertile ground for political extremists. One party waiting in the wings was the Nationalsozialistische Deutsche Arbeiterpartei (NSDAP; National Socialist German Workers' Party or Nazi Party), led by a failed Austrian artist and WWI corporal named Adolf Hitler. In the 1930 elections, the NSDAP gained 18% of the national vote. By January 1933, Hitler had become chancellor.

Hitler moved quickly to consolidate absolute power and to turn the nation's democracy into a one-party dictatorship. He used Berlin's Reichstag fire in March 1933 as a pretext to push through the Enabling Law, allowing him to decree laws and change the constitution without consulting parliament.

The rise of the Nazis had instant, far-reaching consequences. In the 12 short years of what Hitler envisaged as the 'Thousand Year Reich', massive destruction would be inflicted upon German and other European cities; political opponents, intellectuals and artists would be murdered, or forced to go underground or into exile; and a culture of terror and denunciation would permeate almost all of German society.

Jewish Persecution

Jewish people were specifically targeted in what would be a long-term campaign of genocide. In April 1933 Joseph Goebbels, head of the Ministry of Propaganda, announced a boycott of Jewish businesses. Soon after, Jews were expelled from public service and banned from many professions, trades and industries. The Nuremberg Laws (1935) deprived non-Aryans of German citizenship and many other rights. The targeting of Jews reached a peak on 9 November 1938 with the Kristallnacht (Night of Broken Glass) when Nazi thugs attacked synagogues and Jewish cemeteries, property and businesses across the country. While Jews had begun to emigrate after 1933, this event set off a stampede.

The fate of those Jews who stayed behind deteriorated after the outbreak of WWII in 1939. In 1942, at Hitler's request, a conference in Berlin's Wannsee came up with the *Endlösung* (Final Solution): the systematic, bureaucratic and meticulously documented annihilation of European Jews. Of the roughly seven million people who were sent to concentration camps, only 500,000 survived.

World War II

WWII began on 1 September 1939 with the Nazi attack on Poland. France and Britain declared war on Germany two days later, but even this could not prevent the quick defeat of Poland, Belgium, the Netherlands and France. Other countries, including Denmark and Norway, were also soon brought into the Nazi fold.

1935	1936	1939
The Nuremberg Laws are enacted depriving Jews of their German citizenship.	Nazi Germany hosts the Olympic Games.	WWII: Hitler invades Poland; France and Britain declare war on Germany.

In June 1941 Germany broke its non-aggression pact with Stalin by attacking the Soviet Union. Though successful at first, Operation Barbarossa quickly ran into problems, culminating in the defeat at Stalingrad (today Volgograd) the following winter, forcing the Germans to retreat.

With the Normandy invasion of June 1944, Allied troops arrived in formidable force on the European mainland, supported by unrelenting air raids that reduced Germany's cities to rubble and the country's population by 10%. Finally accepting the inevitability of defeat, Hitler killed himself in his bunker along with his wife Eva Braun, whom he'd married just a day earlier, on 30 April 1945. A few days after their deaths, on 8 May, Germany surrendered unconditionally.

Two German States

At conferences in Yalta and Potsdam in February and July 1945 respectively, the Allies (the Soviet Union, the USA, the UK and France) redrew Germany's borders and carved up the country into four occupation zones.

Friction between the Western Allies and the Soviets quickly emerged. While the Western Allies focused on helping Germany get back on its feet by kick-starting the devastated economy, the Soviets insisted on massive reparations and began brutalising and exploiting their own zone of occupation. Tens of thousands of able-bodied men and prisoners of war ended up in labour camps set up deep in the Soviet Union. In the Allied zones meanwhile, democracy was beginning to take root as Germany elected state parliaments (1946–47).

In 1949 the division of Germany was formalised. The western zones evolved into the Bundesrepublik Deutschland (BRD; Federal Republic of Germany or FRG) with Bonn, on the Rhine, as its capital. An economic aid package dubbed the Marshall Plan created the basis for West Germany's *Wirtschaftswunder* (economic miracle), which saw the economy

Night of Long Knives

The brown-shirted SA (Sturmabteilung, or Storm Troopers) was a Nazi organisation charged mainly with policing Nazi Party meetings and disrupting those convened by political opponents. Although it played an important role in Hitler's ascent to power, by 1934 it had become quite powerful in its own right, thanks, in large part, to its leader Ernst Röhm. On 30 June that year, feeling threatened, Hitler ordered the black-shirted SS (Schutzstaffel) to round up and kill the SA leadership (including Röhm and at least 75 others) to bring the organisation to heel. On 13 July, Hitler announced to the Reichstag that the SA would, from that time forth, serve under the command of the army. Justice would be executed by Hitler himself and the black-shirted SS under the leadership of former chicken farmer Heinrich Himmler, effectively giving the SS unchallenged power and making it Nazi Germany's most powerful – and feared – force.

1939–45	1949	1951–61
In addition to millions of Jews murdered during the Holocaust, 62 million civilians and soldiers die during WWII.	West Germany becomes the Federal Republic of Germany (FRG), Soviet-controlled East Germany the German Democratic Republic (GDR).	The economic vision of Ludwig Erhard unleashes West Germany's 'economic miracle'.

East Side Gallery (p43), Berlin

★ History Museums

Deutsches Historisches Museum (p64), Berlin

Jüdisches Museum (p69), Berlin

Römisch-Germanisches Museum (p222), Cologne

Militärhistorisches Museum Dresden (p183)

grow at an average 8% per year between 1951 and 1961. A cornerstone of recovery was the arrival of 2.3 million foreign workers, mainly from Turkey, Yugoslavia and Italy, which laid the foundation for today's multicultural society.

The Soviet zone, meanwhile, grew into the Deutsche Demokratische Republik (German Democratic Republic or GDR), with East Berlin as its capital. A single party, the Sozialistische Einheitspartei Deutschlands (SED; Socialist Unity Party of Germany) dominated economic, judicial and security policy. In order to suppress any opposition, the Ministry for State Security, or Stasi, was established in 1950. Economically, East Germany stagnated, in large part because of the Soviets' continued policy of asset stripping and reparation payments.

The Wall: What Goes Up...

Through the 1950s the economic gulf between East and West Germany widened, prompting 3.6 million East Germans – mostly young and well-educated – to seek a future in the West and thus putting the GDR on the brink of economic and political collapse. Eventually, this sustained brain and brawn drain prompted the East German government – with Soviet consent – to build a wall to keep them in. Construction of the Berlin Wall, the Cold War's most potent symbol, began on the night of 13 August 1961. The intra-German border was fenced off and mined.

The appointment of Erich Honecker as government leader in 1971, combined with the *Ostpolitik* (East-friendly policy) of West German chancellor Willy Brandt, allowed an easier political relationship between the East and West. In September that year, all four Allies signed a Four Power Accord that paved the way to the 1972 Transit Agreement that regulated access between West Berlin and West Germany, guaranteed West Berliners the right to visit East Berlin and the GDR, and even granted GDR citizens permission to travel to West Germany in cases of family emergency.

1954	1961	1971
Germany wins the FIFA soccer World Cup.	The GDR government begins building the Berlin Wall.	Social Democrat chancellor Willy Brandt's *Ostpolitik* thaws relations between the two Germanys.

...Must Come Down

Hearts and minds in Eastern Europe had long been restless for change, but German reunification caught even the most insightful political observers by surprise. The so-called *Wende* (turning point, ie the fall of communism) was a gradual development that ended in a big bang – the collapse of the Berlin Wall on 9 November 1989.

Prior to the Wall's collapse, East Germans were, once again, leaving their country in droves, this time via Hungary, which had opened its borders with Austria. The SED was helpless to stop the flow of people wanting to leave, some of whom sought refuge in the West German embassy in Prague. Meanwhile, mass demonstrations in Leipzig spread to other cities, including East Berlin.

As the situation escalated, Erich Honecker relinquished leadership to Egon Krenz (b 1937). And on the fateful night of 9 November 1989, party functionary Günter Schabowski informed GDR citizens they could travel directly to the West, effective immediately. The announcement was actually supposed to be embargoed until the following day. Tens of thousands of East Germans jubilantly rushed through border points in Berlin and elsewhere in the country, bringing to an end the long, chilly phase of German division. The formal Unification Treaty was signed on 31 August 1990.

The Stasi

In East Germany, the walls had ears. Modelled after the Soviet KGB, the GDR's Ministerium für Staatssicherheit (MfS, or Ministry of State Security, 'Stasi' for short) was founded in 1950. It was secret police, the central intelligence agency and bureau of criminal investigation all rolled into one. Called the 'shield and sword' of the SED, the sole East German party, it put millions of GDR citizens under surveillance in order to suppress internal opposition.

The Stasi grew in power and size and, by the end, had 91,000 full-time employees and 189,000 IMs (*Inoffizielle Mitarbeiter*, unofficial informants). The latter were recruited among regular folks to spy on their coworkers, friends, family and neighbours. There were also 3000 IMs based in West Germany.

When the Wall fell, the Stasi fell with it. Thousands of citizens stormed the ministry's headquarters in January 1990, thus preventing the shredding of documents that revealed the full extent of institutionalised surveillance and repression through wire-tapping, videotape observation, opening private mail and other methods.

Since Reunification

In December 1990, Helmut Kohl was elected Germany's post-reunification chancellor. Under his leadership East German assets were privatised; state industries were trimmed back, sold or closed; and infrastructure was modernised, all resulting in economic growth

1989	**1990**	**1998**
The Berlin Wall comes down; East Germans flood into West Germany.	Berlin becomes the capital of reunified Germany. Helmut Kohl's conservative coalition promises East-West economic integration.	Helmut Kohl's CDU/CSU–FDP coalition is replaced by an SPD and Bündnis 90/Die Grünen government.

of about 10% each year until 1995. The trend slowed dramatically thereafter, however, creating an eastern Germany that consisted of unification winners and losers.

Amid allegations of widespread financial corruption, the Kohl government was replaced with a coalition government of SPD (Social Democratic Party) and Alliance 90/The Greens in 1998. This marked the first time an environmentalist party had governed nationally – in Germany or elsewhere in the world.

The New Millennium

The rise of the Greens and, more recently, the democratic-socialist Die Linke (The Left) has changed Germany's political landscape dramatically, making absolute majorities by the 'big two' (ie the CDU/CSU and SPD) all the more difficult to achieve. In 2005 they formed a grand coalition led by Angela Merkel (b 1954), the first woman, former East East German, Russian speaker and quantum physicist in the job.

When the financial crisis struck in 2008, the German government pumped hundreds of billions of euros into the financial system to prop up the banks. Other measures allowed companies to put workers on shorter shifts without loss of pay and such incentive schemes as encouraging Germans to trade older cars for new ones. The elections of 2009 and 2013 returned Merkel to power but also confirmed the trend towards a five-party political system.

The 2013 election also saw the meteoric rise of a new party, the Euro-skeptic Alternative für Deutschland (AfD, Alternative for Germany). It drew at least some of its supporters from sympathizers with Pegida ('Patriotic Europeans against the Islamisation of the West'), a populist anti-Islam movement founded in Dresden in October 2014. Although under strong criticism for its ties to the far right, Pegida held demonstrations for months that peaked with 25,000 participants in January 2015.

Although AfD and Pegida have since fizzled, the underlying issue providing fodder for both has not gone vanished: the growing wave of economic and political refugees trying to enter Europe. In Germany, the level of immigration reached a 20-year high in 2015 with an expected 300,000 applications for asylum. Xenophobia and frustration with existing immigration laws and policies have led to a number of arson attacks on shelters built for asylum seekers to live in while their applications grind through Germany's complex bureaucratic process.

Amidst all these serious developments came a moment of levity in 2014 when the German national soccer team won the FIFA World Cup for the fourth time.

2005	2009	2011
Angela Merkel becomes Germany's first woman chancellor.	The CDU/CSU and FDP form a new coalition government; Angela Merkel is re-elected as chancellor.	Southern Europe looks to Germany as the crisis in the Eurozone deepens.

The ceiling of the Kölner Dom (p218)

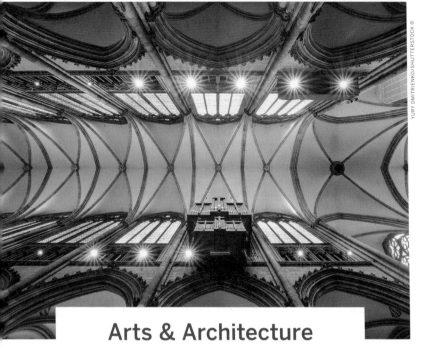

YURY DMITRIENKO/SHUTTERSTOCK ©

Arts & Architecture

Germany's creative population has made major contributions to international culture, particularly during the 18th century when the courts at Weimar and Dresden attracted some of the greatest minds in Europe. With such rich traditions to fall back on, inspiration has seldom been in short supply for the new generations of German artists, despite the upheavals of the country's recent history.

Literary Legacies

German literature in the Middle Ages was written in umpteen dialects, based on the oral tradition and typified by lyrical poetry, ballads and secular epics such as the famous *Nibelungenlied* saga (from the 12th century). Martin Luther's translation of the Bible from Greek to German in 521–22 created a common German language and thus paved the way for modern literature. But this didn't hit its stride until the Enlightenment, two centuries later.

The undisputed literary colossus of the period was Johann Wolfgang von Goethe, most famous for his two-part drama *Faust* about the archetypal human quest for meaning and knowledge. Goethe and his friend Friedrich Schiller were key figures in a celebrated period known as *Weimarer Klassik* (Weimar classicism).

Cuvilliés-Theater (p105), Residenz, Munich

★ Celluloid Classics

The Lives of Others (2006) Stasi unmasked.

Good Bye, Lenin! (2003) Comedy set around the fall of the Wall.

Das Boot (1981) WWII U-boat warfare.

Wings of Desire (1997) An angel in love with a mortal.

In the mid-19th century, realist novels captured the imagination of the newly emerging middle class. Main exponents include Theodor Fontane who's best known for his 1894 society novel *Effi Briest*, and Gerhard Hauptmann whose plays and novels focused on social injustice and the harsh life of the working class.

During the time of the Weimar Republic, Berlin's underworld served as the focus for the novel *Berlin Alexanderplatz* (1929) by Alfred Döblin. Among post-WWII generation writers, Günter Grass became the most celebrated after bursting into the limelight with *Die Blechtrommel* (Tin Drum; 1959). In East Germany, Christa Wolf won high esteem for her 1963 story *Der geteilte Himmel* (Divided Heaven) about a young woman whose fiancé abandons her for life in the West.

After reunification literary achievement stagnated at first, as writers from the East and West began a process of self-examination, but it picked up steam in the late 1990s. Thomas Brussig's tongue-in-cheek *Helden wie Wir* (Heroes Like Us; 1998) was one of the first post-reunification novels and offers an insightful look at East German society. And Russian-born Wladimir Kaminer's amusing, stranger-than-fiction hit *Russendisko* (Russian Disco; 2000) firmly established the author in Germany's light-hearted literary scene.

Caught on Film

Since the foundation of the UFA studios in Potsdam in 1917, Germany has had an active and successful film industry. Marlene Dietrich (1901–92) became the country's first international superstar, starting out in silent films and later moving to Hollywood. Director Fritz Lang made a name for himself with seminal films *Metropolis* (1927) and *M* (1931).

The best-known director of the Nazi era was Leni Riefenstahl (1902–2003), whose *Triumph of the Will* (1934), depicting the Nuremberg rallies, won great acclaim but later rendered her unemployable.

The 1960s and 1970s saw a great revival of German cinema, spearheaded by energetic, politically aware young directors such as Rainer Werner Fassbinder, Wim Wenders, Volker Schlöndorff and Margarethe von Trotta.

A smash hit after reunification was Tom Tykwer's *Run Lola Run* (1998), which established his reputation as one of Germany's best new directors. Wolfgang Becker's GDR comedy *Good Bye, Lenin!* (2003) was another international hit as was Florian Henckel von Donnersmarck's Academy Award–winning *The Lives of Others* (2006) about the work of the Stasi in the 1980s.

Classical to Electronic Sounds

Forget brass bands and oompah music – few countries can claim the impressive musical heritage of Germany, which generated the greatness of Johann Sebastian Bach, Georg

Friedrich Händel, Ludwig van Beethoven, Richard Strauss, Robert Schumann, Johannes Brahms and Richard Wagner, to name a few.

Germany has also made significant contributions to the contemporary music scene. Internationally renowned artists include punk icon Nina Hagen, '80s balloon girl Nena, and rock bands from the Scorpions to Die Toten Hosen and Rammstein.

Kraftwerk pioneered the original electronic sounds, which morphed into techno and became the seminal club music since the 1990s, especially in Berlin and Frankfurt. Today, Germany has the largest electronic music scene in the world, and DJs such as Ellen Allien, Paul Kalkbrenner, Paul van Dyk and Sven Väth have become household names on the global party circuit.

Architecture Through the Ages

The first great wave of buildings came with the Romanesque period (1000–1200), outstanding examples of which include the cathedrals at Worms, Speyer and Mainz. Gothic architecture brought such traits as ribbed vaults, pointed arches and flying buttresses nicely exemplified in Cologne's cathedral, Trier's Liebfrauenkirche and Freiburg's Münster.

For classic baroque, Balthasar Neumann's Residenz in Würzburg, the Passau Cathedral and the Frauenkirche and Zwinger palace in Dresden are must-sees. The neoclassical period of the 19th century was dominated by Karl Friedrich Schinkel, who was especially prolific in Berlin and northern Germany. His Neue Wache and the Altes Museum in Berlin are considered masterpieces of the style.

No modern movement has had greater influence on design than the Bauhaus, founded in 1919 by Walter Gropius. You can still visit the seminal school and private homes of Gropius and his fellow professors in Dresden-Rosslau. For an overview, drop by the Bauhaus Archiv in Berlin. The Nazis shut down the school in 1932 and reverted to the pompous and monumental. Berlin's Olympic Stadium and the party rally grounds in Nuremberg are among the few surviving buildings from that dark period.

For the boldest new architecture head to Berlin where international 'starchitects' including Daniel Libeskind, David Chipperfield and Lord Norman Foster have put their stamp on the city's post-reunification look. Stuttgart, meanwhile, added the stunning Porsche Museum to its cityscape in 2009, while in Hamburg an old docklands area has been turned into a futuristic new city quarter called HafenCity.

Artistic Achievement

German arts' first heyday was during the Renaissance period, which came late to Germany but flourished quickly. The heavyweight of the period is Albrecht Dürer (1471–1528), who was the first to seriously compete with the Italian masters. Dürer influenced court painter Lucas Cranach the Elder (1472–1553) who worked in Wittenberg for more than 45 years.

Two centuries later, the baroque period brought great sculpture, including works by Andreas Schlüter in Berlin. This was followed by neoclassicism in the 19th century, which ushered back interest in the human figure and an emphasis on Roman and Greek mythology. This segued into Romanticism, which drew heavily on emotion and dreamy idealism, nicely captured in the paintings of Caspar David Friedrich and Otto Runge.

In 1905 Ernst Ludwig Kirchner, along with Erich Heckel and Karl Schmidt-Rottluff, founded the artist group *Die Brücke* (The Bridge) in Dresden that turned the art world on its head with ground-breaking visions that paved the way for German expressionism. By the 1920s art had become more radical and political, with artists such as George Grosz,

Contemporary architecture in Hamburg

Otto Dix and Max Ernst exploring the new concepts of Dada and surrealism. Käthe Kollwitz is one of the era's few major female artists, known for her social-realist drawings.

After 1945 abstract art became a mainstay of the German scene, with key figures such as Joseph Beuys, Monica Bonvicini and Anselm Kiefer enjoying worldwide reputations. After reunification, the New Leipzig School achieved success at home and abroad with figurative painters such as Neo Rauch generating much acclaim.

Hitting the Stage

Germany's theatre history began during the Enlightenment in the late 18th century, an epoch dominated by humanistic ideals and authors such as Gotthold Ephraim Lessing, Friedrich Schiller and Johann Wolfgang von Goethe.

Starting in the late 19th century, Berlin emerged as the capital of the German theatre scene. At the Deutsches Theater, Max Reinhardt became the most influential expressionist director, collaborating briefly with dramatist Bertolt Brecht whose *Threepenny Opera* premiered in 1928. Like so many others, both men went into exile under the Nazis. Returning in 1949, Brecht founded the Berliner Ensemble and became East Germany's most important director. In the 1950s Heiner Müller – a Marxist critical of GDR-style socialism – became unpalatable in both Germanys.

In West Germany, directors such as Peter Stein earned contemporary German theatre its reputation for producing classic plays in an innovative and provocative manner. Frank Castorf, meanwhile, is arguably Germany's most dynamic contemporary director, heading up Berlin's Volksbühne since 1992 where he regularly tears down the confines of the proscenium stage with Zeitgeist-critical productions that are somehow populist and elitist all at once. Contemporary playwrights to watch out for include Elfriede Jelinek, Rene Pollesch, Moritz Rinke, Botho Strauss, Rainald Goetz and Roland Schimmelpfennig.

Bavarian Alps

BLUEJAYPHOTO/GETTY IMAGES ©

Germany Outdoors

*No matter what kind of activity gets you off the couch,
you'll be able to pursue it in this land of lakes, rivers,
mountains and forests. Each season offers its own
special delights, be it hiking among spring wildflowers,
swimming in a lake warmed by the summer sun, biking
among kaleidoscopic autumn foliage or schussing
through winter snow. And wherever you go, you'll find
local outfitters eager to gear you up.*

Hiking & Mountaineering

Wanderlust? Germany coined the word. Ramble through romantic river valleys, hike among fragrant pines, bag Alpine peaks or simply go for a walk by the lake or through the dunes. Many of the nicest trails traverse national and nature parks or biosphere reserves. Trails are usually well signposted, sometimes with symbols quaintly painted on tree trunks. To find a route matching your fitness level and time frame, pick the brains of local tourist office staff, who can also supply you with maps and tips.

The Bavarian Alps are Germany's mountaineering heartland, whether for day treks or multiday hut-to-hut clambers. Keep in mind that hiking in the Alps is no walk in the park. You need to be in reasonable condition and come equipped with the right shoes, gear and topographic maps or GPS. Before heading out, seek local advice and instruction on routes, equipment and weather as trails can be narrow and steep with icy patches, even in summer.

The Deutscher Alpenverein (DAV; www.alpenverein.de) is a goldmine of information and maintains hundreds of Alpine mountain huts, many of them open to the public, where you can spend the night and get a meal. Local DAV chapters also organise various courses (climbing, mountaineering etc) and guided treks.

For another excellent resource, see www.wanderbares-deutschland.de for information about dozens of walking trails and a handy interactive map. It's mostly in German, but some routes are also detailed in English.

Cycling

Strap on your helmet! Germany is superb cycling territory, whether you're off on a leisurely spin along the beach, an adrenalin-fuelled downhill ride or a multiday bike-touring adventure. Practically every town and region has a network of signposted bike routes; most towns have at least one bike-hire station (often at or near the train station).

Germany is also criss-crossed by more than 200 long-distance trails covering 70,000km, making it ideal for *Radwandern* (bike touring). Routes combine lightly travelled back roads, forestry tracks and paved highways with dedicated bike lanes. Many traverse nature reserves, meander along rivers or venture into steep mountain terrain.

For inspiration and route planning, check out www.germany.travel/cycling, which provides (in English) an overview of routes and free downloads of route maps and descriptions.

For on-the-road navigation, the best maps are those published by the national cycling organsation Allgemeiner Deutscher Fahrrad Club (ADFC; www.adfc.de). These indicate inclines, track conditions, repair shops and UTM grid coordinates for GPS users. ADFC also offers a useful directory called Bett & Bike (www.bettundbike.de), available online or in bookshops, that lists bicycle-friendly hotels, inns and hostels.

Water Sports

Germany's lakes, rivers, canals and coasts offer plenty of water-based action, even if the swimming season is relatively short (June to September) since water temperatures rarely climb above 21°C. Slip into a canoe or kayak to absorb the natural rhythm of the waterways threading through Bavaria's lush Altmühltal Nature Park. Or drift across Lake Constance to Switzerland and Austria with the Alps on the horizon. The season runs from around April to

---

Long-Distance Cycling Routes

Altmühltal Radweg (160km) Easy to moderate; Rothenburg ob der Tauber to Beilngries, following the Altmühl River through the Altmühltal Nature Park.

Bodensee-Königssee Radweg (418km) Moderate; Lindau to Berchtesgaden along the foot of the Alps with magnificent views of the mountains, lakes and forests.

Donauradweg (434km) Easy to moderate; Neu-Ulm to Passau – a delightful riverside trip along one of Europe's great streams.

Romantische Strasse (359km) Easy to moderate; Würzburg to Füssen – one of the nicest ways to explore Germany's most famous holiday route; busy during summer.

October and a one-/two-person canoe or kayak will set you back around €20/30 per day. Stiff breezes and big waves draw sailors, surfers, windsurfers and kite surfers north. Sylt on the North Sea and Rügen on the Baltic have some of the top conditions and schools in the country for water-based activities.

Winter Sports

Modern lifts, primed ski slopes from 'Sesame Street' to 'Death Wish', cross-country trails through untouched nature, cosy mountain huts, steaming mulled wine, hearty dinners by crackling fires: these are all hallmarks of a German skiing holiday.

The Bavarian Alps, only an hour's drive south of Munich, offer the best downhill slopes and most reliable snow conditions. The most famous resort is Garmisch-Partenkirchen, which regularly hosts international competitions and is but a snowball's toss from the Zugspitze, Germany's highest mountain. It has 60km of slopes, mostly geared towards intermediates.

Picture-book pretty Oberstdorf in the Allgäu Alps has 125km of slopes. It's good for boarders with snow parks and a half-pipe to play on, 75km for cross-country skiers to glide along and 55km of skating tracks. For low-key skiing and stunning scenery there is Berchtesgaden, presided over by the jagged Karwendel range.

Can't or won't ski? All resorts offer snowy fun from tobogganing to ice-skating, snowshoeing and winter walking.

Cycling in Munich (p97)

The Germans

There's much fascination with the German state of mind. The nation and its people have seen two 20th-century wars, carry the memory of the Jewish Holocaust, were on the chilling edge of Cold War division, and now live in a juggernaut-like economy that draws half of Europe in its wake and pumps more goods into the world economy than any other.

National Psyche

It pays to ignore the stereotypes, jingoism and headlines describing Germany in military terms and see the country through its regional nuances. Germany was very slow to become a nation, so look closely to notice the many different local cultures within the one set of borders. You will also find that it's one of Europe's most multicultural countries, with Turkish, Greek, Italian, Russian and Balkan influences.

Germans like to get straight to the point rather than hint or suggest; facing each other squarely in conversation, firm handshakes, and a hug or a kiss on the cheek among friends are par for the course.

Former East

Today around 15 million people live in former East Germany, where until 1989 travel was restricted, the state was almighty and life was secure (but also strongly regulated) from the cradle to the grave. Not surprisingly many former East Germans, who lived well in the former socialist state, had a difficult time coming to terms with a more competitive, unified Germany.

Smoking

Germany was one of the last countries in Europe to legislate smoking and most visitors will notice almost immediately how much more secondhand cigarette smoke is in the air. Almost 29% of German men and 20% of women smoke. Smoking bans are different in each state. See p298 for more information.

Green Germany

Germans are the original Greens. They cannot claim to have invented environmentalism, but they were there at the outset and it was they who coined the word to describe the movement. A few 'Values' and 'Ecology' parties were knocking around beforehand, but it was the group of politicians associated with Rudi Dutschke, Petra Kelly and artist Joseph Beuys who first hit on the name The Greens (Die Grünen) when contesting local and national elections in 1979 and 1980. They gained a strong foothold in Bremen, and other political groups across the world decided they quite liked the moniker.

The Greens' concern for the health of the planet and their strong opposition to nuclear power certainly struck a chord with the local populace. Contemporary Germans recycle vigilantly, often prefer to ride bicycles rather than catch buses, and carry their groceries in reusable cloth shopping bags; all this is simply second nature here.

Football

Football ignites the passion of Germans everywhere and has contributed much to building the confidence of the nation. The national team has won the World Cup four times – in 1954, 1974, 1990 and again in 2014. Germany has also hosted the World Cup twice, in 1974 and 2006.

Domestically, Germany's Bundesliga has fallen behind other European leagues such as England's Premier League but still throws up some exciting duels. On the European stage, Germany's most successful domestic club is the FC Bayern Munich, which has been Deutscher Meister (national champion) 25 times and won the UEFA Champions League five times, the last time in 2012/13.

Bratwurst with *Sauerkraut* and mustard

BRENT HOFACKER/SHUTTERSTOCK ©

German Cuisine

Germany might not have the culinary kudos of some of its neighbours, but its robust, fresh flavours have made it a rising star in Europe's kitchen. You'll never forget your first forkful of black forest gateau, the crisp rieslings sipped in Rhineland taverns, or the roast pork served with foamy Weizen (wheat beer) at a Bavarian beer fest. Bring an appetite, a taste for adventure and get stuck in.

The State of German Cuisine

As in Britain, Germany has redeemed itself gastronomically in the past decade. Of course, if you crave traditional comfort food, you'll certainly find plenty of places to indulge in pork, potatoes and cabbage. These days though, 'typical' local fare is lighter, healthier, creative and more likely to come from organic eateries, ethnic restaurants and gourmet kitchens. In fact in 2015 Germany's Michelin skies twinkled brighter than ever before with 233 one-star, 38 two-star and 11 three-star restaurants.

Top chefs are putting creative spins on tried-and-trusted specialties in a wave that's referred to as the *Neue Deutsche Küche* (New German Cuisine). Many have jumped on the locavore bandwagon, letting the trifecta of 'seasonal-regional-organic' ingredients steer their menus. Many travel to the countryside to source free-range meats, wild-caught fish, farm-fresh fruit and vegetables, handmade cheeses and other delectables, preferably sustainably grown. Menus increasingly champion traditional (and long underrated) ingredients such as root vegetables, old-fashioned grains and game and other meats like goat liver or cheeks.

Price Ranges

The following price indicators are used throughout this book to indicate the costs of one main course:

€ Less than €8

€€ €8 to €15

€€€ More than €15

Traditional Staples

Bread

As German expats living around the world will tell you: the food they miss the most about their homeland is the bread. Indeed, German bread is a world-beater. Its 300 varieties are tasty and textured, often mixing wheat and rye flour.

'Black' rye bread (*Schwarzbrot*) is actually brown, but a much darker shade than the slightly sour *Bauernbrot* – divine with a slab of butter. Pumpernickel bread is steam-cooked instead of baked, making it extra moist, and actually is black. *Vollkorn* means wholemeal, and bread coated in sunflower seeds is *Sonnenblumenbrot.* If you insist on white bread *(Weissbrot),* the Germans have that, too.

Fresh bread rolls (*Brötchen* in the north, *Semmel* in Bavaria, *Wecken* in the rest of southern Germany) can be covered in poppy seeds *(Mohnbrötchen),* cooked with sweet raisins *(Rosinenbrötchen),* sprinkled with salt *(Salzstangel)* or treated in dozens of other, different ways.

Brezeln are traditional pretzels covered in rock salt.

Potatoes

Chipped, boiled, baked, mashed, fried: Germans love their potatoes. The *Kartoffel* is not only vegetable *Nummer Eins* in any meat-and-three-veg dish, it can also be incorporated into any course of a meal, from potato soup (*Kartoffelsuppe*) as a starter, to potato salad (*Kartoffelsalat*) and potato pancakes (*Reibekuchen*).

In between, you can try *Himmel und Erde* (Heaven and Earth), a dish of mashed potatoes and stewed apples served with black pudding; or potato-based *Klösse* (dumplings). *Pellkartoffeln* or *Ofenkartoffeln* are jacket potatoes, usually topped with a dollop of *Quark* (a yoghurt-like curd cheese).

Cabbage

Sauerkraut is a quintessential German side dish that many outside the country find impossible to fathom. Before the 2006 FIFA World Cup, one football magazine suggested: 'It's pickled cabbage; don't try to make it sound interesting.' Okay, we won't. It's shredded cabbage, doused in white-wine vinegar and slowly simmered. But if you haven't at least tried *Rotkohl* (the red-cabbage version), you don't know what you're missing. Braising the cabbage with sliced apples and wine turns it into *Bayrischkraut* or *Weinkraut.*

Sausage

In the Middle Ages German peasants found a way to package and disguise animals' less appetising bits – creating the *wurst*. Today it's a noble and highly respected element of German cuisine, with strict rules determining the authenticity of *wurst* varieties. In some cases, as with the finger-sized Nuremberg sausage, regulations even ensure offal no longer enters the equation.

While there are more than 1500 sausage species, all are commonly served with bread and a sweet (*süss*) or spicy (*scharf*) mustard (*Senf*).

Bratwurst, served countrywide, is made from minced pork, veal and spices, and is cooked in different ways (boiled in beer, baked with apples and cabbage, stewed in a casserole or simply grilled or barbecued).

The availability of other sausages differs regionally. A *Thüringer* is long and spiced, while a *Wiener* is what hot-dog fiends call a frankfurter. Saxony is all about the brain sausage (*Bregenwurst*), Bavaria sells the white, veal-and-pork-based *Weisswurst*, and Berliners swear by their *Currywurst* (slices of sausage topped with curry powder and ketchup).

Seasonal Specialties

While you shall be forgiven for laughing at the unmistakably phallic shape of the chlorophyll-deprived *weisser Spargel* (white asparagus), between late April and late June Germans go nuts for the erotic stalks, which are best enjoyed steamed alongside ham, hollandaise sauce or butter, and boiled potatoes. The stalks also show up as asparagus soup, in quiches and salads and even as ice cream.

Spargelzeit (asparagus season) is a highlight of the culinary calendar that actually kicks off a bit earlier with *Bärlauch* (wild garlic), which starts showing up in salads and as pesto in early spring. Fresh fruit, especially all sorts of berries (strawberries, blueberries, raspberries, gooseberries), red currants and cherries brighten up the market stalls in summer.

In late summer and early autumn, hand-picked mushrooms such as *Steinpilze* (porcini) and earthy *Pfifferlinge* (chanterelles) show up on menus everywhere. A typical winter meal is cooked *Grünkohl* (kale) with smoked sausage, which is often served at Christmas markets. *Gans* (stuffed goose) is a Martinmas tradition (11 November) and also popular at Christmas time.

Dining Tips

Restaurants are often formal places with full menus, crisp white linen and high prices. Some restaurants are open for lunch and dinner only but more casual places tend to be open all day. Same goes for cafes, which usually serve both coffee and alcohol, as well as light meals, although ordering food is not obligatory. Many cafes and restaurants offer inexpensive weekday 'business lunches' that usually include a starter, main course and drink for under €10.

English menus are not a given, even in big cities, though the waitstaff will almost invariably be able to translate for you. The more rural and remote you travel, the less likely it is that the restaurant will have an English menu, or multilingual staff for that matter. It helps to learn a smattering of German.

Handy speed-feed shops, called *Imbiss*, serve all sorts of savoury fodder, from sausage-in-a-bun to doner and pizza. Many bakeries serve sandwiches alongside pastries.

Kaffee und Kuchen

Anyone who has spent any length of time in Germany knows the reverence bestowed on the 3pm ritual of *Kaffee und Kuchen* (coffee and cake). More than just a chance to devour delectable cakes and tortes, Germans see it as a social event. You'll find *Cafe-Konditoreien* (cafe-cake shops) pretty much everywhere – in castles, in the middle of the forest, even on top of mountains. Track down the best by asking sweet-toothed locals where the cake is *hausgebacken* (home-baked).

While coffee in Germany is not as strong as that served in France or Italy, you can expect a decent cup. All the usual varieties are on offer, including cappuccinos and lattes, although you still frequently see French-style bowls of milky coffee *(Milchkaffee)*. Order a *Kanne* (pot) or *Tasse* (cup) of *Kaffee* (coffee) and what you will get is filter coffee, usually with a portion of *Kaffeesahne* (condensed milk).

Sweet Temptations

Lebkuchen Soft gingerbread made with nuts, fruit peel, honey and spices; popular at Christmas.

Black forest gateau A multilayered chocolate sponge, cream and kirsch confection, topped with morello cherries and chocolate shavings.

Aachener Printen Aachen's crunchy spiced cookie, similar to gingerbread.

Lübecker Marzipan A creamy blend of almonds and sugar – from Lübeck.

Stollen Christmas-time spiced cake loaded with sultanas, marzipan and candied peel; the best is from Dresden.

Fast-Food Faves

International fast-food chains are everywhere, of course, but there's plenty of homegrown fast food as well. In fact, some of your best German food experiences are likely to be the snack-on-the-hoof kind. Street food is a tasty way to get versed in wurst and chomp your way around the globe, often with change from a €5 note. In the bigger cities, stalls sizzle up Greek, Italian, Mexican, Middle Eastern and Chinese bites.

The *Imbiss* fast-food stall is a ubiquitous phenomenon, allowing you to eat on the run. Germany's Turkish population invented the modern doner kebab *(Döner)*, adding salad and garlic-yoghurt sauce to spit-roasted lamb, veal or chicken in pita bread. Most kebab joints also do vegetarian versions. In the briny north, snack on fish (usually herring) sandwiches.

Vegetarians & Vegans

Germany was slow in coming but is now embracing meat-free fare with the fervour of a religious convert. Health-conscious cafes and restaurants have been sprouting faster than alfalfa and serve up inspired menus that leave the classic vegie or tofu burger in the dust. With dishes like sweet potato saltimbocca, tandoori seitan, pearl barley strudel with chanterelles, or Parmesan dumplings, chefs strive to push the creative envelope.

Even veganism has made significant inroads: Germany's first all-vegan supermarket opened in Berlin in 2011, followed by the city's first vegan gourmet restaurant the same year. Even many nonvegetarian restaurants now offer more than the token vegetable lasagne. For a comprehensive list of vegan and vegetarian restaurants in Germany, see www.happycow.net/europe/germany.

Berliner Weisse

EPA EUROPEAN PRESSPHOTO AGENCY B.V/ALAMY STOCK PHOTO/GETTY IMAGES ©

Beer & Wine

Few things are as deeply ingrained in the German psyche as the love of beer. 'Hopfen und Malz – Gott erhalt's!' *(Hops and malt are in God's hands) goes the saying, which is fitting given the almost religious intensity with which beer is brewed, consumed and celebrated – not least at the world's biggest festival, Oktoberfest. Brewing here goes back to Germanic tribes, and later to monks, so it follows in a hallowed tradition.*

Beer

The 'secret' of the country's golden nectar dates back to the *Reinheitsgebot* (purity law), demanding breweries use just four ingredients – malt, yeast, hops and water. Passed in Bavaria in 1516, the *Reinheitsgebot* stopped being a legal requirement in 1987, when the EU struck it down as uncompetitive. However, many German brewers still conform to it anyway, seeing it as a good marketing tool against mass-market, chemical-happy competitors. Nevertheless, the craft beer movement, which does not adhere to the *Reinheitsgebot*, has been making inroads in Germany in recent years, most notably in Berlin and Hamburg.

Beer Varieties

Despite frequently tying their own hands and giving themselves just four ingredients to play with, German brewers turn out 5000 distinctively different beers. They achieve this via subtle variations in the basic production process. At the simplest level, a brewer can choose a particular yeast for top or bottom fermenting (the terms indicating where the yeast lives while working – at the top or bottom of the brewing vessel). Bottom fermentation accounts for about 85% of German beers.

The most popular form of brewing is bottom fermentation, which accounts for about 85% of German beers, notably the *Pils* (pilsner), most Bock beers and the *Helles* (pale lager) type found in Bavaria. Top fermentation is used for the *Weizenbier/Weissbier* (wheat/white beer) popular in Berlin and Bavaria, Cologne's *Kölsch* and the very few stouts brewed in the country.

Many beers are regional, meaning that, for example, a Saxon Rechenberger cannot be found in Düsseldorf, where the locally brewed *Altbier* is the taste of choice.

Pils (pilsner) This bottom-fermented full beer, with pronounced hop flavour and creamy head, has an alcohol content of around 4.8%.

Weizenbier/Weissbier (wheat beer) Predominant in the south, especially in Bavaria, this has 5.4% alcohol content. A *Hefeweizen* has a stronger shot of yeast, whereas *Kristallweizen* is clearer with more fizz. These beers are fruity and spicy, often recalling bananas and cloves. Decline offers of lemon as it ruins the head and – beer purists say – the flavour.

Dunkles (dark lager) Brewed throughout Germany, but especially in Bavaria. With a light use of hops, it's full-bodied with strong malty aromas.

Helles (pale lager) *Helles* (pale or light) refers to the colour, not the alcohol content, which is still 4.6% to 5%. Brewing strongholds are Bavaria, Baden-Württemberg and the Ruhr region. It has strong malt aromas and is slightly sweet.

Altbier A dark, full beer with malted barley from the Düsseldorf area.

Berliner Weisse Berlin's top-fermented beer, which comes *rot* (red) or *grün* (green), with a *Schuss* (dash) of raspberry or woodruff syrup respectively. A cool, fruity summer choice.

Bockbier Strong beers with 7% alcohol. There's a '*Bock*' for every occasion, such as *Maibock* (for May/spring) and *Weihnachtsbock* (brewed for Christmas). *Eisbock* is dark and aromatic.

Kölsch By law, this top-fermented beer can only be brewed in or around Cologne. It's alcohol content is about 4.8%; it has a solid hop flavour and pale colour, and is served in small glasses (0.2L) called *Stangen* ('sticks').

Schwarzbier (black beer) Slightly stronger, this dark, full beer has an alcohol content of 4.8% to 5%. It's fermented using roasted malt.

Where to Drink

Up and down this hop-crazy country you will find buzzing microbreweries and brewpubs, cavernous beer halls and chestnut-shaded beer gardens that invite you to linger, quaff a cold one and raise a toast – *Prost!*

Munich offers a taste of Oktoberfest year-round in historic beer halls, where you can hoist a mass litre of *Weizen* and sway to oompah bands, and leafy beer gardens for imbibing and chomping on warm pretzels *(Brez'n)* and *Weisswurst* (herb-veal-pork sausage).

Glühwein (mulled wine)

★ **Beer Gardens**

Braunauer Hof (p126), Munich

Cafe am Neuen See (p77), Berlin

Prater Biergarten (p79), Berlin

Hofbräuhaus (p124), Munich

This festive spirit spills into other Bavarian cities, such as Regensburg and Bamberg, and into villages where monks brew potent dark beers as they have for eons. Breweries offering a peek behind the scenes include Becks's in Bremen.

Wine

For decades the name of German wine was sullied by the cloyingly sweet taste of Liebfraumilch and the naff image of Blue Nun. What a difference a decade can make. Thanks to rebranding campaigns, a new generation of wine growers and an overall rise in quality, German wine is staging a comeback in the 21st century. This triumph was marked in 2014, when 63 medals were awarded to German wines, including Horst Sauer who received two Gold Outstandings for Escherndorfer Lump Riesling Trockenbeerenauslese and Escherndorfer Lump Silvaner.

Even discerning wine critics have been pouring praise on German winemakers of late. According to Master of Wine Tim Atkin (www.timatkin.com), 'Germany makes the best rieslings of all', and, waxing lyrical on the country's Pinot noirs, he muses, 'if only the Germans didn't keep most of them to themselves.'

For a comprehensive rundown of all German wine-growing regions, grape varieties, news of the hottest winemakers, and information on tours or courses, visit www.winesofgermany.co.uk and www.germanwines.de.

Grape Varieties

Having produced wines since Roman times, Germany now has more than 1000 sq km of vineyards, mostly on the Rhine and Moselle riverbanks. Despite the common association with riesling grapes (particularly in its best wine regions) the less acidic Müller-Thurgau (Rivaner) grape is more widespread.

Better than Glühwein

Served in winter and designed to inure you to the sudden drop in temperatures, hot spiced *Glühwein* is a common commodity at Germany's popular Christmas markets. However, a far more spectacular and intoxicating mulled wine is *Feuerzangenbowle* (literally 'fire-tongs-punch'), where a flaming rum-soaked sugar cube falls into the spiced red wine, producing a delicious and heady drink. It's become a cult tipple, thanks to a movie of the same name.

What Germans call *Grauburgunder* is known to the rest of the world as Pinot gris. German reds are light and lesser known. *Spätburgunder* (Pinot noir) is the best of the bunch and goes into some velvety, full-bodied reds with an occasional almond taste.

Wine Regions

There are 13 official wine-growing areas, the best being the Mosel-Saar-Ruwer region. It boasts some of the world's steepest vineyards, where the predominantly riesling grapes are still hand-picked. Slate soil on the hillsides gives the wines a flinty taste. Chalkier riverside soils are planted with the Elbling grape, an ancient Roman variety.

East of the Moselle, the Nahe region produces fragrant, fruity and full-bodied wines using Müller-Thurgau and Silvaner grapes, as well as riesling.

Riesling grapes are also the mainstay in Rheingau and Mittelrhein (Middle Rhine), two other highly respected wine-growing pockets. Rheinhessen, south of Rheingau, is responsible for Liebfraumilch, but also some top rieslings.

Other wine regions include the Pfalz (Rheinland-Palatinate), Hessische Bergstrasse (Hesse), Baden (Baden-Württemberg), Würzburg (Bavaria) and Elbtal (Saxony).

The Württemberg region around Stuttgart produces some of the country's best reds, while Saxony-Anhalt's Saale-Unstrut region is home to Rotkäppchen (Little Red Riding Hood) sparkling wine, a former GDR brand that's been a big hit in reunited Germany.

Hooded beach chairs in Schleswig-Holstein

Survival Guide

Directory A–Z

Accommodation

Germany has all types of places to unpack your suitcase. Standards are generally high and even basic accommodation will likely be clean and comfortable. Reservations are a good idea between June and September, and around major public holidays, festivals, cultural events and trade shows.

Budget stays will generally have you checking in at hostels, *Gasthof* (country inns), *Pensionen* (B&Bs or small hotels), simple family hotels or some Airbnb properties. Facilities may be shared. Midrange properties offer extra creature comforts, such as cable TV,

wi-fi and private bathrooms. Overall, these constitute the best value for money. Top-end places come with luxurious amenities, perhaps scenic locations, special decor or historical ambience. Many also have pools, saunas and business centres.

Costs

Accommodation costs vary wildly between regions, and between cities and rural areas. What gets you a romantic suite in a countryside inn in the Bavarian Forest may only be worth a two-star room in Munich. City hotels geared to the suit brigade often lure leisure travellers with lower rates on weekends. Seasonal variations are common in holiday regions, less so in the cities.

Reservations

Most tourist offices and properties now have an online booking function with a best-price guarantee. When making a room reservation directly with a smaller hotel or a B&B, tell your host what time they can expect you to arrive and stick to your plan or ring again. Many well-meaning visitors have lost rooms by showing up late.

If you've arrived in town and don't have reservations or online access, swing by the tourist office, where staff can assist you in finding last-minute lodgings. After hours, vacancies with contact details and addresses may be posted in the window or in a display ca

Agritourism

Family-friendly farm holidays offer a great opportunity to get close to nature in relative comfort. Kids get to interact with their favourite barnyard animals and maybe help with everyday chores. Accommodation ranges from bare-bones rooms with shared facilities to fully furnished holiday apartments. Minimum stays are common. Farm types include organic, dairy and equestrian farms, as well as wine estates. Note that places advertising *Landurlaub* (country holiday) no longer actively work their farms.

The German Agricultural Association inspects and controls the quality of hundreds of farms. Details are published on www.landreise.de, which also lets you contact individual properties directly. Another source is www.landsichten.de.

Hotels

You'll find the gamut of options in Germany, from small family-run properties to international chains and luxurious designer abodes. Increasingly popular are budget designer chains (eg Motel One) geared towards lifestyle-savvy travellers.

In older, family-run hotels, rooms often vary dramatically in terms of size, decor and amenities. The cheapest may have shared facilities,

My Home is My Castle

If you're the romantic type, consider a fairy-tale getaway in a castle, palace or country manor dripping with character and history. They're typically in the countryside, strategically perched atop a crag, perhaps overlooking a river or rolling hills. And it doesn't take a king's ransom to stay in one. In fact, even wallet-watchers can fancy themselves knight or damsel when staying in a castle converted into a youth hostel (eg Burg Stahleck on the Rhine). More typically, though, properties are luxury affairs, blending the gamut of mod cons with baronial ambience and olde-worlde trappings, like four-poster beds, antique armoires and heavy drapes. Sometimes your hosts are even descendants of the original castle builders – often some local baron, count or prince. For details, see www.thecastles.de or www.germany-castles-hotels.com.

while others come with a shower cubicle installed but no private toilet; only the pricier ones have their own bathrooms. Increasingly, city hotels are not including breakfast in their room rate. Many hotels with a high romance factor belong to an association called Romantik Hotels & Restaurants (www.romantikhotels.com).

A growing number of properties are now entirely nonsmoking; others set aside rooms or entire floors for smokers.

Chain Hotels

Hotel chains stretch from nondescript establishments to central five-star properties with character and the gamut of amenities. Most conform to certain standards of decor, service and facilities (air-con, wi-fi, 24-hour check-in), and offer last-minute and/or weekend deals. International chains like Best Western, Holiday Inn, Hilton and Ramada are now ubiquitous on the German market, but there are also some home-grown contenders.

A&O (www.aohostels.com) Combines hostel and two-star hotel accommodation.

Dorint (www.dorint.com) Three- to five-star properties in cities and rural areas.

InterCity (www.intercityhotel.com) Good-value two-star chain usually located at train stations.

Kempinski (www.kempinski.com) Luxury hotel group with a pedigree going back to 1897.

Leonardo (www.leonardo-hotels.com) Three- to four-star city hotels.

Meininger Well-run hotel-hostel combo for city-breakers on a budget.

Motel One (www.motelone.com) Fast-growing chain of budget designer hotels.

Sorat (www.sorat-hotels.com) Four-star boutique hotels.

Steigenberger (www.steigenberger.com) Five-star luxury often in historic buildings.

Pensions, Inns & Private Rooms

The German equivalent of a B&B, *Pensionen* are small and informal and an excellent low-cost alternative to hotels. *Gasthöfe/Gasthäuser* (inns) are similar, but usually have restaurants serving regional and German food to a local clientele. *Privatzimmer* are guest rooms in private homes, though privacy seekers may find these places a bit too intimate.

Amenities, room size and decor vary, often within a single establishment. The cheapest units may have shared facilities or perhaps a sink and a shower cubicle in the room but no private toilet. What rooms lack in amenities, though, they often make up for in charm and authenticity, often augmented by friendly hosts who take a personal interest in ensuring that you enjoy your stay.

Travellers in need of buckets of privacy, high

Which Floor?

In Germany, as elsewhere in Europe, 'ground floor' refers to the floor at street level. The 1st floor (what would be called the 2nd floor in the US) is the floor above that. Lonely Planet follows German usage.

comfort levels or the latest tech amenities may not feel as comfortable, although wi-fi, cable TV and other mod cons are becoming increasingly available in these places as well.

Some tourist offices keep lists of available rooms; you can also look around for *'Zimmer Frei'* (rooms available) signs in house or shop windows. They're usually quite cheap, with per-person rates starting at €15 and usually topping out at €30, including breakfast.

If a landlord is reluctant to rent for a single night, offer to pay a little extra.

For reservations, try www. bed-and-breakfast.de, www. bedandbreakfast.de or www.bedandbreakfast.com.

Customs Regulations

Goods brought in and out of countries within the EU incur no additional taxes, provided duty has been paid somewhere within the EU and the goods are for personal use. Duty-free shopping is only available if you're leaving the EU.

Duty-free allowances (for anyone over 17) arriving from non-EU countries:

o 200 cigarettes or 100 cigarillos or 50 cigars or 250g of loose tobacco or a proportional combination of these goods

o 1L of strong liquor or 2L of less than 22% alcohol by volume, plus 4L of wine, plus 16L of beer

o other goods up to the value of €300 if arriving by land, or €430 if arriving by sea or air (€175 for under 15 years)

Climate

Berlin

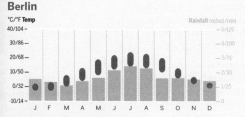

Frankfurt Am Main

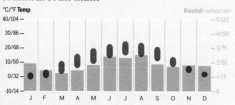

Munich

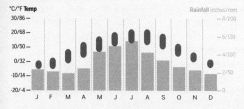

Discount Cards

Concession discounts are widely available for seniors, children and students. In some cases, you may be asked to show ID or prove your age. Tourist offices in many cities sell Welcome Cards, which entitle visitors to discounts on museums, sights and tours, plus unlimited trips on local public transport. They can be good value if you plan on taking advantage of most of the benefits and don't qualify for any of the standard discounts.

If you qualify for one of the following discount cards, you can reap additional benefits on travel, shopping, attractions or entertainment:
Camping Card International (www.campingcardinternational.

com) Up to 25% savings in camping fees and third-party liability insurance while on the campground.

International Student Identity Card (www.isic.org) The most popular discount card, but only for full-time students. Available at ISIC points (see website) and online. Cost varies by country and ranges from US$4 to US$25.

International Youth Travel Card (www.istc.org) Similar to ISIC but for nonstudents under 30 years of age. Available at ISIC points.

Electricity

120V/60Hz

Food

For details on German food and drink, see p284.

Gay & Lesbian Travellers

Germany is a magnet for *schwule* (gay) and *lesbische* (lesbian) travellers, with the rainbow flag flying especially proudly in Berlin and Cologne. There are also sizeable communities in Hamburg, Frankfurt and Munich.

○ Legal stuff: Homosexuality has been legal since the late 1960s. The age of consent is 14. There is no same-sex marriage; only registered partnerships.

○ Attitudes tend to be more conservative in the countryside, among older people and in the eastern states.

○ As elsewhere, Germany's lesbian scene is less public than its male counterpart and is centred mainly on women's cafes and bars.

○ Gay pride marches are held throughout Germany in springtime; the largest, in Cologne and Berlin, draw hundreds of thousands of rainbow revellers and friends.

Publications

Blu (www.blu.fm) Free print and online magazine with searchable, up-to-the-minute location and event listings.

L-Mag (www.l-mag.de) Bi-monthly magazine for lesbians. Available at newsagents.

Spartacus International Gay Guide (www.spartacusworld.com) Annual English-language travel guide for men. Available online, in bookstores and as an app.

Websites & Apps

German National Tourist Office (www.germany.travel/en/ms/lgbt/home/home.html) Dedicated LGBT pages.

BGLAD (www.bglad.com) International online resource and directory with hundreds of links.

Spartacus World (www.spartacusworld.com) Hip hotel, style and event guide.

Patroc Gay Travel Guide (www.patroc.com) Travel information to 25 European destinations.

Health

Germany is a healthy place; your main risks are likely to be sunburn, foot blisters, insect bites, mild stomach problems and hangovers. Tap water is drinkable.

Before You Go

○ A signed and dated letter from your doctor describing your medical conditions and medications, including generic names, is a good idea. It is illegal to import codeine-based medication without a doctor's certificate.

○ No vaccinations are required for travel to Germany, but the World Health

Organization (WHO) recommends that all travellers be covered for diphtheria, tetanus, measles, mumps, rubella and polio.

Availability & Cost of Health Care

○ Excellent health care is widely available from *Rettungsstelle* (emergency rooms) at *Krankenhauser* (hospitals) and at *Arzt* (doctors' offices).

○ For minor illnesses or injuries (headache, bruises, diarrhoea), trained staff in pharmacies can provide advice, sell prescription-free medications and make doctors' referrals if further help is needed.

○ Condoms are widely available in drugstores, pharmacies and supermarkets. Birth control pills require a doctor's prescription.

Pharmacies

○ German *Drogerien* (chemists, drugstores) do not sell any kind of medication, not even aspirin. Even *rezeptfrei* (over-the-counter) medications for minor health concerns, such as a cold or upset stomach, are only available at an *Apotheke* (pharmacy).

○ For more serious conditions, you will need to produce a *Rezept* (prescription) from a licensed physician. If you take regular medication, be sure to bring a supply for your entire trip, as the same brand may not be available in Germany.

○ The names and addresses of pharmacies open after hours (these rotate) are posted in every pharmacy window, or call ☎01141.

Insurance

○ Comprehensive travel insurance to cover theft, loss and medical problems is highly recommended.

○ Some policies specifically exclude dangerous activities, such as motorcycling, scuba diving and even trekking; read the fine print.

○ Check that the policy covers ambulance or an emergency flight home.

○ Before you leave, find out if your insurance plan makes payments directly to providers or reimburses you for health expenditures.

○ Paying for your airline ticket with a credit card sometimes provides limited travel accident insurance – ask your credit-card company what it is prepared to cover.

○ If you have to make a claim, be sure to keep all necessary documents and bills.

○ Worldwide travel insurance is available at www.lonelyplanet.com/travel-insurance. You can buy, extend and claim online anytime – even if you're already on the road.

○ Consider coverage for luggage theft or loss. If you already have a homeowner's or renter's policy, check what it will cover and only get supplemental insurance to protect against the rest.

○ If you have prepaid a large portion of your vacation, trip cancellation insurance is worthwhile.

European Health Insurance Card

Citizens of the EU, Switzerland, Iceland, Norway and Liechtenstein receive free or reduced-cost, state-provided (not private) health-care coverage with the European Health Insurance Card (EHIC) for medical treatment that becomes necessary while in Germany. It does not cover emergency repatriation home. Each family member needs a separate card. UK residents can find information on how to obtain the card at www.ehic.org.uk.

You will need to pay directly and fill in a treatment form; keep the form to claim any refunds. In general you can claim back around 70% of the standard treatment cost.

Citizens of other countries need to check whether there is a reciprocal arrangement for free medical care between their country and Germany.

Smoking Regulations

Germany was one of the last countries in Europe to legislate smoking. However, there is no nationwide law, with regulations left to each of the 16 states, creating a rather confusing patchwork of antismoking laws. Generally, smoking is a no-no in schools, hospitals, airports, train stations and other public facilities. But when it comes to bars, pubs, cafes and restaurants, every state does it just a little differently. Since 2011, Bavaria bans smoking practically everywhere, even in Oktoberfest tents. However, in most other states, lighting up is allowed in designated smoking rooms in restaurants and clubs. One-room establishments smaller than 75 sq metres may allow smoking, provided they serve no food and only admit patrons over 18. The venue must be clearly designated as a *Raucherbar* (smokers' bar).

Internet Access

o Some cafes and bars have wi-fi hot spots that let laptop-toting customers hook up for free, although you usually need to ask for a password.

o Many hotels have an internet corner for their guests, often at no charge. Note that in some properties wi-fi access may be limited to some rooms and/or public areas, so if you need in-room access be sure to specify at the time of booking.

o Internet cafes seem to have the lifespan of a fruit fly, so listings are quickly outdated. Ask staff at your hotel for a recommendation.

o Wi-fi is available for a fee on select ICE train routes, including Berlin to Cologne and Frankfurt to Munich, and in DB Lounges (free in 1st class). Nearly 130 stations, including those in Berlin, Munich, Hamburg and Frankfurt, offer 30 minutes' free wi-fi with registration via Deutsche-Telekom.

o Locate wi-fi hot spots at www.hotspot-locations.com.

Legal Matters

o The permissible blood-alcohol limit is 0.05%; drivers caught exceeding this are subject to stiff fines, a confiscated licence and even jail time. Drinking in public is not illegal, but be discreet.

o Cannabis *consumption* is not illegal, but the possession, acquisition, sale and cultivation of it is considered a criminal offence. There is usually no prosecution for possessing 'small quantities', although the definition of 'small' varies by state, ranging from 6g to 20g. Dealers face far stiffer penalties, as do people caught with any other recreational drugs.

o If arrested, you have the right to make a phone call and are presumed innocent until proven guilty, although you may be held in custody until trial. If you don't know a lawyer, contact your embassy.

Money

The unit of currency in Germany is the euro (€). Euros come in seven notes (€5, €10, €20, €50, €100, €200 and €500) and eight coins (€0.01, €0.02, €0.05, €0.10, €0.20, €0.50, €1 and €2).

ATMs & Debit Cards

o The easiest and quickest way to obtain cash is by using your debit (bank) card at a *Geldautomat* (ATM) linked to international networks such as Cirrus, Plus, Star and Maestro.

o ATMs are ubiquitous and usually accessible 24/7.

o ATM cards often double as debit cards, and many

shops, hotels, restaurants and other businesses accept them for payment. Most cards use the 'chip and pin' system; instead of signing, you enter your PIN. If your card isn't chip-and-pin enabled, you may be able to sign the receipt, but ask first.

○ Deutsche Bahn (DB) ticket vending machines in train stations and local public transport may not accept non-chip-and-pin cards.

Cash

Cash is king in Germany. Always carry some with you and plan to pay cash almost everywhere. It's also a good idea to set aside a small amount of euros as an emergency stash.

Credit Cards

○ Credit cards are becoming more widely accepted, but it's best not to assume you'll be able to use one – ask first. Sometimes a minimum purchase amount applies. Even so, a piece of plastic is vital in emergencies and also useful for phone or internet bookings. Visa and MasterCard are more commonly accepted than American Express or Diner's Club.

○ Avoid getting cash advances on your credit card via ATMs, as fees are steep and you'll be charged interest immediately (in other words, there's no grace period as with purchases).

○ Report lost or stolen cards to the central number ☎116 116 or the following:
American Express ☎069-9797 1000

MasterCard ☎0800-819 1040

Visa ☎0800-814 9100

Moneychanging

○ Commercial banks usually charge a stiff fee (€5 to €10) per foreign-currency transaction, no matter the amount, if they offer exchange services at all.

○ *Wechselstuben* (currency exchange offices) at airports, train stations and in bigger towns usually charge lower fees. Traveller-geared Reisebank (www.reisebank. de) branches are ubiquitous in Germany and are usually found at train stations. They keep longer hours than banks and are usually open on weekends.

○ Exchange facilities in rural areas are rare.

Tipping

Restaurant bills always include a *Bedienung* (service charge), but most people add 5% or 10%, unless the service was truly abhorrent. It's considered rude to leave the tip on the table. When paying, tell the server the total amount you want to pay (say, if the bill is €28, you say €30). If you don't want change back, say '*Stimmt so*' (that's fine). If you order food at a counter, don't tip.

Customary Tips

WHERE & WHO	CUSTOMARY TIP
bar	€1, rounded to nearest euro
hotel porter	€1-1.50 per bag
restaurant	5-10%
room cleaners	€1-2 per day
taxi driver	10%, rounded to nearest euro
toilet attendant	€0.20-0.50
tour guide	€1-2 per person

Opening Hours

The following are typical opening hours in Germany, although these may vary seasonally and between cities and villages. For specifics, see individual listings. Where hours vary across the year, we've provided those applicable in high season.

Banks 9am to 4pm Monday to Friday, extended hours usually on Tuesday and Thursday; some open Saturday

Bars 6pm to 1am

Cafes 8am to 8pm

Clubs 11pm to early morning hours

Post offices 9am to 6pm Monday to Friday, 9am to 1pm Saturday

Restaurants 11am to 11pm (food service often stops at 9pm in rural areas)

Major stores and supermarkets 9.30am to 8pm Monday to Saturday (shorter hours outside city centres)

Practicalities

o **DVD** Germany is DVD region code 2.

o **Laundry** Virtually all towns and cities have a *Waschsalon* (launderette). Hostels often have washing machines for guest use, while hotels offer cleaning services.

o **Newspapers & Magazines** Dailies include the *Süddeutsche Zeitung*, *Die Welt* and *Der Tagesspiegel* (all quite centrist), and the more conservative *Frankfurter Allgemeine Zeitung*. *Die Zeit* is a weekly with in-depth reporting. *Der Spiegel* and *Focus* magazines are popular news weeklies.

o **Radio** Regional stations feature a mixed format of news, talk and music.

o **Weights & Measures** Metric system.

o **Women's Clothing** A German size 36 equals a US size 6 and a UK size 10, then increases in increments of two, making size 38 a US size 8 and UK size 12.

Public Holidays

Germany observes three secular and eight religious public holidays. Banks, shops, post offices and public services close on these days. States with predominantly Catholic populations, such as Bavaria and Baden-Württemberg, also celebrate Epiphany (6 January), Corpus Christi (10 days after Pentecost), Assumption Day (15 August) and All Saints' Day (1 November). Reformation Day (31 October) is only observed in eastern Germany (but not in Berlin).

The following are *gesetzliche Feiertage* (public holidays):

Neujahrstag (New Year's Day) 1 January

Ostern (Easter) March/April; Good Friday, Easter Sunday and Easter Monday

Christi Himmelfahrt (Ascension Day) Forty days after Easter

Maifeiertag/Tag der Arbeit (Labour Day) 1 May

Pfingsten (Whit/Pentecost Sunday & Monday) Fifty days after Easter

Tag der Deutschen Einheit (Day of German Unity) 3 October

Weihnachtstag (Christmas Day) 25 December

Zweiter Weihnachtstag (Boxing Day) 26 December

Telephone

German phone numbers consist of an area code, starting with 📞0, and the local number. Area codes are between three and six digits long; local numbers, between three and nine digits. If dialling from a landline within the same city, you don't need to dial the area code. You must dial it if using a mobile.

Calling Germany from abroad
Dial your country's international access code, then 📞49 (Germany's country code), then the area code (dropping the initial 0) and the local number.

Calling internationally from Germany Dial 📞00 (the international access code), then the country code, the area code (without the zero if there is one) and the local number.

Calling on the Cheap

If you have access to a private phone, you can benefit from cheaper rates by using a 'Call-by-Call' access code (📞01016 or 📞01088). Rates change daily and are published in the newspapers, or online at www.billiger telefonieren.de (in German).

With a high-speed internet connection (preferably a free wi-fi hot spot), you can make free Skype-to-Skype calls anywhere from a mobile or a computer. You can also buy Skype Credit and make inexpensive calls to a mobile or landline number.

Google Talk and FaceTime (for Apple devices only) work similarly.

Mobile Phones

o German mobile numbers begin with a four-digit prefix, such as ☏0151, ☏0157, ☏0170, ☏0178.

o Mobile (cell) phones are called 'Handys' and work on GSM 900/1800. If your home country uses a different standard, you'll need a multiband GSM phone while in Germany. Check your contract for roaming charges.

o If you have an unlocked phone that works in Germany, you may be able to cut down on roaming charges by buying a prepaid, rechargeable local SIM card for €10, including calling time. The cheapest and least complicated of these are sold at discount supermarkets, such as Aldi, Netto and Lidl. Telecommunications stores (eg Telekom, O₂ and Vodaphone) also sell SIMs. Top-up cards are widely available in kiosks and supermarkets.

o If you want to purchase an inexpensive unlocked phone, try the electronics chains Media Markt and Saturn. Prices start at €20.

o Calls made to a mobile phone are more expensive than those to a landline, but incoming calls are free.

o The use of mobile phones while driving is *verboten* (forbidden), unless you're using a headset.

School Holidays

Each state sets its own school holidays but, in general, German children have six weeks off in summer and two weeks each around Christmas, Easter and October. Traffic is worst at the beginning of school holidays in population-rich states like North Rhine–Westphalia and can become a nightmare if several states let out their schools at the same time.

Germans are big fans of miniholidays around public holidays, which are especially common in spring, when many holidays fall on a Thursday or Monday. On those 'long weekends' you can expect heavy crowds on the roads, in the towns and everywhere else. Lodging is at a premium at these times.

Phonecards

o Public pay phones are becoming increasingly rare and only work with Deutsche Telekom (DT) phonecards, available in denominations of €5, €10 and €20 at DT stores, post offices, newsagents and tourist offices. Calling internationally from pay phones is expensive.

o For long-distance or international calls, prepaid calling cards issued by other companies tend to offer better rates than DT's phone cards, although they may charge a per-call connection fee. Read the fine print on the card itself. These cards are widely available at newsagents and telephone call shops. They work from any phone.

Special Numbers

Customer service numbers in Germany often have prefixes that indicate the rate at which they're charged. The following table details the cost for calls made from landlines. Note that the per-minute charge can be as high as €0.42 for calls made from mobile phones.

NUMBER	COST
☏0800	free
☏01801	€0.04 per minute
☏01802	€0.06 per call
☏01803	€0.09 per minute
☏01804	€0.20 per call
☏01805	€0.14 per minute
☏01806	€0.20 per call
☏01807	first 30 seconds free, then €0.14 per minute
☏0900	up to €2 per minute

Time

Clocks in Germany are set to Central European time (GMT/UTC plus one hour). Daylight saving time kicks in at 2am on the last Sunday in March and ends on the last Sunday in October. The use of the 24-hour clock (eg 6.30pm is 18.30) is the norm. As daylight saving times vary across regions, the following time differences are indicative only:

CITY	NOON IN BERLIN
Auckland	11pm
Cape Town	1pm
London	11am
New York	6am
San Francisco	3am
Sydney	9pm
Tokyo	8pm

Toilets

○ German toilets are sit-down affairs. Men are expected to sit down when peeing.

○ Free-standing 24-hour self-cleaning toilet pods have become quite common. The cost is €0.50 and you have 15 minutes. Most are wheelchair-accessible.

○ Toilets in malls, clubs, beer gardens etc, often have an attendant who expects a tip of between €0.20 and €0.50.

○ Toilets in airports are usually free, but in main train stations they are often maintained by private companies like McClean, which charge as much as €1.50 for the privilege.

○ Along autobahns, rest stops with facilities are spaced about 20km to 30km apart.

Tourist Information

○ Just about every community in Germany has a walk-in tourist office where you can get advice and pick up maps and pamphlets, sometimes in English. Many also offer a room- and ticket-reservation service that's usually free. See the destination chapters for local offices.

○ With few exceptions, at least one staff member will speak English and will be happy to make the effort to help you.

○ A useful pre-trip planning source is the **German National Tourist Office** (www.germany. travel), where information is available in almost 30 languages.

Travellers with Disabilities

○ Germany is fairly progressive when it comes to barrier-free travel. Access ramps and/or lifts are available in many public buildings, including train stations, museums, concert halls and cinemas. In historic towns, though, cobblestone streets make getting around difficult.

○ Trains, trams, underground trains and buses are increasingly accessible. Some stations also have grooved platform borders to assist blind passengers in navigating. Seeing-eye dogs are allowed on all forms of public transport. For the hearing impaired, upcoming station names are often displayed electronically on public transport.

○ Newer hotels have lifts and rooms with extra-wide doors and spacious bathrooms.

○ Some car-rental agencies offer hand-controlled vehicles and vans with wheelchair lifts at no charge, but you must reserve them well in advance. In parking lots and garages, look for designated spots marked with a wheelchair symbol.

○ Many local and regional tourist offices have special brochures for people with disabilities, usually in German.

○ Good general resources include the **Deutsche Bahn Mobility Service Centre** (☏ 01806-996 633, ext 9 for English; www.bahn.com), which has train access information and route planning assistance. The website has useful information in English (search for 'barrier-free travel'). The **German National Tourist Office** (www. germany.travel) should be your first port of call, with inspirational information in English.

Visas

o EU nationals only need their passport or national identity card to enter, stay and work in Germany as a tourist. If you plan to stay longer, you must register with the authorities at the *Bürgeramt* (Citizens' Registration Office) within two weeks of your arrival.

o Citizens of Australia, Canada, Israel, Japan, New Zealand, Poland, Switzerland and the US only need a valid passport (no visa) if entering Germany as tourists for up to three months within a six-month period. Passports must be valid for another four months beyond the intended departure date. For stays exceeding 90 days, contact your nearest German embassy or consulate, and begin your visa application well in advance.

o Nationals from other countries need a Schengen Visa, named for the 1985 Schengen Agreement that abolished international border controls between most European countries. Applications for a Schengen Visa must be filed with the embassy or consulate of the country that is your primary destination. It is valid for stays of up to 90 days. Legal residency in any Schengen country makes a visa unnecessary, regardless of your nationality.

o For full details, see www.auswaertiges-amt.de and check with a German consulate in your country.

Transport

Getting There & Away

Most travellers arrive in Germany by air, or by rail and road connections from neighbouring countries. Flights, cars and tours can be booked online at www.lonelyplanet.com/bookings.

Entering the Country

Entering Germany is usually a very straightforward procedure. If you're arriving from any of the 25 other Schengen countries, such as the Netherlands, Poland, Austria or the Czech Republic, you no longer have to show your passport or go through customs in Germany, no matter which nationality you are. If you're coming in from non-Schengen countries, full border procedures apply.

Air

Frankfurt Airport is the main gateway for transcontinental flights, although Düsseldorf and Munich also receive their share of overseas air traffic. Until the opening of the new Berlin Brandenburg Airport, flights to Berlin will arrive at its two smaller international airports, Tegel and Schönefeld. There are also sizeable airports in Hamburg, Cologne/Bonn and Stuttgart, and smaller ones in such cities as Bremen, Dresden, Hanover, Leipzig-Halle, Münster-Osnabrück and Nuremberg.

Lufthansa, Germany's national flagship carrier and a Star Alliance member, operates a vast network of domestic and international flights and has one of the world's best safety records. Practically every other national carrier from around the world serves Germany, along with budget airlines Air Berlin (www.airberlin. com), EasyJet (www.easyjet.com), Flybe (www.flybe. com), airBaltic (www.airbaltic.com), Ryanair (www.ryanair.com) and Germanwings (www.germanwings. com). Note that Ryanair usually flies to remote airports that are often little more than recycled military airstrips. Frankfurt-Hahn, for instance, is actually near the Moselle River, about 110km northwest of Frankfurt proper.

Bus

Long-distance coach travel to Germany from such cities as Milan, Vienna, Amsterdam and Copenhagen has become a viable option thanks to a new crop of companies offering good-value connections aboard comfortable buses with snack bars and free wi-fi. Major operators include **MeinFernbus** (📞0180-515 9915; www.meinfernbus.de), **Flixbus** (📞01807-1239 9123; www.flixbus.com), **Megabus** (📞in the UK 0900 1600 900; www.megabus.com), **Berlin-linienbus** (📞030-338 4480; www.berlinlinienbus.de) and Eurolines (www.eurolines.com). For routes, times and prices, check www.busliniensuche.de (also in English).

A backpacker-geared hop-on, hop-off service, **Busabout** (📞in the UK 08450 267 514; www.busabout.com) runs coaches along three interlocking European loops between May and October. Passes are sold online and through travel agents.

Germany is part of the north loop. Within Germany, the service stops in Berlin, Dresden, Munich and Stuttgart. Loops can be combined. In Munich,

for instance, the north loop intersects with the south loop to Italy.

Trips on one loop start at €569, on two loops €979 and on three €1159. The Flexitrip Pass, which allows you to travel between cities across different loops, costs €489/537/569/599 for six/seven/eight/nine stops.

Car & Motorcycle

When bringing your own vehicle to Germany, you need a valid driving licence, car registration and proof of third-party insurance. Foreign cars must display a nationality sticker unless they have official European plates. You also need to carry a warning (hazard) triangle and a first-aid kit.

There are no special requirements for crossing the border into Germany by car. Under the Schengen Agreement there are no passport controls if entering the country from the Netherlands, Belgium, Lux-

embourg, Denmark, Austria, Switzerland, the Czech Republic and Poland.

From the Eurotunnel

Coming from the UK, the fastest way to the Continent is via the **Eurotunnel** (📞in Germany 01805-000 248, in the UK 08443 35 35 35; www.eurotunnel.com). These shuttle trains whisk cars, motorbikes, bicycles and coaches from Folkestone in England through the Channel Tunnel to Coquelles (near Calais, in France) in about 35 minutes. From there, you can be in Germany in about three hours. Loading and unloading takes about one hour.

Shuttles run daily around the clock, with up to four departures hourly during peak periods. Fares are calculated per vehicle, including up to nine passengers, and depend on such factors as time of day, season and length of stay. Standard one-way tickets start at £55. The website and travel agents have full details.

Climate Change & Travel

Every form of transport that relies on carbon-based fuel generates CO_2, the main cause of human-induced climate change. Modern travel is dependent on aeroplanes, which might use less fuel per kilometre per person than most cars but travel much greater distances. The altitude at which aircraft emit gases (including CO_2) and particles also contributes to their climate change impact. Many websites offer 'carbon calculators' that allow people to estimate the carbon emissions generated by their journey and, for those who wish to do so, to offset the impact of the greenhouse gases emitted with contributions to portfolios of climate-friendly initiatives throughout the world. Lonely Planet offsets the carbon footprint of all staff and author travel.

Train

Rail services link Germany with virtually every country in Europe. In Germany ticketing is handled by Deutsche Bahn (DB; www.bahn.com). Long-distance trains connecting major German cities with those in other countries are called EuroCity (EC) trains. Seat reservations are essential during the peak summer season and around major holidays, and are recommended at other times.

Deutsche Bahn's overnight service is called **City Night Line** (☎0180-699 6633; www.nachtzugreise.de) and offers three levels of comfort:

Schlafwagen (sleeping car; €46 to €176 supplement) Private, air-conditioned compartment for up to three passengers; the deluxe version (*1. Klasse*) has a shower and toilet.

Liegewagen (couchette; €21 to €70 supplement) Sleeps up to six people; when you book an individual berth, you must share the compartment with others; women may ask for a single-sex couchette at the time of booking but are advised to book early.

Sitzwagen (seat carriage; €10 to €49 supplement) Roomy reclining seat.

Resources

www.raileurope.com Detailed train information and ticket and train-pass sales from Rail Europe.

www.railteam.eu Journey planner provided by an alliance of seven European railways, including Eurostar, Deutsche Bahn and France's SNCF. No booking function yet.

www.seat61.com Comprehensive trip-planning information, including ferry details from the UK.

Eurostar

Thanks to the Channel Tunnel, travelling by train between the UK and Germany is actually a fast and enjoyable option. High-speed **Eurostar** (☎from outside the UK +44 1233 617 575, in the UK 03432 186 186; www.eurostar.com) passenger trains hurtle at least 10 times daily between London and Paris (the journey takes 2½ hours) or Brussels (two hours). In either city you can change to regular or other high-speed trains to destinations in Germany.

Eurostar fares depend on carriage class, time of day, season and destination. Children, rail-pass holders and those aged between 12 and 25 and over 60 qualify for discounts. For the latest fare information, including promotions and special packages, check the website.

Rail Passes

If you want to cover lots of territory in and around Germany within a specific time, a rail pass is a convenient and good-value option. Passes cover unlimited travel during their period of validity on national railways as well as on some private lines, ferries and river-boat services.

There are two types: the Eurail Pass, for people living outside Europe, and the InterRail Pass, for residents of Europe, including residents of Russia and Turkey.

Eurail

Eurail Passes (www.eurail.com) are valid for travel in up to 28 countries and need to be purchased – on the website, through a travel agent or at www.raileurope.com – before you leave your home country. Various passes are available:

Global Pass Unlimited 1st-class travel for 15 or 21 consecutive days, or one, two or three months. There are also versions that give you five days of travel within a 10-day period or 10 or 15 days of travel within a two-month period. The 15-day continuous version costs €580.

Select Pass Five, six, eight or 10 days of travel within two months in four bordering countries in 1st class; a five-day pass in three countries costs €413.

Regional Pass Gets you around two neighbouring countries on four, five, six, eight or 10 days within two months. The Germany–Austria Pass for five days costs €263 in 2nd class or €328 in 1st class.

Groups of two to five people travelling together save 15% off the regular adult fares. If you're under 26, prices drop 35%, but you must travel in 2nd class. Children aged between four and 11 years get a 50% discount on the adult fare. Children under four years travel free.

The website has details, as well as a ticket-purchasing function allowing you to pay in several currencies.

InterRail

InterRail Passes (www.interrail.eu) are valid for unlimited travel in 30 countries. As with the Eurail Pass, you can choose from several schemes:

Global Pass Unlimited travel in 30 countries, available for 15 days (€414), 22 days (€484) or one month (€626) of continuous travel; for five travel days within

Low-Emission Stickers

To decrease air pollution caused by fine particles, most German cities now have low-emissions environmental zones that may only be entered by cars displaying an *Umweltplakette* (emissions sticker, sometimes also called *Feinstaubplakette*). And yes, this includes foreign vehicles. No stickers are needed for motorcycles.

The easiest way to obtain the sticker is by ordering it online from www.green-zones.eu, a handy website in many languages. The cost is €29.95. You can cut this amount in half if you order from the TÜV (Technical Inspection Authority) at www.tuev-sued.de or www.tuev-nord.de, both of which provide easy instructions in English. Once in Germany, stickers are also available from designated repair centres, car dealers and vehicle-licensing offices. Drivers caught without one will be fined €80.

a 10-day period (€264) or for 10 travel days within a 22-day period (€374).

Germany Pass Buys three/four/six/eight days of travel within a one-month period for €205/226/288/319. This pass is not available if you are a resident of Germany.

Prices quoted are for one adult travelling in 2nd class. Different prices apply to 1st-class tickets and for travellers under 26 or over 60. Children under four travel for free and do not need a pass. Up to two children under 11 travel free with a child pass if accompanied by at least one person with an adult pass.

Boat

Germany's main ferry ports are Kiel and Travemünde (near Lübeck) in Schleswig-Holstein, and Rostock and Sassnitz (on Rügen Island) in Mecklenburg–Western Pomerania. All have services to Scandinavia. Timetables change from season to season.

Return tickets are often cheaper than two one-way tickets. Some ferry companies now set fares the way budget airlines do: the earlier you book, the less you pay. Seasonal demand is a crucial factor (school holidays and July and August are especially busy), as is the time of day (an early-evening ferry can cost much more than one at 4am). For overnight ferries, cabin size, location and amenities affect the price. Book well in advance if you're bringing a car.

People under 25 and over 60 may qualify for discounts. To get the best fares, check out the booking service offered by Ferry Savers (www.ferrysavers.com).

Getting Around

Air

Most large and many smaller German cities have their own airports and numerous carriers operate domestic flights within Germany. Unless you're flying from one end of the country to the other, say Berlin to Munich or Hamburg to Munich, planes are only marginally quicker than trains once you factor in the time it takes to get to and from airports.

Lufthansa has the densest route network. The other main airlines offering domestic flights are:

Air Berlin (www.airberlin.com) Flies to Berlin-Tegel, Cologne-Bonn, Dresden, Düsseldorf, Frankfurt, Friedrichshafen, Hanover, Karlsruhe-Baden-Baden, Leipzig-Halle, Memmingen, Münster-Osnabrück, Munich, Nuremberg, Paderborn, Saarbrücken, Stuttgart, Sylt.

Germanwings (www.germanwings.com) Destination cities are Berlin-Schönefeld, Berlin-Tegel, Cologne-Bonn, Dortmund, Dresden, Düsseldorf, Hamburg, Hanover, Karlsruhe-Baden-Baden, Leipzig-Halle, Nuremberg, Rostock, Stuttgart, Usedom.

Bicycle

Cycling is allowed on all roads and highways but not on the autobahns (motorways). Cyclists must follow the same rules of the road as cars and motorcycles. Helmets are not compulsory (not even for children), but wearing one is common sense. Dedicated bike lanes are common in bigger cities.

Bicycles may be taken on most trains but require a separate ticket (*Fahrradkarte*), costing €9 per trip on long-distance trains (IC and EC and City Night Line). You need to reserve a space at least one day ahead and leave your bike in the bike compartment, which is usually at the beginning or end of the train. There may be a fee on some services. Bicycles are not allowed on high-speed ICE trains.

Many regional bus companies have vehicles with special bike racks. Bicycles are also allowed on practically all boat and ferry services.

Boat

Considering that Germany abuts two seas and has a lake- and river-filled interior, don't be surprised to find yourself in a boat at some point. For basic transport, ferry boats are primarily used when travelling to or between the East Frisian Islands in Lower Saxony; the North Frisian Islands in Schleswig-Holstein; Helgoland, which also belongs to Schleswig-Holstein; and the islands of Poel, Rügen and Hiddensee in Mecklenburg–Western Pomerania.

Scheduled boat services operate along sections of the Rhine, the Elbe and the Danube. There are also ferry services in river sections with no or only a few bridges, as well as on major lakes such as the Chiemsee and Lake Starnberg in Bavaria and Lake Constance in Baden-Württemberg.

From around April to October, local operators run scenic river or lake cruises lasting from one hour to a full day.

Bus
Local & Regional

Buses are generally slower, less dependable and more polluting than trains, but in some rural areas they may be your only option for getting around without your own vehicle. This is especially true of the Harz Mountains, sections of the Bavarian Forest and the Alpine foothills. Separate bus companies, each with its own tariffs and schedules, operate in the different regions.

The frequency of services varies from 'rarely' to 'constantly'. Commuter-geared routes offer limited or no service in the evenings and at weekends, so keep this in mind or risk finding yourself stuck in a remote place on a Saturday night. Make it a habit to ask about special fare deals, such as daily or weekly passes or tourist tickets.

In cities, buses generally converge at the Busbahnhof or Zentraler Omnibus Bahnhof (ZOB; central bus station), which is often near the Hauptbahnhof (central train station).

Long-Distance Coaches

Thanks to the 2013 lifting of an anachronistic ban on long-distance domestic bus travel (passed in 1931 to protect the then state-owned railway system), the route network has grown enormously, making exploring Germany by coach easy, inexpensive and popular. Buses are modern, clean, comfortable and air-conditioned. Most companies offer snacks and beverages as well as free onboard wi-fi.

Fierce competition has kept prices extremely low. A trip from Berlin to Hamburg costs as little as €8, while the fare from Frankfurt to Munich averages €15.

MeinFernbus (www.meinfernbus.de), Flixbus (www.flixbus.com), Postbus (www.postbus.de), Berlinlinienbus (www.berlinlinienbus.de) and Eurolines (www.eurolines.com) are the biggest operators, but there are dozens of smaller, regional ones as well. A handy site for finding out which operator goes where, when and for how much is www.busliniensuche.de.

From April to October, special tourist-geared service the **Romantic Road Coach** (☏09851-551 387; www.romantic-road.com) runs one coach daily in each direction between Frankfurt and Füssen (for Schloss Neuschwanstein) via Munich; the entire trip takes around 12 hours. There's no charge for breaking the journey and continuing the next day. Note that buses get incredibly crowded in summer. Tickets are available for the entire route or for short segments. Buy them online or from travel agents, **EurAide** (Map p112; www.euraide.de; Desk 1, Reisezentrum, Hauptbahnhof; ◷10am-7pm Mon-Fri Mar-Apr & Aug-Dec, to 8pm May-Jul; 🚃Hauptbahnhof, Ⓤ Hauptbahnhof, Ⓢ Hauptbahnhof) in Munich or *Reisezentrum* offices in larger train stations.

Car & Motorcycle

German roads are excellent and motoring around the country can be a lot of fun. The country's pride and joy is its 11,000km network of autobahns (motorways, freeways). Every 40km to 60km, you'll find elaborate service areas with petrol stations, toilet facilities and restaurants; many are open 24 hours. In between are rest stops *(Rastplatz),* which usually have picnic tables and toilet facilities. Orange emergency call boxes are spaced about 2km apart.

Autobahns are supplemented by an extensive network of *Bundesstrassen* (secondary 'B' roads, highways) and smaller *Landstrassen* (country roads). No tolls are charged on any public roads.

If your car is not equipped with a navigational system, having a good map or road atlas is essential, especially when negotiating the tangle

of country roads. Navigating in Germany is not done by the points of the compass. That is to say that you'll find no signs saying 'north' or 'west'. Rather, you'll see signs pointing you in the direction of a city, so you'd best have that map right in your lap to stay oriented. Maps cost a few euros and are sold at bookstores, train stations, airports and petrol stations. The best are published by Freytag & Berndt, ADAC, Falk and Euromap.

Driving in the cities can be stressful thanks to congestion and the expense and scarcity of parking. In city centres, parking is usually limited to parking lots and garages charging between €0.50 and €2.50 per hour. Note that some parking lots *(Parkplatz)* and garages *(Parkhaus)* close at night and charge an overnight fee. Many have special parking slots for women that are especially well lit and close to exits.

Many cities have electronic parking-guidance systems directing you to the nearest garage and indicating the number of available spaces. Street parking usually works on the pay-and-display system and tends to be short term (one or two hours) only. For low-cost or free long-term and overnight parking, consider leaving your car outside the centre in a Park & Ride (P+R) lot.

Automobile Associations

Germany's main motoring organisation, the **ADAC** (Allgemeiner Deutscher Automo-

bil-Club; 🖉information 0800 510 1112, roadside assistance 0180 222 2222; www.adac.de), has offices in all major cities and many smaller ones. Its roadside-assistance program is also available to members of its affiliates, including British (AA), American (AAA) and Canadian (CAA) associations.

Driving Licence

Drivers need a valid driving licence. International Driving Permits (IDP) are not compulsory, but having one may help German police make sense of your home licence (always carry that, too) and may simplify the car- or motorcycle-hire process.

Car Hire

As anywhere, rates for car hire vary considerably, but you should be able to get an economy-size vehicle from about €40 to €60 per day, plus insurance and taxes. Expect surcharges for rentals originating at airports and train stations, additional drivers and one-way hire. Child or infant safety seats may be hired for about €5 per day and should be reserved at the time of booking.

Rental cars with automatic transmission are rare in Germany and will usually need to be ordered well in advance.

To hire your own wheels, you'll need to be at least 25 years old and possess a valid driving licence and a major credit card. Some companies lease to drivers between the ages of 21 and 24 for an additional charge (about €12 to €20 per day). Younger people or those without a credit card are usually out of luck. For insurance reasons, driving into an Eastern European country, such as the Czech Republic or Poland, is often a no-no.

All the main international companies maintain branches at airports, major train stations and towns. These include the following:

Alamo (☏0800 723 9253; www.alamo.com)

Avis (☏01806-217 702; www.avis.de)

Europcar (☏040-520 187 654; www.europcar.com)

Hertz (☏01806-333 535; www.hertz.com)

National (☏0800-723 8828; www.nationalcar.com)

Sixt (☏01806-25 25 25; www.sixt.de)

Pre-booked and prepaid packages arranged in your home country usually work out much cheaper than on-the-spot rentals. The same is true of fly-drive packages. Deals can be found on the internet and through companies including **Auto Europe** (☏in Germany 0800-560 0333; www.autoeurope.com), **Holiday Autos** (☏in the UK 020 3740 9859; www.holidayautos.co.uk) and **DriveAway Holidays** (☏in Australia 1300 723 972; www.driveaway.com.au).

Peer-to-Peer Rentals

Peer-to-peer car rental is still in its infancy in Germany. The main service is Drivy (www.drivy.de). You need to sign up on its website, find a car you'd like to rent, contact the owner and sign the rental agreement at the time you're handed the keys. Renters need to be at least 21 years old and to have had a driving licence for at least two years. If your licence was not issued in an EU member country, Norway, Iceland or Liechtenstein, you need to have an International Drivers' License. Payment is by credit card or PayPal. Rentals include full insurance and roadside assistance. For full details, see the website.

Insurance

German law requires that all registered vehicles, including those brought in from abroad, carry third-party-liability insurance. You could face huge costs by driving uninsured or underinsured. Germans are very fussy about their cars, and even nudging someone's bumper when jostling out of a tight parking space may well result in your having to pay for an entirely new one.

Normally, private cars registered and insured in another European country do not require additional insurance, but do check this with your insurance provider before leaving home. Also keep a record of who to contact in case of a breakdown or accident.

When hiring a vehicle, make sure your contract includes adequate liability insurance at the very minimum. Rental agencies almost never include insurance that covers damage to the vehicle itself, called Collision Damage Waiver (CDW) or Loss Damage Waiver (LDW). It's optional, but driving without it is not recommended. Some credit-card companies cover CDW/LDW for a certain period if you charge the entire rental to your card; always confirm with your card issuer what it covers in Germany. Note that some local agencies may refuse to accept your credit-card coverage as proof of insurance.

Road Rules

Driving is on the right-hand side of the road and standard international signs are in use. If you're unfamiliar with these, pick up a pamphlet at your local motoring organisation or visit www.adac.de (search for 'traffic signs'). Obey the road rules and speed limits carefully.

Speed- and red-light cameras as well as radar traps are common and notices are sent to the car's registration address wherever that may be. If you're renting a car, the police will obtain your home address from the rental agency. There's a long list of fineable actions, including some perhaps surprising ones such as using abusive language or gestures and running out of petrol on the autobahn.

The usual speed limits are 50km/h on main city streets and 100km/h on highways, unless otherwise marked.

Limits drop to 30km/h in residential streets. And yes, it's true: there really are no speed limits on autobahns... in theory. In fact, there are many stretches where slower speeds must be observed (near towns, road construction), so be sure to keep an eye out for those signs or risk getting ticketed. And, obviously, the higher the speed, the higher the fuel consumption and emissions.

Other important driving rules:

○ The highest permissible blood-alcohol level for drivers is 0.05%, which for most people equates to one glass of wine or two small beers.

○ Seat belts are mandatory for all passengers, including those in the back seat, and there's a €30 fine if you get caught not wearing one. If you're in an accident, not wearing a seat belt may invalidate your insurance. Children need a child seat if under four years and a seat cushion if under 12; they may not ride in the front until age 13.

○ Motorcyclists must wear a helmet.

○ Mobile phones may be used only if they are equipped with a hands-free kit or speakerphone.

○ Pedestrians at crossings have absolute right of way over all motor vehicles.

○ Always watch out for cyclists when turning right; they have the right of way.

○ Right turns at a red light are only legal if there's a green arrow pointing to the right.

Local Transport

Germany's cities and larger towns have efficient public-transport systems. Bigger cities, such as Berlin and Munich, integrate buses, trams, U-Bahn (underground, subway) trains and S-Bahn (suburban) trains into a single network.

Fares are determined by zones or time travelled, sometimes by both. A multi-ticket strip (*Streifenkarte* or *4-Fahrtenkarte*) or day pass (*Tageskarte*) generally offers better value than a single-ride ticket. Normally, tickets must be stamped upon boarding in order to be valid. Fines are levied if you're caught without a valid ticket.

Bicycle

Germans love to cycle, be it for errands, commuting, fitness or pleasure. Many cities have dedicated bicycle lanes, which must be used unless obstructed. There's no helmet law, not even for children, although using one is recommended, for obvious reasons. Bicycles must be equipped with a white light at the front, a red one at the back and yellow reflectors on the wheels and pedals.

Bus & Tram

Buses are a ubiquitous form of public transport and practically all towns have their own comprehensive network. Buses run at regular intervals, with restricted services in the evenings and at weekends. Some cities operate night buses along popular routes to get night owls safely home.

Occasionally, buses are supplemented by trams (*Strassenbahn*), which are usually faster because they travel on their own tracks, largely independent of other traffic. In city centres they sometimes run underground. Bus and tram drivers generally sell single tickets and day passes only.

S-Bahn

Metropolitan areas, such as Berlin and Munich, have a system of suburban trains called the S-Bahn. They are faster and cover a wider area than buses or trams but tend to be less frequent. S-Bahn lines are often linked to the national rail network and sometimes connect urban centres. Rail passes are generally valid on these services. Specific S-Bahn lines are abbreviated with 'S' followed by the number (eg S1, S7).

Taxi

Taxis are expensive and, given the excellent public-transport systems, not recommended unless you're in a real hurry. (They can actually be slower than trains or trams if you're stuck in traffic.) Cabs are metered and charged at a base rate (flag fall) plus a per-kilometre fee. These charges are fixed but vary from city to city. Some drivers charge extra for bulky luggage or night-time rides. It's rarely possible to flag down a taxi; more typical is to order one by phone (look up *Taxiruf* in the phone book) or board at a taxi rank. If you're at a hotel or restaurant, ask staff to call one for you. Taxis also often wait outside theatres or performance venues. Smartphone owners can order a taxi via the Mytaxi app (downloadable for free via iTunes or Google Play) in over 30 German cities.

Uber (www.uber.com), an app that allows private drivers to connect with potential passengers, is not widely used in Germany after a court ruled in May 2015 that the services UberPop and UberBlack violate German transportation laws. Uber reacted by creating UberX, which uses only professionally licensed drivers and is available in Düsseldorf, Frankfurt, Hamburg and Munich. Trip costs tend to be between 3% and 12% less than regular taxi fares. Exclusive to Berlin as of now is UberTaxi, which hooks passengers up with regular taxis. Normal rates apply.

U-Bahn

Underground (subway) trains are known as U-Bahn in Germany and are the fastest form of travel in big cities. Route maps are posted in all stations, and at many you'll be able to pick up a printed copy from the stationmaster or ticket office. The frequency of trains usually fluctuates with demand, meaning there are more trains during commuter rush hours than in the middle of the day. Tickets bought from vending machines must usually be validated before the start of your journey. Specific U-Bahn lines are abbreviated with 'U' followed by the number (eg U1, U7).

Train

Germany's rail system is operated almost entirely by Deutsche Bahn (DB; www.bahn.com), with a variety of train types serving just about every corner of the country. The DB website has detailed information (in English and other languages), as well as a ticket-purchasing function with detailed instructions.

There is a growing number of routes operated by private companies but integrated into the DB network, such as the Ostdeutsche Eisenbahn in Saxony and the Bayerische Oberlandbahn in Bavaria.

Tickets may be bought using a credit card up to 10 minutes before departure at no surcharge. You will need to present a printout of your ticket, as well as the credit card used to buy it, to the conductor. Smartphone users can register with Deutsche Bahn and download the ticket via the free DB Navigator app.

Tickets are also available from vending machines and agents at the *Reisezentrum* (travel centre) in train stations. The latter charge a service fee but are useful if you need assistance with planning your itinerary (if necessary, ask for an English-speaking clerk).

Children under 15 travel for free if accompanied by at least one parent or grandparent. The only proviso is that the names of children aged between six and 14 must be registered on your ticket at the time of purchase. Children under six always travel free and without a ticket.

Smaller stations have only a few ticket windows and the smallest ones are equipped with vending machines only. English instructions are usually provided.

Tickets sold on board incur a surcharge and are not available on regional trains (RE, RB, IRE) or the S-Bahn. Agents, conductors and machines usually accept debit cards and major credit cards. With few exceptions (station unstaffed, vending machine broken), you will be fined if caught without a ticket.

Most train stations have coin-operated lockers (*Schliessfach*) costing from €1 to €4 per 24-hour period. Larger stations have staffed left-luggage offices (*Gepäckaufbewahrung*), which are a bit more expensive than lockers. If you leave your suitcase overnight, you'll be charged for two full days.

A Primer on Train Types

Here's the low-down on the alphabet soup of trains operated by Deutsche Bahn (DB):

InterCity Express (ICE) Long-distance, high-speed trains that stop at major cities only and run at one- or two-hour intervals.

InterCity (IC), EuroCity (EC) Long-distance trains that are fast, but slower than the ICE; also run at one- and two-hour intervals and stop in major cities. EC trains run to major cities in neighbouring countries.

InterRegio-Express (IRE) Regional trains connecting cities with few intermediary stops.

City Night Line (CNL) Night trains with sleeper cars and couchettes.

Regional Bahn (RB) Local trains, mostly in rural areas, with frequent stops; the slowest in the system.

Regional Express (RE) Local trains with limited stops that link rural areas with metropolitan centres and the S-Bahn.

S-Bahn Local trains operating within a city and its suburban area.

Reservations

o Seat reservations for long-distance travel are highly recommended, especially if you're travelling anytime on Friday, on a Sunday afternoon, during holiday periods or in summer. Choose from window or aisle seats, row or facing seats, or seats with a fixed table.

o Reservations are €4.50 (free if travelling 1st class) and can be made online and at ticket counters until 10 minutes before departure. You need to claim your seat within 15 minutes of boarding the train.

Classes

German trains have 1st- and 2nd-class cars, both of them modern and comfortable. If you're not too fussy, paying extra for 1st class is usually not worth it, except perhaps on busy travel days (Friday, Sunday afternoon and holidays), when 2nd-class cars can get very crowded. Seating is either in compartments of up to six people or in open-plan carriages with panoramic windows. On ICE trains you'll also enjoy reclining seats, tables, and audio systems in your armrest. Newer-generation ICE trains also have individual laptop outlets, mobile-phone reception in 1st class and, on some routes, wi-fi access.

Trains and stations are nonsmoking. ICE, IC and EC trains are air-conditioned and have a restaurant or self-service bistro.

Tickets

Standard, non-discounted train tickets tend to be quite expensive. On specific trains, a limited number of tickets is available at the discounted *Sparpreis* (saver fare), costing €29 to €99 in 2nd class and €49 to €149 in 1st. You need to book early or be lucky to snag one of these tickets, though. There's a €5 service charge if tickets are purchased by phone, from a travel agent or in the station ticket office. Other promotions, discounted tickets and special offers become available all the time. Check www.bahn.com for the latest deals.

German Rail Pass

If your permanent residence is outside Europe (which for this purpose includes Turkey and Russia), you qualify for the German Rail Pass (GRP). Tickets are sold through www.germanrailpasses.com and www.raileurope.com and by agents in your home country.

o The **GRP Flexi** allows for three, four, five, seven or 10 days of travel within one month.

o The **GRP Consecutive** is available for five, 10 or 15 consecutive days.

○ Passes are valid on all trains within Germany, including ICE trains, and IC buses to Strasbourg, Prague, Krakow, Antwerp, Brussels, London, Zagreb and Copenhagen; and on EuroCity trains to Kufstein, Innsbruck, Bolzano, Trento, Verona, Bologna, Liège and Brussels.

○ Sample fares: three-day pass €255/189 in 1st/2nd class, seven-day pass €363/269 in 1st/2nd class. Children between six and 11 pay half fare. Children under six travel free.

○ Those aged 12 to 25 qualify for the **German Rail Youth Pass**, starting at €204/151 in 1st/2nd class for three days of travel within one month.

○ Two adults travelling together can use the **German Rail Twin Pass**, starting at €382/284 in 1st/2nd class for three days of travel within one month.

Language

German pronunciation is very similar to that of English, and if you read our pronunciation guides below as if they were English, you'll be understood just fine. Note that in our guides 'ew' is pronounced like 'ee' with rounded lips, and that 'kh' and 'r' are both throaty sounds. Stressed syllables are in italics.

To enhance your trip with a phrasebook, visit **lonelyplanet.com**. Lonely Planet iPhone phrasebooks are available through the Apple App store.

Basics

Hello.
Guten Tag.   goo·ten taak
How are you?
Wie geht es Ihnen?   vee geyt es ee·nen
I'm fine, thanks.
Gut, danke.   goot dang·ke
Excuse me./Sorry.
Entschuldigung.   ent·shul·di·gung
Yes./No.
Ja./Nein.   yaa/nain
Please./You're welcome./That's fine.
Bitte.   bi·te
Thank you.
Danke.   dang·ke
Goodbye.
Auf Wiedersehen.   owf vee·der·zey·en
Do you speak English?
Sprechen Sie   shpre·khen zee
Englisch?   eng·lish
I don't understand.
Ich verstehe nicht.   ikh fer·shtey·e nikht
How much is this?
Was kostet das?   vas kos·tet das
Can you reduce the price a little?
Können Sie mit dem   ker·nen zee mit dem
Preis heruntergehen?   prais he·run·ter·gey·en

Accommodation

I'd like to book a room.
Ich möchte bitte ein   ikh merkh·te bi·te ain
Zimmer reservieren.   tsi·mer re·zer·vee·ren

How much is it per night?
Wie viel kostet es   vee feel kos·tet es
pro Nacht?   praw nakht

Eating & Drinking

I'd like ..., please.
Ich hätte gern..., bitte.   ikh he·te gern... bi·te
That was delicious!
Das hat hervorragend   das hat her·fawr·
geschmeckt!   rah·gent ge·shmekt
Bring the bill/check, please.
Die Rechnung, bitte.   dee rekh·nung bi·te
I don't eat ...
Ich esse kein ...   ikh e·se kain ...

I'm allergic to ...
Ich bin allergisch   ikh bin a·lair·gish
gegen ...   gey·gen ...
   fish   *Fisch*   fish
   poultry   *Geflügelfleisch*   ge·flew·gel·flaish
   red meat *Rind-und*   rint·unt
                 Lammfleisch   lam·flaish

Emergencies

Help!
Hilfe!   hil·fe
I'm ill.
Ich bin krank.   ikh bin krangk
Call a doctor!
Rufen Sie einen Arzt!   roo·fen zee ai·nen artst
Call the police!
Rufen Sie die Polizei!   roo·fen zee dee po·li·tsai

Directions

Where's a/the ...?
Wo ist ...?   vaw ist ...
   ATM
   der Geldautomat   dair gelt·ow·to·maat
   bank
   eine Bank   ai·ne bangk
   market
   der Markt   dair markt
   museum
   das Museum   das mu·zey·um
   restaurant
   ein Restaurant   ain res·to·rahng
   toilet
   die Toilette   dee to·a·le·te
   tourist office
   das Fremden-   das frem·den·
   verkehrsbüro   fer·kairs·bew·raw

Behind The Scenes

Acknowledgements

Climate map data adapted from Peel MC, Finlayson BL & McMahon TA (2007) 'Updated World Map of the Koppen-Geiger Climate Classification', *Hydrology and Earth System Sciences*, 11, 163344.

This Book

This guidebook was curated by Marc Di Duca, who also researched and wrote for it along with Kerry Christiani, Catherine Le Nevez, Tom Masters, Andrea Schulte-Peevers, Ryan Ver Berkmoes and Benedict Walker.

This guidebook was commissioned in Lonely Planet's Melbourne office, and produced by the following:

Destination Editor Gemma Graham
Series Designer Campbell McKenzie
Cartographic Series Designer Wayne Murphy
Associate Product Directors Sasha Baskett, Liz Heynes
Product Editor Kate Mathews
Senior Cartographers Corey Hutchison, Anthony Phelan
Book Designer Wendy Wright
Assisting Editor Gabrielle Stefanos
Cartographers Julie Dodkins, Gabriel Lindquist
Cover Researchers Brendan Dempsey-Spencer, Naomi Parker

Thanks to Andrew Bigger, Katie Coffee, Daniel Corbett, Ruth Cosgrove, James Hardy, Anna Harris, Kerrianne Jenkins, Elizabeth Jones, Indra Kilfoyle, Valentina Kremenchutskaya, Georgina Leslie, Dan Moore, Jenna Myers, Darren O'Connell, Katie O'Connell, Kirsten Rawlings, Diana Saengkham, Dianne Schallmeiner, Ellie Simpson, Lyahna Spencer, John Taufa, Angela Tinson, Lauren Wellicome, Juan Winata

Send Us Your Feedback

We love to hear from travellers – your comments keep us on our toes and help make our books better. Our well-travelled team reads every word on what you loved or loathed about this book. Although we cannot reply individually to postal submissions, we always guarantee that your feedback goes straight to the appropriate authors, in time for the next edition. Each person who sends us information is thanked in the next edition, the most useful submissions are rewarded with a selection of digital PDF chapters.

Visit lonelyplanet.com/contact to submit your updates and suggestions or to ask for help. Our award-winning website also features inspirational travel stories, news and discussions.

Note: We may edit, reproduce and incorporate your comments in Lonely Planet products such as guidebooks, websites and digital products, so let us know if you don't want your comments reproduced or your name acknowledged. For a copy of our privacy policy visit lonelyplanet.com/privacy.

Index

A

accommodation 293-5
  language 314
activities 279-81, *see also
  individual activities*
air travel 303, 306
aquariums 117
archaeological sites, *see* Cold
  War sites, Roman sites, WWII
  sites
architecture 79, 277
art galleries, *see* museums &
  galleries
arts 275-8
ATMs 298-9
Augsburg 209

B

Bacharach 236
Baden-Baden 19, 160-1, 169-71
beer 122, 226, 254, 288-90
beer festivals 100-1
beer gardens 290
Beilstein 257
Berlin 6, 35-83, **36**, **44-5**, **65**,
  66-7, **71**, **72**, **83**
  accommodation 83
  climate 37
  drinking 76-9
  entertainment 79-80
  events 36
  festivals 36
  food 74-6
  information 80
  itineraries 2, 22, 37, 44-5,
    60-1, 62-3, **44-5**, **61**, **63**
  nightlife 76-9

planning 37
shopping 73
sights 64-71
tours 72-3
travel to/from 81
travel with 37
travel within 81-2
Berlin Wall 42-5, 272-3, **44-5**
bicycle travel, *see* cycling
Bingen 234-5
Black Forest, the 10, 156-73, **157**
  travel to/from 156
boat travel 306, 307
  Moselle Valley 253
  Rhine Valley 235
  Starnberg 128
books 29, 275-6
Boppard 238-9
Brandenburger Tor
  (Brandenburg Gate) 40-1
Brandt, Willy 272
Braubach 241
breweries 153, 254
Burg Reichenstein 235
bus travel 303-4, 307-8, 310
business hours 33, 299-300

C

cakes 287
car travel 304, 308-10, *see also*
  drives
castles & palaces 25
  accommodation 294
  Belvedere auf dem
    Pfingstberg 95
  Burg Eltz 258
  Burg Landshut 255
  Burg Metternich 257
  Burg Maus 237
  Hohes Schloss 140
  Kaiserburg 194
  Marksburg 241
  Marmorpalais 93
  Mäuseturm 235

Potsdamer Stadtschloss
  (Landtag Brandenburg) 92
Reichsburg 252
Residenz 102-5
Residenzschloss 180-1
Schloss Charlottenburg 52-5
Schloss Cecilienhof 93
Schloss Heidelberg 148-9
Schloss Hohenschwangau
  138-9
Schloss Neuschwanstein 9,
  18, 133-41
Schloss Nymphenburg 107
Schloss Sanssouci 88-91
Schloss Stolzenfels 240
Zwinger 182
cathedrals, *see* churches &
  cathedrals
cell phones 32, 301
Checkpoint Charlie 64
children, travel with 30-1
Christmas markets 28
  Berlin 36
  Munich 127
  Nuremberg 199
churches & cathedrals 24
  Asamkirche 107
  Berliner Dom 49
  Frauenkirche 178-9
  Heiliggeistkirche 146
  Jacobskirche 210
  Jesuitenkirche 150
  Kaiser-Wilhelm-
    Gedächtniskirche 70
  Kölner Dom 24, 218-19, 220
  Konstantin Basilika 247
  Liebfrauenbasilika 257
  Michaelskirche 110-11
  Nikolaikirche 92
  Peterskirche 236
  Pfarrkirche St Michael 255
  St Peterskirche 107
  St Sebalduskirche 194
  Stiftskirche 170
  Theatinerkirche 111

Map Legend & Symbols Key

Look for these symbols to quickly identify listings:

- ◎ Sights
- ✪ Activities
- ⊙ Courses
- ⊙ Tours
- ✪ Festivals & Events
- ✖ Eating
- ⊙ Drinking
- ✪ Entertainment
- ⊙ Shopping
- ❶ Information & Transport

These symbols and abbreviations give vital information for each listing:

- 🍃 Sustainable or green recommendation
- **FREE** No payment required

- ☎ Telephone number
- ⊘ Opening hours
- Ⓟ Parking
- ⊖ Nonsmoking
- ❄ Air-conditioning
- @ Internet access
- 🛜 Wi-fi access
- 🏊 Swimming pool
- 🚌 Bus
- ⛴ Ferry
- 🚋 Tram
- 🚆 Train
- 📖 English-language menu
- 🌱 Vegetarian selection
- 👪 Family-friendly

Find your best experiences with these Great For... icons.

- Budget
- Food & Drink
- Drinking
- 🚲 Cycling
- Shopping
- Sport
- Art & Culture
- Events
- 📷 Photo Op
- 🔭 Scenery
- Family Travel

- Short Trip
- Detour
- Walking
- Local Life
- History
- Entertainment
- Beaches
- ❄ Winter Travel
- ☕ Cafe/Coffee
- Nature & Wildlife

Sights

- 🏖 Beach
- 🐦 Bird Sanctuary
- 🕎 Buddhist
- 🏰 Castle/Palace
- ✝ Christian
- 🕌 Confucian
- 🕉 Hindu
- ☪ Islamic
- 🕉 Jain
- ✡ Jewish
- ❶ Monument
- 🏛 Museum/Gallery/ Historic Building
- 🏚 Ruin
- ⛩ Shinto
- 🪯 Sikh
- ☯ Taoist
- 🍷 Winery/Vineyard
- 🐾 Zoo/Wildlife Sanctuary
- ◎ Other Sight

Points of Interest

- Ⓒ Bodysurfing
- 🏕 Camping
- ☕ Cafe
- 🛶 Canoeing/Kayaking
- ● Course/Tour
- 🤿 Diving
- 🍸 Drinking & Nightlife
- ✖ Eating
- 🎭 Entertainment
- ♨ Sento Hot Baths/ Onsen
- 🛍 Shopping
- 🎿 Skiing
- 🛏 Sleeping
- 🤿 Snorkelling
- 🏄 Surfing
- 🏊 Swimming/Pool
- 🚶 Walking
- 🏄 Windsurfing
- ⊙ Other Activity

Information

- 🏦 Bank
- 🏛 Embassy/Consulate
- ✚ Hospital/Medical
- @ Internet
- 👮 Police
- 📮 Post Office
- ☎ Telephone
- 🚻 Toilet
- ❶ Tourist Information
- ● Other Information

Geographic

- 🏖 Beach
- ⊢ Gate
- 🏠 Hut/Shelter
- 🗼 Lighthouse
- 🔭 Lookout
- ▲ Mountain/Volcano
- 🌴 Oasis
- 🌳 Park
-)(Pass
- ⛱ Picnic Area
- 💧 Waterfall

Transport

- ✈ Airport
- Ⓑ BART station
- ⊗ Border crossing
- Ⓣ Boston T station
- 🚌 Bus
- ⊶⊶ Cable car/Funicular
- ⊶🚲⊷ Cycling
- ⊖ Ferry
- Ⓜ Metro/MRT station
- ⊷Ⓜ⊷ Monorail
- Ⓟ Parking
- ⛽ Petrol station
- Ⓢ Subway/S-Bahn/ Skytrain station
- 🚕 Taxi
- ⊶🚆⊷ Train station/Railway
- ⋈⋈⋈⋈ Tram
- Ⓣ Tube Station
- Ⓤ Underground/ U-Bahn station
- ● Other Transport

Germany in that time. On this trip, he particularly enjoyed discovering Leipzig's secret life beyond the Altstadt, the gorgeousness that is Görlitz and getting to know Dresden. More of Tom's work can be found at www.tommasters.net.

Andrea Schulte-Peevers

Born and raised in Germany and educated in London and at UCLA, Andrea has travelled the distance to the moon and back in her visits to some 75 countries, but her favourite place in the world is still Berlin. She's written about her native country for two decades and authored or contributed to over 80 Lonely Planet titles, including *Germany, Berlin,* and *Pocket Berlin*.

Ryan Ver Berkmoes

Ryan Ver Berkmoes once lived in Germany for three years, in Frankfurt, during which time he edited a magazine until he got a chance for a new career with Lonely Planet. One of his first jobs was working on Lonely Planet's Germany coverage. He loves smoked fish, which serves him well in the north, and beer, which serves him pretty well everywhere in Germany. Follow him at ryanverberkmoes.com and @ryanvb.

Benedict Walker

Currently hanging by the beach near his mum in hometown Newcastle, Ben is living his dreams, travelling the world for Lonely Planet. So far, Ben has co-written Lonely Planet's *Japan, Canada, Florida* and *Australia* guidebooks. This is his first time writing for the Germany team, soon to be followed with Vietnam. Otherwise, he's written and directed a play, toured Australia managing travel for rockstars and is an avid photographer toying with his original craft of film-making. He's an advocate of following your dreams – they can come true. For updates, see www.wordsand journeys.com.

Our Story

A beat-up old car, a few dollars in the pocket and a sense of adventure. In 1972 that's all Tony and Maureen Wheeler needed for the trip of a lifetime – across Europe and Asia overland to Australia. It took several months, and at the end – broke but inspired – they sat at their kitchen table writing and stapling together their first travel guide, *Across Asia on the Cheap*. Within a week they'd sold 1500 copies. Lonely Planet was born.

Today, Lonely Planet has offices in Franklin, London, Melbourne, Oakland, Beijing and Delhi, with more than 600 staff and writers. We share Tony's belief that 'a great guidebook should do three things: inform, educate and amuse'.

Our Writers

Marc Di Duca

A well-established travel-guide author, Marc has explored many corners of Germany over the last 25 years, but it's to the quirky variety and friendliness of Bavaria that he returns most willingly. When not hiking Alpine valleys, eating snowballs in Rothenburg ob der Tauber or brewery-hopping in Bamberg, he can be found in Sandwich, Kent, where he lives with his wife, Tanya, and their two sons.

Kerry Christiani

Having lived for six years in the Black Forest, Kerry returned to this neck of the woods (her second home) to write her content. Summer hikes in the forest, bike rides on Lake Constance and going on the trail of Mozart and Maria in Salzburg kept her busy. She tweets @kerrychristiani and lists her latest work at www.kerrychristiani.com.

Catherine Le Nevez

Catherine's wanderlust kicked in when she first roadtripped across Europe – including Germany – aged four, and she's been road-tripping here ever since, completing her Doctorate of Creative Arts in Writing, Masters in Professional Writing, and post-grad qualifications in Editing and Publishing along the way. Catherine has worked as a freelance writer for many years and over the last decade-plus she's written scores of Lonely Planet guides and articles covering destinations all over Germany, Europe and beyond.

Tom Masters

Tom hails from London, but has lived in Berlin since 2009 and has travelled widely all over

--- **More Writers** ---

STAY IN TOUCH
lonelyplanet.com/contact

AUSTRALIA Levels 2 & 3, 551 Swanston St, Carlton, Victoria 3053
☏ 03 8379 8000, fax 03 8379 8111

USA 150 Linden St, Oakland, CA 94607
☏ 510 250 6400, toll free 800 275 8555, fax 510 893 8572

UK 240 Blackfriars Rd, London SE1 8NW
☏ 020 3771 5100, fax 020 3771 5101

 twitter.com/ lonelyplanet
 facebook.com/ lonelyplanet
 instagram.com/ lonelyplanet
 youtube.com/ lonelyplanet
 lonelyplanet.com/ newsletter